Rainbow Green Live-Food Cuisine

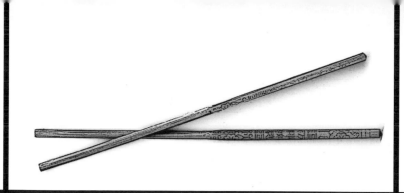

# Rainbow
# Green
# Live-Food
# Cuisine

## Gabriel Cousens, M.D.
### and the Tree of Life Café Chefs

**North Atlantic Books**
**Berkeley, California**

Published by
North Atlantic Books
P.O. Box 12327
Berkeley, California 94712
and
Essene Vision Books
P.O. Box 1080
Patagonia, Arizona 85624

Cover and book design by Maxine Ressler

Printed in Canada

*Rainbow Green Live-Food Cuisine* is sponsored by the Society for the Study of Native Arts and Sciences, a nonprofit educational corporation whose goals are to develop an educational and crosscultural perspective linking various scientific, social, and artistic fields; to nurture a holistic view of arts, sciences, humanities, and healing; and to publish and distribute literature on the relationship of mind, body, and nature.

ISBN-13: 978-1-55643-465-5

**Library of Congress Cataloging-in-Publication Data**

Cousens, Gabriel, 1943-
    Rainbow green live-food cuisine / by Gabriel Cousens and chefs of the Tree of Life Cafe.
        p. cm.
Includes bibliographical references and index.
    ISBN 1-55643-465-0
    1. Raw food diet—Recipes.  2. Nutrition.  3. Health.  I. Tree of Life Cafe. II. Title.
    RM237.5.C68 2003
    613.2'6—dc21                                    2003012499


6  7  8  9  10  11  12  Transcontinental  12  11  10  09  08  07

# DEDICATION

To our brothers and sisters throughout the world who have made a commitment to themselves to live and eat in a way that creates the highest physical, emotional, mental, and spiritual expression and helps to heal the planetary ecology and Earth's inhabitants.

# ACKNOWLEDGMENTS

*Rainbow Green Live-Food Cuisine* has been a joyful collective effort. We wish to acknowledge and thank the many people who are a part of the Tree of Life, who participated and shared recipes as they were taught on site and tested at the Tree of Life Café. These people include: Shanti, Karen, Philip, Chad, Sita, Heather, Ren, Rebecca, Rose Lee, Aaron, Lucas, Alison, Isaiah, and Tsiona.

Deep thanks to Ivri who served as the Tree of Life's *Rainbow Green Live-Food Cuisine* project manager and in-house editor. She also compiled the recipes, as well as wrote the section "Raising Rainbow Babies."

Much appreciation to Philip, the Tree of Life Café Manager and Chef, who took the photographs of the cuisine, edited the recipes, and wrote "The Secrets to Rainbow Green Live-Food Cuisine Preparation" and the "Resources Directory."

Thanks to Shanti who contributed all the recipes for the "Essential Oil Delicacies" and the Café staff who wrote the "Traveling in the Raw" section.

Thanks to Susan, Tree of Life Administrative Assistant, who generated some of the charts and helped with the details in a few pinches.

Gratitude to Kaliji for the wisdom of Kali Ray TriYoga,® and for writing about airplane Yoga for the section "Preventing Jet Stress."

We also thank Richard Harvey for the excellent phase-contrast and dark-field slides he contributed to this book, and his partner Mary Houston, who helped Richard prepare the slides and inspired me to probe more deeply into Dr. Robert Young's research.

Special thanks to David Wolfe and Eliot Rosen who gave their support, energy, and their gift of words in writing the Foreword and Preface, respectively.

We also are very grateful for the enduring support of the folks at North Atlantic Books, especially Kathy Glass, who served as editor, and Sarah Serafimidis, the Project Manager.

# Table of Contents

## SECTION 1

## RAINBOW GREEN LIVE-FOOD CUISINE IS THE WAY TO LIVE

# SECTION 2

## Rainbow Green Live-Food Cuisine Recipes

# PREFACE

The teachings of the Greek physician Galen (129–199 A.D.) held such indomitable sway over Western medicine that until the European Renaissance a full 1,400 years later, those who challenged Galen's pre-scientific legacy faced professional ridicule, public banishment, and even death.

Refusing to blindly believe unproven doctrine, Leonardo Da Vinci, Dr. William Harvey, and others autopsied human corpses so they might see empirically, with their own eyes, the poetic architecture of human anatomy.

In like manner, Dr. Gabriel Cousens relies on his "own eyes" and not upon unsubstantiated dietary theories or idealistic ideologies of how things "should be."

Having treated thousands of patients during his thirty-plus years as a holistic physician, Dr. Cousens time and again saw intriguing patterns emerge in positive response to his therapeutic interventions. As his patient data grew, the logical next step was to conduct clinical studies. This book represents the results of Dr. Cousens' latest clinical exploration.

Dr. Cousens enlisted the aid of his residential staff at the Tree of Life Rejuvenation Center, who initially adopted a low-glycemic (low-sweet) therapeutic diet for three months, and then voluntarily continued on the maintenance phase to this day. Dr. Cousens monitored clinical progress by way of dark-field microscopic blood samples and other diagnostic measures.

Before this dietary experiment, the residents had already been eating a 100% live-food diet but with no restrictions on fruit intake. On this no- to low-fruit live-food program, they felt better and better with each passing day. Blood samples revealed dramatically fewer pathogenic microorganisms, directly corroborating glowing subjective reports of their increased physical energy and mental clarity. Clearly something wonderful was occurring. Based on this successful experience, Dr. Cousens began offering the program to his clients.

Dr. Cousens believes that in today's world, most of us are laboring under a toxic load of pathogenic microorganisms, heavy metal deposits, and pesticide residues. These substances enter the body mostly from what we eat. Paradoxically, even "wholesome foods"—grains, fruits, and high-glycemic vegetables—can be literally "feeding the problem."

High-glycemic foods are not the only problem, however. A typical modern-day meal featuring a main course of beef, poultry, or fish may contain up to 750 million pathogenic microorganisms per serving, compared to a typical vegan meal containing only 500 pathogenic microorganisms per meal.

These same foods were not as troublesome for past generations as they are for us today. Our ancestors had stronger genetic inheritance and constitutional strength because they weren't exposed to excessive antibiotic intake, foodless foods stripped of their essential nutrients, or poisonous pesticides, hormones, and food additives.

Other major offenders that induce fermentation and increase toxin-producing microbes—what Dr. Cousens calls "self-composting"—are eggs, mushrooms, brewer's and nutritional yeast, peanuts, alcohol, dairy, corn, white rice, white sugar, and anything that contributes to excess acidity and a low-oxygen state.

There is a fascinating historical footnote illustrating the school of medical thought behind Rainbow Green Live-Food Cuisine. In the late 1800s, French microbiologists Dr. Antoine Béchamp and Dr. Claude Bernard waged a much-publicized ongoing debate with Nobel Prize laureate Dr. Louis Pasteur, the creator of the "germ theory" of disease. On his deathbed, Pasteur shocked his attendants by changing his lifelong position. With all his remaining strength, he whispered (in French, of course): "Claude Bernard was right. The microbe is nothing. The terrain is everything."

By this parting utterance, Pasteur acknowledged that external germs weren't the primary root-cause of disease, only opportunistic scavengers that appear when the body is weak and out of balance. The primary underlying etiology of disease was a disruption of what Béchamp referred to as the "biological terrain." By this he meant the overall condition of the host organism's cells, fluids, organs, etc. Factors that improve or maintain the health of the biological terrain include 1) low levels of toxicity and fermentation; 2) the proper range of acid/alkaline balance; 3) strong electromagnetic potential; 4) high cellular oxygenization; and 5) a high number of pro-biotic beneficial bacteria and a low number of pathogenic microorganisms.

There is over 100 years of microscopic evidence supporting the validity of the biological terrain approach. In this book, Dr. Cousens provides convincing visual illustrations that include microscopic dark-field, dry field, and phase-contrast photographic slides showing "protits"—minute non-pathogenic organisms—mutating or "morphing" into full-blown toxin-producing fungi, molds, yeast, and viruses.

Modern-day exponents of the biological terrain school presently number only a few thousand worldwide, yet their size is steadily growing. This is typical in the history of scientific progress: Paradigm-shifting breakthroughs often hit cul-de-sac dead-ends in societal acceptance due to the vagaries of vested economic interest, political intrigue, and pride of ego. It is ironic that the pharmaceutical-based healthcare delivery system—staunch advocates of Pasteur's opposing germ theory—has somehow forgotten Pasteur's very own dying words: "The germ is nothing. The terrain is everything."

The Rainbow Green Live-Food Cuisine regimen is divided into three phases. The Healing Phase I permits no fruit or high-glycemic foods whatsoever. The Stabilizing Phase I.5 allows a few mildly sweet foods, but one might need to revert to Healing Phase I if negative symptoms return. The Maintenance Phase II is what one eats on a long-term basis. This last stage permits occasional higher glycemic foods, but only if one's biological terrain can handle the microbe-stimulating effects of these foods.

For some health seekers, having to abstain from some of their favorite foods may come as an unwelcome shock. However, to reclaim their health-birthright, Dr. Cousens says the following three factors may first need to be addressed:

1. Despite the belief that they are eating relatively wholesome foods, in actual fact their bodies are burdened with toxin-producing microbes that are being fed by the very foods that people think are good for them.

2. Switching from inorganic to organically grown foods will dramatically reduce the food-borne intake of pesticides and heavy metals. As an added bonus, the inherent internal cleansing properties of a live-food diet will further help to detoxify the body.

   In this connection, Dr. Gunther Enderlein conducted a lifetime of biological terrain microscopic research spanning sixty years. He concluded, "The most powerful diet for bringing a diseased biological terrain back to normal is live foods." Dr. Cousens is himself a student of Dr. Maria Blecker, one of Dr. Enderlein's protégés.

3. Individualizing the Rainbow Green Live-Food Cuisine to fit one's dominant metabolic type as either a fast or slow oxidizer is a critical piece of this dietary approach. Dr. Cousens also teaches how to assess one's basic Ayurvedic constitutional type—vata, pitta, kapha, or hybrid—and to partake of only those recipes that specifically support unique bio-individuality.

"Those who apply these guiding principles enjoy more physical energy, sharper mental clarity, and a richer, more loving emotional life," says Dr. Cousens. He reports a 99% success rate in helping others maintain a live-food vegan diet.

For these and other reasons, Rainbow Green Live-Food Cuisine creates a direct passageway to radiant health as well as a solid foundation for building an ecologically conscious, fulfilling way of life. Rainbow Green Live-Food Cuisine is destined to save many present and would-be vegetarians/vegans from falling off the dietary wagon.

If you're wondering why Dr. Cousens put so much emphasis on becoming a live-food vegan, it's because he believes that internal warfare on the battlefield of the biological terrain cannot be separated from disharmony in the external world. Indeed, conflicts between nations, races, and creeds have made much of the world a festering compost heap. Rainbow Green Live-Food Cuisine is the fastest and most effective way of putting a stop to internal self-composting. Therefore, if we transform our inner environment, the outer world will change as well.

While I was interviewing Dr. Cousens in 1987 in connection with his first book, *Spiritual Nutrition and the Rainbow Diet,* he shared in a thoughtful, humble tone, "Eliot, the further up the mountain I travel, the more I can help my patients and students." As a vegan myself for thirty years, I'm convinced that Dr. Cousens is 100% dedicated to helping people attain glowing health, deeper happiness, and accelerated spiritual growth. His vegan-based Rainbow Green Live-Food Cuisine program will be an important step towards experiencing these expansive states.

In a world where healthy, peaceful, loving humans increasingly reflect their inherent divine nature, this gift of a book is your invitation to live what Dr. Cousens calls a "new paradigm of awakened living." And a great way to start is with your next healthy bite of Rainbow Green Live-Food Cuisine!

Eliot Jay Rosen, QCSW, CNC

Nutrition-oriented psychotherapist and author of the *Los Angeles Times* best-selling book and video documentary, *Experiencing the Soul: Before Birth, During Life, After Death*

# FOREWORD

We are so blessed to have access to the information shared in this book.

Dr. Cousens has established himself as the leading holistic medical doctor in the United States and, in my opinion, the leading physician in the world. I consider Dr. Gabriel Cousens to be the foremost medical authority in the field of nutrition and particularly in the area of raw- and living-food, vegetarian nutrition. In this landmark, groundbreaking book, Dr. Gabriel Cousens presents *the* cutting-edge research in nutritional healing.

As a leading researcher and developer of raw-food products for the marketplace, I rely on Dr. Cousens' expertise in the health and nutrition field in order to make educated decisions that affect consumers interested in the best health possible. I consult with Dr. Cousens on a regular basis about various ideas and approaches. Many times I believed that I had come across something so unique or exotic that I was sure he did not know about it, only to discover that he had known about it for years.

Dr. Cousens' research is extraordinary. He is constantly seeking more and more subtle refinement in his approach in order to allow more people to succeed with their diet strategy. I certainly have greatly benefited from some of the key insights I first learned from Dr. Cousens over the years.

Having conducted many retreats and workshops with Dr. Cousens and served as a professor for the Master's program at Dr. Cousens' school of vegan and live-food nutrition, I am intimately familiar with the meticulous level of quality that goes into every project Dr. Cousens undertakes.

Throughout these pages, Dr. Cousens elaborates and expands a long line of research beginning with biochemist Antoine Béchamp through Dr. Enderlein into the present day with Gaston Naessens' and Dr. Robert Young's work.

Dr. Cousens has meticulously combed this vast body of research and drawn from it a startling conclusion: that sugar is the primary culprit behind disease, because sugar feeds mold, fungus, yeast, and viruses (nature's composting tools). An excess of sugar in our diet causes our "composting button" to be pushed. It causes us to begin to slowly, yet perceptibly, be compromised from the inside.

We know that the amount of sugar (carbohydrates) present in the Western diet today has never been seen before in the whole of human history. Yearly consumption of refined sugar in the United States was no more than about ten pounds per person in the early 1800s. The U.S. Department of Agriculture reported that this had risen to 152 pounds per person by 1996. Reading Dr. Cousens' book reminded me of the wake-up call I received when I read William Duffy's classic book *Sugar Blues.*

We have such an enormous amount of sugar in our present diet that many indigenous peoples, upon adopting a Western diet, immediately develop sugar diabetes because they have never seen such a high carbohydrate diet in their entire genetic history.

We have artificially increased the levels of sugars in foods by protecting foods from natural predators and nature's recyclers (viruses, bacteria, fungus, mold). Even though plant domestication techniques, fence lines, and pesticides may keep nature's recyclers away for a moment, they will not protect us after we ingest sugary/starchy plants, whether eaten raw, cooked, or refined.

Our technological ability to protect plants from natural predators has become extraordinarily sophisticated in the last hundred years, increasing our exposure to sugars far beyond our capacity to adapt. As Dr. Cousens demonstrates, this is a primary cause of the epidemic of disease and ill health currently experienced in Western civilization.

Sugar is not the only challenge we face. Fungal-infected food (especially grains and corn) and the animals that eat this food (cattle, pigs, chicken) introduce an enormous quantity of foreign organisms in the body that break down overall immunity.

Dr. Cousens presents a three-phase program incorporating the leading-edge technology in the field to guide us away from high starch/sugar foods and fungal-contaminated animal foods and toward a mineral-rich, live-food diet.

The wide spectrum of recipes provided in Part 2 will assist anyone in adopting and adapting to a low-sugar, living-food regime. Dr. Cousens and his Tree of Life staff have compiled an enormous array of fantastic, 100% healthy, simple recipes. I know they are delicious because I have had the privilege to sample many myself!

Of additional and great value is the discussion of nutrition for children, healthy jet travel, and the latest research in gardening and farming. I have paid close attention to Dr. Cousens' knowledge in all of these areas and have shifted the advice I give to others and my own approach accordingly.

The Tree of Life staff is also to be applauded. They have done a fantastic job organizing this project with Dr. Cousens.

Overall, this book covers a wide spectrum of fascinating ideas and intelligent, well-thought-out strategies for healing. What Dr. Cousens presents you are ideas and concepts that allow you to get a wider understanding of diet, health, emotional poise, and spiritual balance.

One of the key themes in the book *A Course In Miracles* is that "a miracle is created simply by a shift in perception." Following the diet plan in this book engenders a transformation within you that allows you to gain a new perception—to ask a new question, get a new answer, and, with applied creativity, have more choices. Essentially, we create miracles in our lives if we have enough choices.

I consider Dr. Gabriel Cousens a dear friend, a seeker of truth, a pillar of health, and someone who leads by example. Dr. Cousens' relentless search for ecological health solutions indicates how much he cares about the health and well-being of his patients, friends, and the planet. *Rainbow Green Live-Food Cuisine* represents a culmination of his key teachings and research in the health and nutrition field.

As you discover that you are enjoying the contents of *Rainbow Green Live-Food Cuisine* and that you would like to make it part of your lifestyle, I recommend visiting Dr. Cousens' Tree of Life Rejuvenation Center in Patagonia, Arizona, and trying this food out for yourself! I look forward to every trip there, so I can eat the most extraordinary, healthy, organic food available anywhere!

Enjoy the Rainbow Green Live-Food Cuisine and have the best day ever!

David Wolfe
www.davidwolfe.com
David Wolfe is the author of *Eating For Beauty: The Sunfood Diet Success System,* and he is CEO of Nature's First Law Inc., CEO of Genesis 129 LLC, and founder of The Fruit Tree Planting Foundation.

# Introduction

This book represents a paradigm shift in the live-foods movement. It is the next step in my personal research and service to work out how to develop a healthy diet that supports all levels of a person's function, from basic physical health to one's spiritual evolution. In 1975, I began my path toward searching for a diet that would be the best for serving all of these purposes. In 1987, I wrote my first book, *Spiritual Nutrition and the Rainbow Diet,* which specifically highlights how live foods are the healthiest food approach on the planet and by far the most powerful for supporting spiritual life. In 1991, I came out with the book *Conscious Eating,* which took this approach further with the principle that we are all individuals and must be able to select a diet that best fits our constitution. In 2000, the revised and expanded edition was published. It contains further details of (1) how to develop an individualized diet that best serves our constitution; (2) the breakthrough theory of the origins of the biologically altered brain; (3) a complete live-food approach for pregnancy and nursing; and (4) many new recipes. In the present book, with the collaboration of the Tree of Life Café staff and my wonderful wife and partner, Shanti GoldsCousens, we are presenting the next step in the development of the healthiest maintenance diet for supporting your physical, emotional, mental, and spiritual life. The final book in the series, the next one I will write, is on spiritual fasting.

The spark of the idea for this book was furnished by Robert Young, Ph.D., D.Sc., in his book *Sick and Tired.* He made the point, based on a great deal of microscopic dark-field and dry-field research, that a diet low in fungus and mycotoxins (toxins that are produced by fungus) is best for our overall health. I have a better appreciation of Robert Young's work since studying pleomorphic science for the last ten-plus years (the microscope-based science dating from the late 1800s that describes the transmutation of organisms in our blood from one non-pathogenic form to a variety of pathogenic forms). His insight and understanding into this whole process enables us to use pleo-morphic theory in a practical way to understand our health. No one else has put this information together like Robert Young. The information from *Sick and Tired* has a heavy influence throughout the initial chapters of this book. For this I want to express my gratitude, appreciation, and acknowledgment.

In my usual scientific way, I felt that before I even shared these ideas with any-one else, I needed to personally explore this diet, which is essentially a low-glycemic fruit, vegetable, nut, seed, sea vegetable, algae-based diet. But within a few days, most of the staff had followed Shanti and me on this, particularly the café staff, and three months later, most had experienced very significant positive changes in their energy levels and sense of well-being. I began to explore this diet with clients who were suffering from mycotoxicosis (which is not just toxicity from candida infection, but from mycotic infection in gen-eral). This, of course, included most of my clients, as I began to realize that most people, in this day and age, have an excess of fungal growth in their sys-tem. Again, much to my surprise, people who were able to follow this diet for a period of three months showed remarkable positive changes in their blood picture, as well as in the quality of their health and energy.

As I looked at the results, I could not help but say, "We need to make some changes" because most of the live-food preparation in North America cer-tainly includes a fair amount of natural sweets. Sweet foods, which have a high glycemic index even if they are natural and raw, are still very mycosis-producing. Over the period of the next year at the Tree of Life Café (part of the Tree of Life Rejuvenation Center), we began to develop a series of recipes for people to use in their everyday lives, incorporating the Rainbow Green Live-Food Cuisine: a low-sweet, low-fungus, and low mycotoxin-producing, delicious, gourmet, vegan, live-food cuisine.

We are pleased to share this exciting revolutionary breakthrough in quality of health and delightful taste.

Gabriel Cousens, M.D., M.D.(H),
Diplomate in Ayurveda,
www.treeoflife.nu
e-mail: healing@treeoflife.nu

Rainbow Green Live-Food Cuisine

is

# The Way to Live

*Chapter*

# To Compost or Not:
# The Theory Behind the
# Rainbow Green
# Live-Food Cuisine

The theory that I am sharing with you is what is presently known as the pleomorphic theory, developed over a period from the late 1800s to early 1900s by several people who have influenced my understanding of holistic health. The first is Antoine Béchamp (1816–1908), who was a master of pharmacy, doctor of science, doctor of medicine, professor of medical chemical pharmacy, professor of physics and toxicology, and professor of biological chemistry. What he discovered was the process of fermentation, which he described as the process of digestion by microscopic ferments or life forms. As a genius in his field, he saw that blood is not a liquid but a flowing tissue. In his work, he discovered what he called "microzymas" or ferments in the blood. The mycrozymas are living microscopic and colloidal elements capable of fermenting the sugar in our system. The microzyma is the smallest living unit in nature and in our bodies; it is much smaller than the cells.

The cornerstone of Béchamp's theory was that maintaining a healthy terrain and biological physiology is the key to health. When the biological terrain was disrupted, when people got too acid, then the natural fermentation process in the body was accelerated, and a morbid evolution of these microzymas would take place. They would coagulate and pleomorphically permutate into bacteria, yeast, fungus, and eventually mold. As these morbid pleomorphic forms from the microzymas developed, they fed on our vital body substances and produced more toxins, which we call mycotoxins. This toxic process resulted in a degenerative disease symptomology.

Another great researcher who came a bit later and based some of his work on Béchamp was a physician, Professor Gunther Enderlein (1872–1968). (I had the opportunity to study with one of Dr. Enderlein's German students, Dr. Maria Blecker.) Dr. Enderlein proved the pleomorphic theory postulated by Béchamp, through his sixty years of observations of living human blood. He also proved that the cell was not the smallest unit of life, and that within the cell are protits, which is the tiniest unit of life. Perhaps most important of all, he validated Béchamp's theory of pleomorphism, which states that these protit-microorganisms change in their form according to the conditions of the blood and its tenor in general. Instead of calling them microzymas, Dr. Enderlein referred to them as protits, but the principle is essentially the same. For the purpose of this book, I am choosing to use the word "protit," as that is the term I am accustomed to using. Dr. Gasten Naessens in Canada has also discovered these pleomorphic forms, and he calls them somatids.

Fundamentally, what these researchers have discovered, which can be readily seen in a microscope, is that these protits, which are of very small size (.001 micron), form a colloidal energetic field, not only in our human system within the cells, but also in extra-cellular fluid and the lymph and the blood. This is, essentially, everywhere in the body. This colloidal field, if it is healthy, helps to create health. If the living colloid field is disrupted by toxic influences, then the energetic and physiologic electromagnetic field changes in the direction of pathology, and we move to progressively poorer health.

This theory was further developed by Dr. Robert Young. In my discussions with him, I added my theory of Tachyon energy and subtle organizing energy fields (SOEF) (as explained in *Spiritual Nutrition and the Rainbow Diet, Conscious Eating,* and *Tachyon Energy: A New Paradigm in Holistic Healing*), which he felt comfortable with. In essence, the combined Tachyon, SOEF, living colloid theory is key for understanding this new concept in nutrition. The subtle organizing energy field (SOEF), which is energized by the Tachyon energy (energy just faster than the speed of light), creates an energetic matrix from the protits' colloid suspension on the physical plane. This manifests first as a living colloidal field in the space between and within the cells. This protit colloidal field is affected by the environment, as well as by the normalizing SOEF matrix. Acid food, acid thoughts, low oxygen, environmental toxins, heavy metals, and lack of exercise all have the power to distort this living protit colloidal field. They can shift it from a healthy, creative, energetic matrix for cells and tissues into a morbid pleomorphic expression: an unhealthy field. These negative environmental stresses create a morbid pleomorphic change from the healthy protit energetics of life to bacteria and higher forms of yeast, mold, and fungus, as the protits pleomorphically transmute and coagulate. These higher morbid pleomorphic forms give off mycotoxins, which tend to break down our living tissues. These morbid pleomorphic forms, for which I use the word "mycosis," also eat the sugar in our systems, the DNA, the proteins, the enzymes, and the hormones. They live off our tissues and vital fluids, and as they increasingly give off mycotoxins (in essence, their fecal waste), they further imbalance and acidify the system and create favorable conditions for more of these pleomorphic organisms to grow and, therefore, increase the state of mycosis.

In an undisturbed, healthy state there is a clear and full expression of the vital subtle-organizing, high-energy fields into the colloidal field. Undisturbed by toxic influences, this energetic continuum—from Tachyon energy, to SOEF vital life pattern, to a healthy energetic protit colloidal system—is the foundation of optimum health. The living colloidal system is the first level of physical manifestation of life energies. This healthy protit colloidal field is needed for a healthy coagulation system and for proper building blocks for all cellular, lymph, blood, and intra-cellular structures. When this protit colloidal field, which is very sensitive to morbid effects, is energetically healthy, then we have a perfect, supportive field for a healthy matrix for the creation and life force of our cells and tissues. When the subtle organizing energy field matrix on the colloid field is disrupted by degenerative influences, then this protit colloidal field acts as a sensor to the physiological imbalance. It reacts to the environment and creates a morbid energetic field to compensate. This shift to a morbid field takes us toward degenerating health.

The protits—independent living elements—seem to have critical roles of being a builder as well as a recycler of organisms. In essence, "from dust to dust." This recycling is the dying and death process. As long as the subtle organizing energy field imprint of the colloidal matrix of the protits is not too significantly disturbed, then the protit colloidal system acts as a builder and restorer of life. When the colloidal energetic matrix is disturbed significantly, then the "recycling button" or "composting button" is pushed and the protits begin their function as recyclers of whatever organism they are in. In essence, they begin to accelerate the rate of fermentation of the system. At the turn of the nineteenth century, candida was primarily seen in people who were dying of cancer or other very serious diseases. What was going on was that the recycle button had been pushed and they had already begun the cycle of degeneration.

The process of chronic disease is activated in a person who is toxic enough to push the "composting button." Depending on the degree of toxicity, this composting process leads to chronic disease, misery, and ultimately death. The key to restoring health is minimizing or eliminating the toxic conditions so that the composting button is turned off. A low-sweet, live-food, non-acidic diet and a healthy mind are the key factors in turning off the composting button and reestablishing vibrant health. These reverse the forces of entropy or composting. Activities that enhance the flow of the energetic continuum, from enhancing the flow of Tachyon energy, to energizing the SOEFs, to all forms of positive lifestyle habits, all help to reverse entropy or the aging-degeneration process.

This diet is designed to turn off the self-composting button. Today we have a great many more morbid influences on us including hybrid, high-sweet fruits, radiation, intense pollution, heavy metal toxicity, and an accelerated amount of stress in the environment and within our minds, as well as the use of genetically engineered food, irradiated food, processed food, fast food, junk food, refined white flour food, white sugar food, and canned foods. All of these foods specifically are morbid influences on the protit colloidal field as it attempts to express the pure subtle organizing energetic matrix in our cells and tissues. Whereas a diet high in fruit was considered an excellent diet fifty years ago, because of the greatly increased physical, emotional, mental, and spiritual toxicity in ourselves and the world, we now need to shift to a diet with lower sugar content. The purpose of this, of course, is to have less fermentation and therefore not feed the morbid pleomorphic evolving organisms. In addition, because of the conditions in our environment (and I see this as a global issue), I have had to look at adjusting the live-food diet to counterbalance the toxic conditions of our planet and the conditions that all of us human beings are facing. It is in this context that I am offering and explaining the Rainbow Green Live-Food Cuisine.

As we delve deeper into this theory, which helps us more profoundly understand the process of disease, we enter into a debate that has been going on for the last hundred years, which is the theory that the terrain is of primary importance in establishing conditions that then create disease. This is, in essence, the pleomorphic theory. Once the terrain becomes disease-inducing, the organisms that are in us (the protits) pleomorphically change into morbid forms and create the actual conditions of disease. The opposing theory is that we catch bacteria or viruses, and that they then become the cause of disease. Somewhere there is an in-between place that combines both concepts. However, there is an old statement that "The swamp breeds mosquitoes. Mosquitoes do not breed a swamp." If your terrain (your basic physiology) is strong and healthy and in proper pH from eating the right foods, you are less likely to get any exogenous acute disease, and you are likely to be better able to fight disease. Chronic disease is more easily understood when one's framework is the pleomorphic theory. Most chronic diseases are not an acute invasion in an immunologically and pleomorphically weakened terrain, but a chronic break-down that can degenerate or devolve all the way to cancer. It is hard for any disease to invade a person who has a strong terrain. That is why some people do not get sick when there is an epidemic going around, and why other people are always getting sick. Usually those people who do not get sick are those with a very strong physiology or basically strong biological terrain.

We are all hooked up by the subtle organizing energy fields to an optimal terrain. However, by disrupting the acid-alkaline balance (most usually by becoming too acid: eating acid-promoting foods, living an acid-promoting stressful lifestyle, and thinking acid thoughts), we shift the terrain. Another factor that shifts the terrain significantly is the level of toxicity to which we are exposed. Heavy-metal toxicity, environmental pollution, lack of oxygen, poor nutritional status, mineral depletion, poor lymphatic flow, loss of electrical charge in the cells, and exposure to electromagnetic pollution all increase toxicity. Drugs that encourage yeast and fungus, which imbalance the biological terrain, include steroids, antibiotics, birth control pills, alcohol, and cigarettes. Lack of exercise, lack of rest, flesh and dairy products, white sugar, and white flour have the same effect.

As a result of all these acid-producing conditions (or any one of them, but usually it's collectively all), the red blood cells actually lose the normal, healthy negative charge that keeps them repelled from one another and prevents clumping. The cells living in these conditions become invaded by mold and fungus, lose their charges and turn positive, and begin to clump. They also clump to healthy cells, which have a negative charge, infecting them as well. As the electromagnetic field changes more and more, cells are disrupted. There is more and more clumping. The bacteria-yeast-mold sequence beginning to take place because of a lack of oxygen also promotes clumping. The more clumping you have, the less oxygen is getting to the tissues and cells in the terrain. This whole cycle can be easily identified with dark-field microscopy.

The fungal toxins that are given off are called mycotoxins. When people are very toxic as a result of fungal growth, their condition is called mycotoxicosis or mycosis. These mycotoxins further increase the acidity, acting as acids that eat away at the tissue. Symptoms are experienced as one's body attempts to deal with the poisons that result from the action of the acid toxins on the cells and tissues. They produce metabolic waste called exotoxins, as well as endotoxins, which are poisons within the organism.

One of the main mycotoxins is acid aldehyde, which converts to alcohol. The acid aldehyde causes the liver to increase the production of low-density lipoproteins, which are called LDL cholesterol. These low-density lipoproteins help bind and deactivate the mycotoxins. They also raise the cholesterol level. Acid aldehyde can decrease our strength and stamina, cloud our mind, decrease immunity, destroy neurotransmitters, and bind to red blood cells to make them less flexible and therefore decrease oxygenation of the tissues. Some of the other pathological results of excess acid aldehyde are pancreatitis, cardiomyopathy, general brain atrophy and dementia, atrophy of the interior spaces of the brain (called the ventricles), jaundice, splenomegaly (enlarged spleen), stomach ulcers, cirrhosis, and fetal edema. Acid aldehyde destroys essential enzymes and decreases cell energy.

Another powerful mycotoxin is called cyclosporin, which suppresses the immune system and can cause cancer. Uric acid is another mycotoxin. It can cause gout and also uses up the body minerals, particularly potassium, magnesium, sodium, zinc, and calcium, to neutralize the uric acid. Oxalic acid is a mycotoxin associated with kidney stones.

There is another mycotoxin called alloxan, which is a metabolic breakdown by-product of uric acid. It directly destroys pancreatic cells. Some research shows that rats given high-uric-acid foods (a diet that had about 10% uric acid) all developed diabetes.

These mycotoxins and the breakdown they cause eventually exhaust the immune system. As this whole process continues, the biological terrain is increasingly and chronically changed to an abnormal fermentative metabolic condition, which has often been identified as a pre-condition or condition of cancer. In many of my clients who have significant mycosis, their cancer profile (done at an outside laboratory) shows a pre-cancer condition. When the systemic condition localizes, like in a tumor, we call it cancer. In my theory, the tumors show up where the body is constitutionally the weakest.

Other results of a systemic mycosis (this is more than just candida), secondary to an exhausted immune system, are allergies, irritation and inflammation, eczema, runny nose (which are ways the body tries to eliminate the toxins), environmental sensitivities, fungal infections in the heart, lungs, and sinuses, fatigue, neurological problems, depression, anxiety, PMS, paranoia, panic attacks, headaches, poor concentration, poor memory, and mental confusion. These are just some of the effects. In children, we often see the mycotoxic symptoms appearing in autism, diaper rash, thrush, urinary infections, upper respiratory infections, colic, constipation, diarrhea, hyper-activities, and learning disabilities.

Additional problems that we see with mycosis are: weight problems, bloating, mycotoxic conditions of the colon and liver, a tendency towards parasites, rectal itch, urinary tract infections with itching and burning, vaginitis, increased colds and flu, cellulitis, fungus in the mouth, jock-itch, athlete's foot, and fungus of the skin. Other results of mycosis include: tendency to infection, fatigue, adrenal and thyroid weakness (which I see very often in my clients), indigestion, diarrhea, food cravings, intestinal pain, chronic fatigue syndrome, asthma, hemorrhoids, cold and flu, dry and itchy skin, receding gums, dizziness, joint pain, bad breath, diabetes, heartburn, dry mouth, PMS and menstrual problems, irritable nervous system, puffy eyes, decreased sex drive, vaginal yeast infections, hay fever, acne, gas and bloating, low blood-sugar imbalances, muscle aches and pains, and a general feeling of ill health. Mycotoxic stress and fermentation in the blood and lymph also increase free radicals in the system.

As part of the circle of degeneration, there is a collapse of the colloid system in the biological terrain that causes further aggravation of red blood cells and loss of charge of energy in the cells. We need to understand that the protits are the colloids of life, which we need to function appropriately. The living colloid system holds the state of balance, because it maintains the electrical

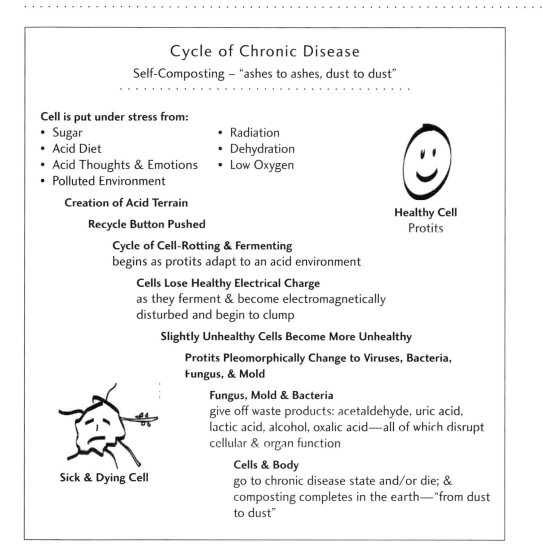

## Cycle of Chronic Disease
### Self-Composting – "ashes to ashes, dust to dust"

**Cell is put under stress from:**
- Sugar
- Acid Diet
- Acid Thoughts & Emotions
- Polluted Environment
- Radiation
- Dehydration
- Low Oxygen

**Healthy Cell**
Protits

**Creation of Acid Terrain**

**Recycle Button Pushed**

**Cycle of Cell-Rotting & Fermenting**
begins as protits adapt to an acid environment

**Cells Lose Healthy Electrical Charge**
as they ferment & become electromagnetically
disturbed and begin to clump

**Slightly Unhealthy Cells Become More Unhealthy**

**Protits Pleomorphically Change to Viruses, Bacteria,
Fungus, & Mold**

**Fungus, Mold & Bacteria**
give off waste products: acetaldehyde, uric acid,
lactic acid, alcohol, oxalic acid—all of which disrupt
cellular & organ function

**Sick & Dying Cell**

**Cells & Body**
go to chronic disease state and/or die; &
composting completes in the earth—"from dust
to dust"

charge in the system and, therefore, stops excessive coagulation. Excessive coagulation is not only more clumping but is merging together to create higher forms. The colloids of life, the protits, will sense any electrical compromise and be affected by it. We depend on our colloids for life force and health. By creating a proper alkaline balance in our biological terrain, via proper diet and lifestyle, we maintain a state of optimal health, because in this process we are maintaining an optimal living colloid or protit system.

Lack of harmony with the colloids creates a menu for disease. To grasp this, we just need to understand that the negative charge in the cells, especially the red blood cells, is the first line of defense, because it keeps the cells from clumping. When the charge is lost, the cells become susceptible to external organisms as well as infestation by yeast and fungus, which feed on the hemoglobin in the red blood cells.

Most of the people I see in my clinical practice have had "their recycle button pushed" and are working on returning to health, which can take anywhere from two months to three years. It depends on being able to turn off the button. I would like to note that I am not an oncologist. It is increasingly common knowledge among natural healers who treat cancer that there is a connection between the degree of fungus in the blood and body and the increasing potential for cancer. This theoretical view established by Dr. Antoine Béchamp and Dr. Enderlein is not part of the educational system in allopathic medical schools, where the germ theory of Louis Pasteur, Antoine Béchamp's rival, prevails. It is interesting to note that on his deathbed, Louis Pasteur said, "Claude Bernard was right. The microbe is nothing. The terrain is everything." (This is according to pleomorphic physicians I have studied with and Robert Young, Ph.D., in *Sick and Tired.*) It is the biological terrain that is most important. Extreme pleomorphic mycosis may generate the conditions that manifest as cancer. This has not been proven, but there is strong theoretical evidence to support this idea.

# SUMMARY

Based on her clinical observations, Florence Nightingale, a nurse known for her work during the American Civil War, asserted, "There are no specific diseases, only specific disease conditions." In other words, in health the protits act harmoniously. In disease, they become disturbed. They change their form and function, and they evolve morbidly in a sequence that we can call coagulation, because they grow from a colloidal size (very, very small—.001 microns) and change to become viruses and then bacteria, and then yeast, and then fungus, and then mold. Everybody has a little bit of all this. Eventually it reaches a critical amount and your composting switch is turned on. This occurs when the terrain has enough deranged cells. This is the theoretical onset of chronic disease.

In summary, the role of the protits is either to keep us healthy, building us up, or to turn us to compost and recycle us. Because of all the complexities in the conditions of the world, in the generally poor diet—the very high-sugar, acidifying, and junk-food diet that people are on—as well as the use of specific allopathic drugs that seem to set this degenerative process off, there are more and more people in the compost process of being recycled. This manifests very clearly as chronic disease. At this point, the protits are just doing their job. The Rainbow Green Live-Food Cuisine shows us how to do our job of keeping healthy.

*Please see the color section for microscope images of blood showing the pleomorphic theory in action.*

A picture is worth a thousand words. The dark-field, dry-field, and phase-contrast slides reveal the pleomorphic transformation from normal healthy red blood cells and protits to degenerating red blood cells and mutating protits that have become pathogenic forms called chondrites and various stages of mycotic (fungal and possible pre-cancer) forms called ascits. These pictures illustrate what it really means to have the self-composting button pushed.

Through the healing power of the Rainbow Green Live-Food Cuisine, after three months we often see the return to a normal blood picture, as in the first slide, and the reversal of the pathogenic dry-field picture back to a healthy dry-field picture, as illustrated by the second picture in each of the dry-field sequences.

*Chapter*

# Preventing
# the Composting of
# Western Civilization

Now that we have developed a theory to understand a major cause of chronic degenerative disease, that is, a deranged biological terrain, we need to identify the specific foods that disrupt the biological terrain. Factors other than diet can contribute to an acid-producing lifestyle, and while they are obviously important as part of any holistic viewpoint, they are not the subject of this book. A lifestyle that is overextended, filled with anxiety, fear, negativity, and stress; lacking adequate sleep; without proper exercise, breathing, and oxygenation, and proper work to move the lymph; and with the use of allopathic drugs as mentioned in the previous chapter that tend to disrupt the healthy balance—all of this certainly enhances the potential for deranging the biological terrain. This book focuses on foods that disrupt the biological terrain—and the foods that heal it. The upcoming chapters are intended to motivate and prepare you for fully appreciating the incredibly tasty, gourmet Rainbow Green Live-Food Cuisine that awaits you.

We start our discussion with the foods that clearly disrupt the biological terrain and diminish the negative charge of the red blood cells. These are foods that are high in fungal forms and mycotoxins, high in sugar content, animal fats, mushrooms, commercial salt, saturated vegetable oils, margarine, butter, soy sauce, dairy products, pastries, creams, and commercial irradiated, genetically engineered, microwaved fast foods. In essence, these high-sugar, fatty, salty, pastry foods, although they taste good to many people, accelerate the process of rotting or the composting of all of Western civilization.

In my opinion, the number-one type of food that deranges the biological terrain is any food that is high in **sugar.** This sugar is not limited to white sugar but includes fruits that contain a high amount of sugar or have a high glycemic index. A high-glycemic index food is one that converts rapidly to sugar in the blood. It includes processed beet and corn sugar, sorbital, fructose, maple syrup, dried and sweet fruits, melons, and all refined carbohydrates, such as white flour, white sugar, white rice, rice cakes, some grains, and white potatoes. It is absolutely essential to eliminate these from the diet in order to restore the biological terrain to normal and to decrease and eliminate the mycosis that most people have. Some questions have been raised about the herb stevia that is used to provide a sweet taste. It has no calories or carbohydrates, and according to a study in Brazil (*J. Medical Biological Res* 1986; 19(6):771-4), stevioside, the active ingredient, does not raise blood glucose. In all subjects in the study, it lowered blood glucose.

Because of the overall shift in our environment to one of significant mycotoxic stress, we have developed the Rainbow Green Live-Food Cuisine to provide a contemporary optimal diet: the diet of choice for the evolutionary healing of the individual and the planet, as well as for the awakening of consciousness in the twenty-first century. It has a minimum of fruits and only includes moderate- to low-glycemic fruits. Fruits tend to ferment very easily and to develop fungus, yeast, and mold. If you cut leafy greens and you cut open a fruit, there would be no question about which would ferment first; it would be the fruit. This is a minimal fruit diet which does not include any high-glycemic fruit juice. One of the worst offenders of all is apple juice, because it contains a mycotoxin called patulin, which has been shown to induce mammary tumors in mice according to the *British Journal of Cancer,* 1965. I am not saying that one should never have diluted apple juice on occasion, or when doing a juice fast, but this is not something one should have on a regular basis, and absolutely not when one is in the first phase of the treatment program to undo the mycosis.

**Grains** constitute the next class of yeast/fungi/mold-stimulating foods after the high-sugar foods and fruits in particular. Research shows that stored grains ferment in ninety days. Within that time many mycotoxins are produced. In essence, stored grains are a mycotoxic hazard. A correlation was found between 112 patients with esophageal cancer and eating of stored grains (*Cancer,* 1987). There was a particular risk factor for stomach cancer among Scandinavian and German men eating stored grains reported in *The Fungal/Mycotoxin Etiology of Human Disease,* vol 2. Stored potatoes also represent a mycotoxic risk. The black spots on them are caused by the fungi aspergillus and fusarium, which produce the mycotoxins aflatoxin and fumosium. Some grains are *not* stored and therefore are not a mycotoxic hazard. These include spelt, amaranth, quinoa, millet, buckwheat, and wild rice. Buckwheat is often thought of as a seed, but it is actually classified as a grain. Buckwheat and quinoa are the only grain-like foods that we use on a regular basis at the Tree of Life Café because they can be sprouted and served live. Our latest research shows that wild rice, widely believed to be raw, apparently is not. (See "The Secrets of Preparing Rainbow Green Live-Food Cuisine" for more on wild rice.)

In discussing this topic, I do not want to be in a position of going "against the grain" of society, but as I look closely at this issue, I need to point out the effect of grain on our society and our health. For five million years, humans thrived without using grains. Explorers have found that many societies world-wide never really used grains, including the Polynesians and early Africans. As we look at global food needs, it is clear that compared to meat-eating, switching to grains would meet our worldwide food problems. You can feed forty times more people on grains before the grains are eaten by livestock than once they have been converted to meat. Grain consumption is certainly better for the world and personal health than eating animals and dairy. However, eating grains does not take us to the highest octave of health that we can achieve.

Historical records suggest that humanity thrived on a diet primarily composed of vegetables, fruits, nuts, and seeds. Grains were not included in this. The only natural grain eaters are birds. In hard-core reality, bread does not exist in nature. To eat grains, we usually have to cook them. Some grains, however, can be sprouted, and we can make some adjustments to make the grains taste good—but the question is: *"Do we need to make adjustments so we can eat grains?"* Foods that require cooking to be consumed probably are not very good nutritionally for humans, even before cooking. By cooking them, we further compromise their nutritional value, because the vitamins, minerals, enzymes, co-enzymes, carbohydrates, proteins, and fats are damaged or destroyed by the heat of cooking. What we get with grains after they have been cooked is the maximum amount of calories with the minimum amount of nutrients.

Most grains create acidity except for buckwheat and millet. Grains contain very little calcium and are also low in sodium, chlorine, iodine, sulfur, and other minerals. In fact, vegetables as well as fruits contain from ten to a hundred times more calcium and other base minerals per calorie than grains. But grains do contain high amounts of acid-forming minerals. Grains are primarily acid-forming. We must remember that acidity is one of the main things that push the recycle or rotting button. In order to neutralize some of the uric acid from grains, our bodies use up available calcium and must pull calcium from our bones to replace the loss. In order to deal with the poor or bland taste of cooked or even raw sprouted grains, we end up having to add flavoring agents such as salt, fats, oils, refined sugar, dried fruits, or other fruits and spices. Many of these condiments contribute to the pushing of the recycling button. There is a tendency to balance the grains with fats in our diet, and again we run into a bit of a problem because many of these fats tend to support fungal growth. We often see jelly or butter on toast, or sour cream on corn chips, or a cheese sandwich; all are things that we use to balance the taste of grain. So we find ourselves living through a high-grain and -fat diet. Neither is particularly good for health. Grains are especially noted for their high fiber content. However, humans have more sensitive systems, and we require what is given to us naturally in nature, which is the soft, soluble fiber found in fruits and vegetables. Grain fiber is coarse and sharp non-soluble fiber. While it helps to clear things out, it also acts as an irritant in our system, and irritating the colon can actually worsen certain conditions, such as irritable bowel. The presence of non-soluble grain fiber in the intestines causes food to move from the bowels more rapidly than usual. This reduces nutrient absorption.

Grains do not rot like fruit, but they do ferment. This fermentation is the mixture of the starch, sugar, and sometimes the yeast. The result of these products is alcohol and gas. The alcohol is a mycotoxic by-product and can create what we refer to by the phrase "food drunk." Alcohol is a protoplasmic poison, which means that it has a negative effect on any cell in the body. Grains generally have been associated with a series of problems: allergies, asthma, gluten and gliadin intolerance, digestive disturbances, yeast infections, various mucous and congestive conditions, and several types of arthritis. These are, of course, linked with mycosis, either directly by eating grains, or indirectly through eating the animals that feed on them and drinking the animals' milk. A high percentage of my clients have grain allergies and get much better when they stop eating grains. Grain allergies not only cause the typical mucous membrane irritation, congestion, asthma, and sinusitis, but can have an effect on the mental state as well. Gluten, an ingredient in many grain products, has been associated with several forms of mental and neurological disorders. Some research has found that gluten contains fifteen different opioid sequences (morphine-like molecules). These can add to the addictiveness and neurotoxic effect of the grains. I believe that these opioids are in some way connected to the addictive eating patterns associated with grains, as well as to some learning disorders and to schizophrenic reactions in some people.

Not only do grains on their own create problems, but many toxic chemicals are used in the processing of grains. These include mercury, cyanide, ammonium, salt, chlorine, fluorine, mineral oil, alum, and aspartame.

In my experience as a psychiatrist and holistic physician, I see many people with eating disorders. Many have problems with starches, especially the white-flour, white-sugar starches that we call pastries. The eating of these foods seems to be very much connected with blood-sugar imbalances, depression, and short-term highs. It seems that most people do not binge on vegetables, but they do binge on starches. Starchy foods are the number-one choice to "calm and comfort." One name for this addiction is "starchaholic." Additional symptoms of starchaholics include an immediate clarity that they feel when they have their sweet or starch, which moves to confusion; and changes in mental state from well-being to negativity and depression, from cooperative to uncooperative, from peaceful to aggressive, from a sensitive, tuned-in person to one who is numb, from energetic (which may happen initially for a few minutes to one half-hour or an hour) to lethargic. These symptoms are very common. As people begin to withdraw from these starches there often is emotional pain associated with the withdrawal, which creates a tremendous drive to have that piece of cake or pizza in order to feel better. Sometimes after stuffing themselves with their pastries, starchaholics fall asleep. The most common tip-off sign of being a starchaholic is the frequent use of and powerful cravings for starches. In America, people may be having starchy foods as often as three times a day, and then even more often as snacks. There is also a tendency to overeat starchy foods such as pasta and pizza, because we get such a slow rise in the blood sugar that the appetite control is not turned off until we have already overeaten. There is a tendency in starchaholics to put on a significant amount of weight.

From an ecological point of view, grain consumption is significantly better than consuming livestock, but when compared to fruit orchards and vegetable growth we see that almost 250% more people can be fed with an acre of orchard than with an acre of grain. So even though it is an improvement, it is still not the most beneficial path. It is really the same with health: from the vegetarian and vegan point of view, clearly grains are a more healthy food than flesh and dairy. But compared to live, raw vegetables and a little bit of fruits, nuts, and seeds, grains are a very poor second choice. Not only are most grains stored, which is why we have the mycotoxin problem, but once the grains are harvested and milled, they lose a significant amount of their nutritive value. There is no such thing as "fresh bread." Most flour may be years old before it is used. Not only am I concerned about the mold and fungus in storage, but infestation of insects and rodents. The freshest foods are, of course, vegetables, nuts, fruits, and seeds that are picked directly from the garden.

The bottom line is simply this: from the perspective of how to create a low-mycotoxic diet, stored grains feed the mycotoxicity and therefore create a highly mycotoxic diet. They do this because: (1) most grains create acidity, which further alters the biological terrain, and (2) most grains are kept in storage, giving them the chance to begin the fermentation process and, therefore, are filled with mold and fungus and a high amount of mycotoxins. For these two reasons, the Rainbow Green Live-Food Cuisine does not include grains, except for a moderate amount of sprouted quinoa and sprouted buckwheat.

**Flesh and dairy foods** represent another class of foods that seem to be closely associated with mycotoxins. One of the main reasons is that these animals and their milk are heavily affected by their fungally infected feed—grains that have been kept in long-term storage. Meat and dairy are also acidifying to the system. I had an interesting experience discovering this with two live-food clients. I often observe people's blood with a dark-field microscope, and one of my clients who was on 100% live foods had very clean blood. One day, however, when I looked at his blood, it was full of all kinds of yeast and fungal forms. I asked him, "What's going on?" He told me that for a few weeks he had been drinking raw goat's milk. Since that was the only change and because he wasn't particularly sick, I said, "Let's do an experiment. No raw goat's milk for a few weeks, and let me look at your blood again." After three weeks, I saw him again and his blood was back to normal. This was a very strong message to me because I had assumed that most of the mycotoxic evidence in the dark-field exam was from cattle and cow's milk. I don't know if this goat was being fed grain, but it makes me aware that all animal products—no matter how organic, raw, or homegrown—are likely to have this mycotoxic effect.

*The Fungal/Mycotoxin Etiology of Human Disease,* Vol. 2, 1994, lists the amounts of pathogenic microorganisms found in various foods. Grade A pasteurized milk has 5,000,000 microorganisms/pathogens per cup; cheese has 100,000,000 per serving; a single egg has 37,000,000; beef, poultry, lamb, and seafood have 336,000,000 per serving. The average American meal of animal products has approximately 750 million to 1 billion pleomorphic pathogenic microorganisms. The average vegan meal (only plant foods) contains less than 500 pleomorphic pathogenic microorganisms. In other words, the average vegan meal has between one and two million times less pleomorphic pathogenic microorganisms than a dairy-, egg-, or flesh-based meal.

When meat is aged, it is partially fermented and thus has many more mycotoxins in it. Actually, once an animal is killed, the recycling begins instantly. These protits do their job. They move from health to breaking the system down and composting it. One particularly strong piece of research to this effect that Robert Young cites in his book is that mutton (which is aged, fermented lamb) was found to be associated with "an epidemic" of juvenile diabetes in newborns following Christmas holidays. My theoretical explanation of this is that the uric acid, given off as part of the mycotoxins, breaks down to alloxan. Alloxan has been found to specifically destroy the beta cells, or insulin-producing cells, in the pancreas.

As far as I am concerned, almost any commercial meat is filled with mycotoxins, due to how the animals are fed, the storage of the meat, and because it is already in the rotting cycle. Research suggests that eggs from grain-fed chickens also contain much higher mycotoxin content. Many animal products contain fatty streaks, which tend to ferment more quickly and produce uric acid and other mycotoxins. There are many reasons not to eat dairy and meat, but from the point of view of this book, we are focusing on the mycotoxic aspect in particular. In terms of global and human ecology, the whole livestock industry is a significant disaster. In my book *Conscious Eating,* I go into great detail about the deleterious effects of eating meat and dairy.

Foods with a notably high mycotoxin and fungal count are corn, peanuts,

## Pathogenic Microorganisms

| | |
|---|---|
| Honey | 5 million per cup |
| Milk | 5 million per cup |
| Butter | 7 million per cup |
| Eggs | 37 million per egg |
| Cheese | 100 million per serving |
| Ice Cream | 225 million per serving |
| Beef, Poultry, Fish | 336 million per serving |
| Average American Meal | 750 million to 1 billion per meal |
| Average Vegan Meal | 500 per meal |

From: *The Fungal/Mycotoxin Etiology of Human Disease*, Vol. 2, 1994.

cottonseed, cashews, barley, oats, wheat, and malted products. Peanuts on the average contain twenty-six different carcinogenic fungi, especially aflatoxin. Research presented in *Cancer* (1971) showed a connection with liver cancer and peanuts containing aflatoxins. Corn contains twenty-five mycotoxic fungi. Research reported in several published studies (*International Journal of Cancer*) shows that corn ingestion is associated with cancer of the esophagus and gastric cancer. Corn is a particularly difficult food to avoid because so many cultures use it, but in the context of the mycotoxic-free diet, corn is a hazard. It is important to understand that most of these mycotoxins are heat-insensitive, and therefore are not affected or diminished by the heat of cooking.

One of the main foods to avoid is **yeast,** baker's yeast, nutritional yeast, and brewer's yeast. The classification we are talking about is *Saccharomyces cerevisiae*. As discussed earlier, wheat itself has a high mycotoxic level. Baked goods like bread, muffins, pies, cakes, and pastries increase the degree of mycotoxicosis, because now we have added the yeast content to it.

Regular consumption of brewer's yeast, according to Dr. Young's research, has been associated with breast and prostate cancer and liver problems, as well as Crohn's disease, colitis, heart and kidney disease, cirrhosis, and osteo-arthritis. Japanese research has linked breast cancer with ingestion of baked goods. Researchers have also found that breast secretions in breast cancer patients are high in mycotoxins.

I strongly recommend avoiding **alcohol,** which is a primary mycotoxin, and it turns out that alcohol can also convert back into acid aldehyde. **Soy sauce,** which is fermented by *Aspergillus flavus,* is another food on the mycosis black list. In all soy products that are heated, MSG is naturally created as a by-product. This includes nama shoyu, which is a cooked soy-wheat-barley combination that is then fermented, though not pasteurized. It is both an MSG and high-mycotoxin product.

**Edible mushrooms** are another common food that is highly mycotic. Mushrooms are acid-forming and full of mycotoxins. All contain various lev-els of amanitin. Some are immediately poisonous and others with lower con-centrations may cause slower-moving chronic diseases. One cancer researcher, Dr. B. Toth, found that the mycotoxins in mushrooms were associated with can-cer in the lungs, liver, thyroid, nasal cavity, stomach, colon, and gallbladder in mice. According to *Sick and Tired,* all mushrooms contain a minimum of five active ingredients that have been shown to cause cancer in animals.

**Coffee** and **caffeine** create acidification of the tissues. **Tobacco,** which for many reasons we do not advise using, is a problem if the tobacco is cured (fermented) because the commercial companies use sugar and yeast in the curing process. The tobacco then has very high levels of yeast, fungus, and mycotoxins, which are taken directly into the lungs. Some people believe that cancer is not so much caused by the nicotine as by the fermented tobacco with the yeast and fungus and mycotoxins. In *Fungal/Mycotoxin Etiology of Human Disease,* Vol. 2, the mycotoxic fungi *Alternaria* and *Aspergillus niger* were found in six brands of commercial cigarettes. It is interesting to note that cigars, which are not cured, do not seem to cause cancer and do not seem to have much fun-gus. (I am not recommending, however, that people take up cigar smoking.) Research in *Fungal/Mycotoxin Etiology of Human Disease,* Vol. 2, found that in some

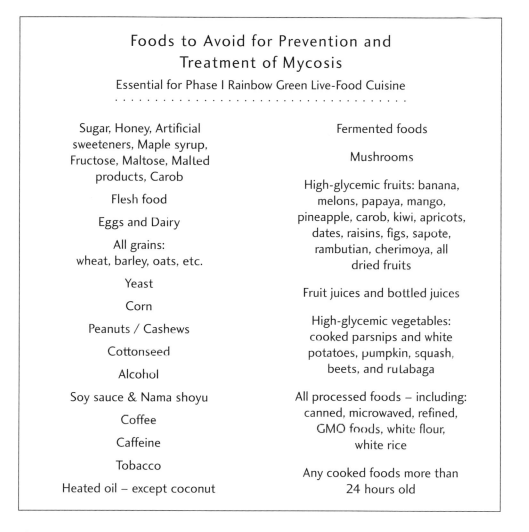

## Foods to Avoid for Prevention and Treatment of Mycosis

### Essential for Phase I Rainbow Green Live-Food Cuisine

Sugar, Honey, Artificial sweeteners, Maple syrup, Fructose, Maltose, Malted products, Carob

Flesh food

Eggs and Dairy

All grains: wheat, barley, oats, etc.

Yeast

Corn

Peanuts / Cashews

Cottonseed

Alcohol

Soy sauce & Nama shoyu

Coffee

Caffeine

Tobacco

Heated oil – except coconut

Fermented foods

Mushrooms

High-glycemic fruits: banana, melons, papaya, mango, pineapple, carob, kiwi, apricots, dates, raisins, figs, sapote, rambutian, cherimoya, all dried fruits

Fruit juices and bottled juices

High-glycemic vegetables: cooked parsnips and white potatoes, pumpkin, squash, beets, and rutabaga

All processed foods – including: canned, microwaved, refined, GMO foods, white flour, white rice

Any cooked foods more than 24 hours old

chewing tobacco, there are nine species of *Aspergillus,* providing a variety of cancer-producing mycotoxins including ochratoxin, patulin (also found in apple juice), aflatoxin, and sterigmatocystin. Research found that cigarette smokers also have a higher amount of fungi in their mouth; *Candida albicans* is especially increased.

Another food to be aware of is **heated oils** because they are disorganized from their original, biological, natural state and become loaded with myco-toxins. Non-heated, virgin olive oil does not seem to have mycotoxins in it.

Foods that I consider anti-mycotic are primarily vegetables, grasses, sea vegetables, nuts, seeds, low-glycemic fruits, and algae. They are alkalinizing and do not have yeast in them. Greens are low-calorie, low-sugar, and high-nutrient-rich foods. The vegetables and grasses contain high fiber and no sugar.

In summary, in the anti-mycotic diet we have eliminated a great many foods. A part of my work at the Tree of Life has been to answer the following question: how does the Tree of Life Café create a cuisine that gives us optimal health and optimal support to our natural living colloid system, and is a joy to eat? This is the magic of the recipes of the Rainbow Green Live-Food Cuisine.

## THE PHASES OF RAINBOW GREEN LIVE-FOOD CUISINE

The Rainbow Green Live-Food Cuisine is divided into two major phases. Phase I, usually for the first three months, is for people who are highly mycotoxic. This phase is essentially greens, vegetables, nuts and seeds, and grasses. It includes sprouted foods, particularly if one sprouts them oneself and is careful to spray them with hydrogen peroxide in order to minimize the chance of fungal growth. It also includes high-colloidal foods that are rich in the super-colloid minerals: iridium, rhodium, and gold. These are aloe leaf, grape seeds, slippery elm, watercress, St. John's wort, bloodroot, bilberry and sheep sorrel, as well as leafy greens in general. The Phase I diet does not include any fruits (except salad fruits such as tomato, avocado, and cucumber), grains, mushrooms, dairy, flesh foods, or any high-sugar foods.

A subphase of the diet called Phase I.5 is the primary phase of the diet for people with a mild to moderate mycosis. In addition to all of the Phase I foods, it includes low-glycemic fruits, fermented foods, and non-stored grains. Recent research has shown, surprisingly, that carrots have a relatively low glycemic index, contrary to the taste, which is often sweet. So we feel very good about using carrots in Phase I.5.

We have included a sweetener that has been a breakthrough for us, which is coconut. Research shows that fresh coconut is high in caprylic acid and lauric

---

## PHASE I - Rainbow Green Live-Food Cuisine
### Organic - Raw - Whole

Nuts and Seeds

Most Raw Vegetables
(those NOT on the high-glycemic list,
or Phase I.5 or Phase II list)

Vegetable Fruits
such as Avocados, Tomatoes,
Cucumbers, Summer Squashes,
Red Bell Pepper

Lemon & Lime

Sea Vegetables such as Nori,
Wakame, Kelp, Hijiki, Dulse

Oils:
Flax, Hemp, Olive,
Sesame, Coconut, Almond,
Sunflower

Coconut Pulp

Chlorella and Spirulina

Klamath Lake Algae

Legumes

Stevia

---

acid. (This does not apply to dried coconut, which can tend to be mycotoxic like many things that are dried and stored.) Caprylic acid is extremely effective as an anti-fungal and anti-mycotic substance. Lauric acid is particularly good as an anti-viral substance. So, in this balance, coconut, which does have carbohydrate, also has caprylic acid, which minimizes its potential mycotoxic effect. I have found that people are able to do very well on the diet with the addition of coconut pulp on Phase I and coconut water on Phase I.5 because it adds a sense of sweetness and therefore the minimum of taste balancing for this cleansing diet.

Phase II of the Rainbow Green Live-Food Cuisine is what we offer at the Tree of Life Café as our normal diet, although Phase I is always available too. Phase II of the Rainbow Green Live Food Cuisine is the life-long health maintenance and joy-cultivating diet. This, in essence, is a high life-force energy and mycotoxic prevention diet. For those of you who need to be on Phase I for three months, it is relatively easy to pick out the recipes in the book that are most appropriate for your needs, as they are marked as Phase I, Phase I.5, or Phase II. (Entries listing the recipes according to phase may be found in the

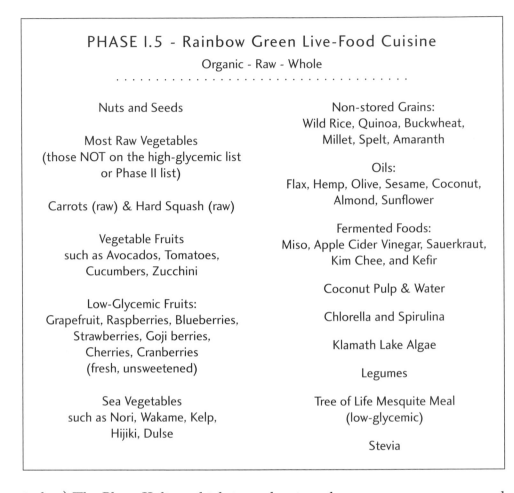

## PHASE I.5 - Rainbow Green Live-Food Cuisine
### Organic - Raw - Whole

Nuts and Seeds

Most Raw Vegetables
(those NOT on the high-glycemic list
or Phase II list)

Carrots (raw) & Hard Squash (raw)

Vegetable Fruits
such as Avocados, Tomatoes,
Cucumbers, Zucchini

Low-Glycemic Fruits:
Grapefruit, Raspberries, Blueberries,
Strawberries, Goji berries,
Cherries, Cranberries
(fresh, unsweetened)

Sea Vegetables
such as Nori, Wakame, Kelp,
Hijiki, Dulse

Non-stored Grains:
Wild Rice, Quinoa, Buckwheat,
Millet, Spelt, Amaranth

Oils:
Flax, Hemp, Olive, Sesame, Coconut,
Almond, Sunflower

Fermented Foods:
Miso, Apple Cider Vinegar, Sauerkraut,
Kim Chee, and Kefir

Coconut Pulp & Water

Chlorella and Spirulina

Klamath Lake Algae

Legumes

Tree of Life Mesquite Meal
(low-glycemic)

Stevia

index.) The Phase II diet, which is predominantly greens, grasses, nuts, and seeds and a moderate amount of low- and moderate-glycemic fruits, offers a very healthy, enjoyable, long-term health-building and -maintaining, delicious cuisine. This is a health breakthrough cuisine that one can enjoy and feel good about for the rest of one's life. Phase II does include a certain amount of low-glycemic fruits, including apples, pears, citrus (not orange juice, but whole citrus). These all seem to be low- to moderate-glycemic foods. My observation has been that once people have significantly diminished their mycotoxic load, they are able to handle this addition of low- and moderate-glycemic fruit to their diet.

## PHASE II - Rainbow Green Live-Food Cuisine
### Organic – Raw – Whole

Nuts and Seeds

All Raw Vegetables

Vegetable Fruits
such as Avocados, Tomatoes,
Cucumbers, Zucchini

High-Glycemic Vegetables
(in raw form only):
Yams, Sweet Potatoes, Beets, Parsnips,
Pumpkin, Squash, Rutabaga

Low-Glycemic Fruits:
Lemon, Lime, Grapefruit, Strawberries,
Cherries, Fresh Cranberries

Moderate-Glycemic Fruits:
Oranges, Apples, Pears, Peaches,
Plums, Pomegranates, Goji Berries,
Blackberries

High-Glycemic Fruits
(in strict moderation only)

Grapefruit & Orange Juice
(diluted)

Sea Vegetables
such as Nori, Wakame, Kelp,
Hijiki, Dulse

Non-stored Grains:
Quinoa, Buckwheat, Millet,
Amaranth, Spelt, Wild Rice

Oils:
Flax, Hemp, Olive, Sesame,
Coconut, Almond, Sunflower

Coconut Pulp & Coconut Water

Non-Fermented Soy Products
(as a transition food)

Fermented Foods:
Miso, Apple Cider Vinegar, Sauerkraut,
Kim Chee, and Kefir

Chlorella and Spirulina

Klamath Lake Algae

Tree of Life Mesquite & Raw Carob

Stevia

Bee Pollen

The following is a well-researched glycemic list that is based on several studies.

High-glycemic fruits may be used occasionally after the "composting switch" is turned off. Most vegetables are low-glycemic. Certain vegetables are high-glycemic when cooked—parsnips, rutabaga, pumpkin, squash, and beets—but they are part of the Phase II diet in moderate amounts in their raw form.

## Glycemic Levels of Fruits and Vegetables

| HIGH | MODERATE | LOW |
|---|---|---|
| Apricot | Carrots | Most Vegetables |
| Melons (all) | Oranges | Grapefruit |
| Kiwi | Peaches | Lemon |
| Mango | Pears | Lime |
| Papaya | Apples | Cherries |
| Pineapple | Pomegranate | Strawberries |
| Banana | Plums | Cranberries |
| Date | Some Berries | Raspberries |
| Fig | Peas | Gogi Berries |
| Raisins | Yams | Blueberries |
| Grapes | Sweet Potatoes | |
| Most Dried Fruits | Parsnip (raw) | |
| Parsnip (cooked) | Rutabaga (raw) | |
| Rutabaga (cooked) | Pumpkin & Squash (raw) | |
| Pumpkin & Squash (cooked) | Beet (raw) | |
| Beet (cooked) | | |
| White Potato | | |

Good data are not yet available on berries, but I suspect most are low- to moderate-glycemic, depending on the berry.

There are certain foods that one should avoid completely or use rarely. They are foods that deplete health, are too high in sugar, or high in molds and fungi. The following is a list of foods to avoid on Rainbow Green Live-Food Cuisine.

For fast and easy reference, we have provided a summary table below of Phase I, Phase I.5, and Phase II foods, as well as foods to avoid.

## Foods to Avoid for Optimal Health
on Rainbow Green Live-Food Cuisine

all cooked foods

all processed foods including:
canned, microwaved, refined,
non-organic, GMO foods

all animal products:
flesh, dairy, eggs

grains:
wheat, barley, oats, etc.
(except non-stored grains)

corn

white potatoes, white rice, white flour

sugar, honey, artificial sweeteners,
maple syrup, fructose, maltose

yeast

alcohol

coffee

caffeine

tobacco

heated oil
(except coconut)

all soy products
including nama shoyu

mushrooms

peanuts & cashews

cottonseed

bottled fruit juices

# TRANSITIONING TO RAINBOW GREEN LIVE-FOOD CUISINE

Transitioning to the Rainbow Green Live-Food Cuisine requires a certain level of thoughtfulness, patience, and trial and error. Phase I of the diet is meant for people who have a variety of chronic degenerative diseases and any form of significant mycosis including candida. Phase I is truly a low-glycemic diet that has the highest level of anti-mycosis effect. After a minimum of three months in Phase I, usually the candida or other levels of chronic disease improve so that one's sense of well-being and health grows. When this is so it is time to move to Phase I.5 or Phase II. Phase II is a maintenance diet. It is very important to distinguish between an intense anti-mycosis diet, which

# Summary of Food Phases Chart

| Phase I | Phase I.5 | Phase II | Phase II Minimal Use | Rainbow Green Live-Food Cuisine Foods to Avoid |
|---|---|---|---|---|
| nuts & seeds | coconut water (diluted with other ingredients) | yams (raw) sweet potatoes (raw) pumpkin (raw) | yams (cooked) sweet potatoes (cooked) pumpkin (cooked) | all processed foods |
| coconut pulp | | | | all animal products: flesh |
| all greens | carrots (raw) | parsnips (raw) | parsnips (cooked) | dairy |
| all vegetables (excepted those listed elsewhere) | hard squash (raw) grapefruit | beets (raw) rutabaga (raw) | beets (cooked) rutabaga (cooked) hard squash (cooked) | eggs all grains (except those listed) |
| | | oranges | summer squash (cooked) | |
| summer squash (raw): zucchini patti pan yellow summer squash | raspberries blueberries strawberries cherries cranberries (fresh, unsweetened) goji berries | apples pears peaches plums pomegranates blackberries | straight carrot juice straight orange juice high-glycemic fruits: apricots figs | corn white potatoes white rice white flour honey |
| sea vegetables | low-glycemic Tree of Life | grapefruit juice (diluted with water) | grapes raisins | sugar alcohol |
| tomatoes avocados cucumber red bell pepper | mesquite meal non-stored grains: wild rice | raw carob bee pollen | melons mangos bananas papaya | coffee caffeine tobacco |
| flax oil hemp oil olive oil sesame oil almond oil sunflower oil coconut oil (butter) | quinoa buckwheat millet amaranth spelt | unfermented soy products (as a transition food) | pineapple kiwi sapote cherimoya rambutian durian | heated oil (except coconut oil) soy sauce & nama shoyu |
| | fermented foods: apple cider vinegar | | dates | yeast brewer's yeast |
| lemons limes | miso sauerkraut kefir | | dried fruits fresh, raw, fruit juices | nutritional yeast mushrooms |
| Klamath Lake algae | | | seed cheese | peanuts |
| super green powders | | | cooked, organic, whole foods | cashews cottonseed |
| stevia | | | | bottled juices |

is Phase I, and the maintenance diet, which is easier to follow. The word "Phase" implies that if one really takes care of one's health and all the aspects of life, one will move from the first phase to the next phase of maintenance. Phase II is a diet appropriate for the rest of one's life. Some people need to stay on Phase I or Phase I.5 for as much as six months. If you are committed to the diet, it takes from three to six months for most chronic disease to become reversed enough that you can move to the maintenance phase. The idea of maintenance still includes a high-quality anti-mycosis diet, as explained already in this chapter. It does not mean you can slip back into sweets and junk food.

During the transition to Phase I, which most people need to go on immediately because most people are actively composting, there is often an increase in food cravings and some detoxification experience. It is very important to understand that this is part of the process. Although some people have no trouble being on Phase I—comfortable and happy and feeling tremendously healthy on the diet—other people, because of their psychological attachment to foods or physical toxicity, really do suffer from tremendous food cravings or physical discomfort. Another cause of food cravings is the fact that fungus loves sugar and will subtly push you to eat sweets so it can survive. When you go on the Phase I diet, it is death to the fungi, and they do not like it. Part of the issue is mastering the basic will power it requires to stay on the Phase I diet when you have a strong mycosis infection, and you really want to turn off the compost button.

The "Foods to Avoid for Optimal Health on Rainbow Green Live-Food Cuisine" Table notes that all **cooked foods** should be avoided to attain *optimal health.* However, in the process of transitioning to a live-food diet we need to be gentle and peaceful with ourselves. During the transition it may be necessary to create a ratio of 80% live foods to 20% organic, whole, cooked foods. Most of these cooked foods may be non-stored grains.

One of the truly positive things about transitioning to the Rainbow Green Live-Food Cuisine is the quality of life experience that one begins to have. There is an increase in joy, well-being, happiness, and energy; depression lifts, and the mind begins to open up to higher potentialities. This really helps to encourage and support the change. An important thing to remember is that it may not happen right away. It may take three months or more.

What is really helpful, if possible, is to get plenty of group support from the people around you. If that means joining a live-food group, connecting with the Tree of Life in some sort of supportive way, or working with loved ones who really care about you returning to the highest quality of life, do it. This can be the most important factor in making this step toward health. Other supportive lifestyle changes include moderate exercise, Yoga, meditation, and breathing exercises, all of which increase that feeling of well-being. The choice to go on the Rainbow Green Live-Food Cuisine has to do with loving yourself and caring enough about yourself to go through the transition time of turning off the compost button so that you can live the life of joy and health and well-being.

There are really no other secrets to this, except to Do It. This book is about how to do it. It gives you the technology and the reasoning, but ultimately, only you the reader can make that decision and develop the will power. One does not need to have a chronic disease and to be in a heavy state of composting to go on the Rainbow Green Live-Food Cuisine. It really applies to most everyone in Western civilization who has been eating a fungus-supporting, composting diet.

Phase I is explained as the phase that shuts off the composting button. Phase II is the part that keeps it shut off. Occasionally we slip on the maintenance program and need to go back to Phase I. It sometimes takes up to two years or more to permanently turn off the composting button. After three months we often shut it down, but to permanently switch it off one needs to be very solid on the Phase II diet for at least two years. It seems to be the human condition to occasionally go back to the composting diet and turn the button on again. In that case, we simply go back to Phase I and then stay there for three months. Then, moving back to Phase II again, we maintain it for several years at least. After those several years are up, one really still needs to stay on Phase II, but when there is a slip, because the system has shifted its biological terrain back to relatively normal, we don't turn on the composting button again so read-ily. In other words, there is more of a buffer for occasional times of imbalance. This is an important, subtle observation I have noticed in clients—once they were able to maintain a live-food diet for a period of time, when they went off it in periods of relapse, they were able to come back on it. They did not particularly undermine their health if they did not stay off a live-food diet for too long. After a body has re-equilibrated its biological terrain, one can vary from the Phase II Rainbow Green Live-Food Cuisine protocol for short periods of time without turning on the composting button. This is the good news. But we need to remember that it takes between one and one-half to two years to firmly establish the turning off of the composting button, and a con-tinually healthy life requires basic adherence to the live-food diet and lifestyle.

The abundant joy, health, and quality of life that people experience on the Phase I and Phase II Rainbow Green Live-Food Cuisine is really worth the journey that you have the opportunity to begin.

*Chapter*

# How to Develop the Best Diet for Yourself

The key to creating the optimal diet for yourself is to understand that there is no single best diet for everyone. This is contrary to the fallacy of allopathic thinking which, as a rule, does not address the person's underlying biochemical individuality. Recently the human genome research by the federal government's National Institutes of Health (NIH) found as many as 1.4 million variations in the human DNA. With this data, it is not surprising that those of us living in the human condition should have at least several different basic diets to choose among, according to our genetic physiology. The point is, there is no single diet nor a specific supplement regimen that works for everyone and every disease.

At present, the shortcomings of allopathic thinking have permeated the health marketplace. Dietary systems have been outlined, many with opposing philosophies, and all sporting thousands of faithful testimonies by their adherents, who shout from the rooftops that their diet is the right way for everyone who would just try it, whether it be cooked foods, macrobiotics, raw foods, the low-protein vegetarian diet, Fit for Life diet, the Atkins diet, a high-protein and fat flesh-food diet, the McDougal-Pritikin high-complex-carbohydrate diet, or the Sears Zone diet. The question one has to raise is: how could these different systems be right for everybody? Of course, the answer is—they are not.

If we look closely at all of these diets, and the people who follow them, we find a curious phenomenon. All of these diets do seem to work, but only for about one-third to one-half of the people—the ones who give the glowing testimonials. Each diet guru has all kinds of reasons for why their diet is the best, but they do not explain why it doesn't work for the other two-thirds of the population. The answer is very simple. It is found in the concept of biochemical individuality. In chapters 3, 4, and 5 of *Conscious Eating*, I go through in great detail the different types of diets and the process of how to individualize your diet. One aspect of the future of nutrition lies in continuing to discover the principles that determine metabolic bio-individuality. In this book, which is focused on understanding and putting into action the Rainbow Green Live-Food Cuisine, I will briefly mention several main concepts. To fully implement your own specific balancing diet, you will want to read about these topics in greater detail.

The first concept is a high-protein versus a low-protein diet. The second concept is the Ayurvedic approach, which involves the doshas. The third concept is the role of blood type in fine-tuning a diet.

## FAST- AND SLOW-OXIDIZER DIETS

Different physiological types require different "fuel mixtures" in order to create the right conditions for maximum cellular energy and expression of health. When we give our body the correct balance of proteins, fats, carbohydrates, vitamins, and minerals for our own physiologic pattern, we enter our personal "zone."

In this approach, the key principles of physiologic constitutions are as follows:

1. any nutrient and food can have opposite biochemical effects in different individuals;

2. any symptoms or degenerate conditions can be caused by opposite biochemical imbalances;

3. diseases are the result of underlying metabolic imbalances, and so the treatment of disease is the treatment of the underlying metabolic imbalance;

4. in a particular individual there is one homeostatic regulatory system that dominates these other systems;

5. which system dominates will determine how a particular diet or nutrient behaves in one's system;

6. to accurately select a proper diet and nutrients, one needs to know the dominant system and metabolic type.

Individual variations in the body's different homeostatic systems lead to ways of classifying physiologic types. The principle of metabolic dominance states that for each person, one constitutionally driven physiologic system is the ruling or most influential system in determining how the body will function on a particular nutritional regimen. Determining your dominant physiologic constitution is one of the keys to conscious eating.

Two of the most significant systems that control how food and supplements affect one's homeostatic mechanism are the oxidative system (fast, slow, and mixed oxidizer) and the autonomic system (sympathetic, parasympathetic, and balanced). By knowing one's dominant system, the choice and combination of foods is most effectively determined.

One basic diet is for those people who need to consume a higher percentage of protein. I want to make it clear that this does not require a flesh-based diet. People of this type have a variety of options. The basic way that we increase the ratio of protein intake in the Rainbow Green Live-Food Cuisine is with a variety of seed or nut pâtés, which are made from soaked nuts and seeds, sometimes with vegetables mixed in. This has been very successful for many people.

Those needing a diet with a high percentage of protein ("fast oxidizers" and "parasympathetics") can also add concentrates like spirulina or chlorella, which are extremely high (60–70%) in protein, or the various green drinks that are mixtures of high-protein algae. These algae are higher in protein than any other food in bulk in the market. In leafy greens, you also have a high concentration of protein, but you need to eat a whole lot of leafy greens to get the effect that a high-protein-diet person needs. The blue-green algae from Klamath Lake, called *Aphanizomenonon flos-aquae,* is 60–70% protein, but it is a very expensive source for bulk protein.

The high-protein-diet person requires about 50% protein. They need about 30% carbohydrate, which is very easy to get from the leafy greens and all of the other Rainbow Green Live-Food Cuisine vegetables. The high-protein diet also requires about 20% oil; again, this is very easy to get with avocados, nuts, and seeds. For these people, I usually recommend two to three tablespoons twice a day of ground flax seed. Flax seed is about 24% omega-3 fatty acid, which is extremely good. People can also use hemp seed, which has a similar percentage of omega-3. Unfortunately, most hemp seeds are irradiated, but the Tree of Life is able to supply hemp seeds and hemp protein that are raw and not irradiated.

By grinding the flax seeds fresh each day, we get a high percentage of fresh oils, which cannot be matched by getting it out of a package or bottled oil, and we get the protein from the seed. Flax seeds are also high in lignins. They have a hundred times more lignin production than any other oil seeds. The bacteria in the bowel convert these lignins into two phytoestrogens: entero-diol and enterolactone. Studies have shown that high levels of lignins can inhibit both the synthesis of estrogen and estrogen-stimulated breast cancer cell growth. These are just some of the advantages of flax seed. Other things to keep in mind include the fact that the lignins boost the immune system, and flax seed supplies healthy fiber. Flax supplies the short- and medium-chain omega-3 fatty acids. DHA (decosahexaenoic acid) can also be obtained commercially from concentrated forms of golden algae. DHA is the essential long-chain omega-3 fatty acid needed for brain development and the fatty acid found in highest concentration in the brain. A deficiency of DHA is associated with post-partum depression in women and lower IQ in DHA-deficient babies.

The one long-chain omega-3 fatty acid that is not available in a concentrated form is EPA (eicosapentanoic acid). For healthy vegans it is available in herbs such as purslane. For extreme metabolic situations such as manic depression, it is not available in commercial concentrated vegan form and must be obtained through fish oil.

Those people who require a relatively low percentage of protein and a higher complex-carbohydrate diet with a moderate or low amount of fat may be either a "slow oxidizer" or "sympathetic." The low-protein, high-carbohydrate diet is approximately 50% carbohydrate, 30–35% protein, and 10–15% oils. For these people, the traditional vegan diet that we think about—which is high in vegetables, with a little bit of fruit, a few nuts and seeds, and half an avocado a day—provides a fine balancing diet. The slow oxidizers/sympathetics really do not need to eat very big meals. Two moderate meals a day and a light snack may be sufficient. In contrast, fast-oxidizers/parasympathetics usually need to have a snack in between meals, totaling five to six meals and snacks per day. Slow-oxidizers/sympathetics also benefit from approximately one to two table-spoons of ground flax seeds, twice a day. The sympathetics/slow-oxidizers do not necessarily need to supplement with any other protein source, such as spirulina or chlorella. However, one of the easiest protein sources for them are the pâtés, as well as eating leafy greens that are moderately high in protein as compared to other vegetables. I discuss these concepts in detail in *Conscious Eating*.

A key concept in this dietary system is that the ratio needs to be the same for each meal. For example, if you are a person who requires a higher ratio of protein, it should be in the same ratio with carbohydrates and oils at each meal. At breakfast, lunch, and dinner, no matter how much you eat, it is best to keep it around 50% protein, 30–35% carbohydrate, and 20–25% oils. As mentioned above, fast oxidizers require the highest ratio of protein. The parasympathetic requires less protein and a little more carbohydrate. Some people classify vegetables as high-protein foods. The ratio of carbohydrates to protein in most vegetables is about 4 to 1, with the exception of carrots and beets, in which the ratio is about 8–1 to 9–1. Slow oxidizers and sympathetics need the lowest ratio of protein, ideally about 50–55% carbohydrate, 30–35% protein, and 10–15% oil.

There is a third type, which we call the "mixed oxidizer." This is essentially a mix between the fast and slow oxidizer. Their diet will be in the middle, a 40–40–20 ratio. When you have 1.4 million genetic variations, even these ratios should be considered guidelines or starting points for you to find the best mix for yourself. My clinical experience is that, aside from the extreme of high or low protein and mixed, there exists a variety of shades. These poles and middle realms are starting points from which one can fine-tune a diet through intuition and trial and error to reach an optimal dietary potential.

# AYURVEDIC DIETARY CONSIDERATIONS

The next major way to organize the personalization of your diet is the Ayurvedic system of *doshas.* Doshas are defined as "things that go out of balance." The three major doshas and combinations thereof comprise the equivalent of psychophysiological constitutional types, revealing that the ancients had insight and appreciation of the inherent differences and respective dietary prescriptions for the various constitutional or "mind-body" types. Ayurvedic medicine has been successfully used for thousands of years. It recognizes the importance of the specific energies of foods and herbs in balancing and healing the body. This system also acknowledges seasonal and other environmental influences. The Ayurvedic tridosha system offers another way to understand how the foods we eat directly affect our health and well-being. The three doshas are called **vata, kapha,** and **pitta.**

To give us a feeling for the different psychophysiological types, we can think of the vata dosha as the air-ether type. These are people with a tremendous amount of kinetic energy and movement in the mind, intestines, muscles, and nerve impulses. They tend to have more difficulties with the nervous system, more aches and pains in muscles and joints, and more large intestine problems than other types. The second type is called kapha, which represents the water-earth elements. They are like potential energy. They have an excess of body fluids and mucus. Their digestion is usually slow. They tend to have problems with their lungs, upper respiratory congestion, colds and flus. The next type is called pitta, which is represented by fire and metabolism. They are hot-blooded individuals with strong, fast digestive systems.

People with a vata constitution are generally thin, flat-chested, have protruding veins and muscle tendons, and have difficulty gaining weight. They have a quality of dryness in their system with dry cracked skin and thinness of body. The vata people tend to have very irregular bowel function—sometimes constipation, sometimes diarrhea. They have a tendency to be irregular and dry and to have irregular menstrual periods.

The vata people in the culture-bound traditional Ayurvedic medicine are told that they should not eat a raw-food diet. But once you break out of the cultural biases in Ayurveda, in my clinical experience, pure vatas can do extremely well on a raw-food diet if they understand that it is composed of more than just salads, which are indeed vata-aggravating. If they follow the dietary balancing principles that are good for vatas, they can be quite successful on a live-food diet using the Rainbow Green Live-Food Cuisine approach. The key balancing concept for vatas who eat a raw-food diet is to eat heavier, oily foods such as avocados, soaked nuts and seeds, and seed pâtés. Nuts and seeds that have been soaked have the water to balance their dryness and the oil to balance their lightness. Heating herbs, such as ginger or cayenne, help vatas by giving their raw food needed warmth.

Since vatas have the tendency to run cold, there is a variety of ways to warm the food to approximately 110°F, which does not destroy the enzymes. You can do this in the sun, or put the food on top of a stove with a pilot light, or literally take a blended food and heat it lightly on the stove until it is warm to the finger-touch, which is approximately 110°F. Vatas are unbalanced by dehydrated, cold, dry, pungent, bitter, and astringent foods. Vatas should eat at regular intervals. It is good if they blend the raw vegetables into liquid soup. The soups have the water element that helps to keep the vatas from drying out. Soaking and blending nuts and seeds helps to minimize the gas that vata people tend to have with dry nuts and seeds. In general, vata people do very well on a live-food diet if they create soupy, oily, sea-salty, and warm foods. Particularly good for vatas are sea vegetables in quantity, and the addition of Celtic salt to their foods as well as warming herbs and spices. Vata people benefit from warm, oily, sweet, salty, watery soupy cuisine, with the use of moderate pungent spices. Any taste in excess may eventually imbalance vata, and any food in excess may aggravate vata. Foods that particularly aggravate vata are cold foods and ice water. A little warm water with ginger at the beginning or end of a meal is very soothing. It is generally thought that ginger is the best spice for vatas. Sweet spices such as cinnamon, fennel, and cardamom are also good, as are coriander, safflower, parsley, cayenne, cumin, and fenugreek. Hot spices should not be used in excess. Asafoetida (*hing*) is particularly good for excess gas. Also important for vatas is that they eat in a warm, comfortable, calm setting and perhaps meditate before eating. It is particularly important for them not to rush or talk through their meals.

Contrary to traditional Ayurvedic thinking, vatas can enjoy a full range of vegetables and salads if they combine it with high-oil-content foods such as avocado and soaked nuts and seeds, or use a blended nut or seed salad dressing. It is useful for vatas to combine watery vegetables such as cucumber or squash with the drier, bitter, and astringent ones such as the leafy greens to balance the effects of these bitter herbs. Making soups with the combination of avocado and leafy greens is a very good thing for vatas. Also such dishes as our *Avocado Kale Salad* are particularly good for the vata constitution. Specific vegetables that balance vata are asparagus, beets, carrots, celery, cucumber, green beans, okra, parsnips, radishes, turnips, sweet potatoes, and zucchini. The cabbage family tends to produce gas, and nightshades can also be difficult for vatas. Vegetables with a lot of roughage should be minimized or blended into the raw soups for vata raw-food people. The blending creates more water in the food and releases cellulose enzymes stored in the vegetables to aid in digestion. Raw fermented cabbage is an excellent way to take in the healing power of cabbage, and an option for getting these useful brassicas into the system. In its fermented form, there is better nutrient assimilation of cabbage. Although no fermented foods are used in the Phase I Rainbow Green Live-Food Cuisine, sauerkraut is one of the few that we allow in Phase I.5. The fermented cabbage has high amounts of lactobacillus, which have predigested the cabbage for us. These microorganisms aid in the general digestive process and strengthen colon function. The lactobacilli create an intestinal environment that is unfriendly to candida. Raw cultured vegetables have been found to be effective in the treatment of a number of disease processes including candida, peptic ulcers, ulcerative colitis, colic, food allergies, cystitis, and constipation. Cultured vegetables also seem to have an anti-radiation effect. At the Tree of Life Café, we serve cultured vegetables on a regular basis, because of their important healing benefits. In summary, although traditionally prepared raw vegetables could be unbalancing to vatas, blending them in soups, juicing them and warming them, culturing them, adding spices that are warming or adding digestive stimulants, and using oily or creamy dressings make it possible to eat most raw vegetables without aggravating the vata dosha.

Fruits are generally easy for vatas to handle. The most balancing fruits for vatas include avocados, berries, cherries, coconuts, citrus, and plums. The Rainbow Green Live-Food Cuisine eliminates or reduces a significant number of fruits that have higher sugar content and therefore a higher glycemic index. These include bananas, dates, figs, melons, papayas, and mangos. Some fruits are balancers of all the doshas and therefore recommended, including cherries and berries.

Kapha people tend to be those who gain weight easily. Females tend to gain weight in the lower part of their bodies such as the hips and buttocks, and to have more water retention particularly with their menstrual period, but their periods are usually regular without excessive flow. Kaphas tend to have a heavy bone structure with wide shoulders and hips. The skin of kaphas is more oily and smooth. Their sleep is usually deep and long.

The digestion in a kapha is slow and regular. Their digestion is especially slow if they eat a lot of oil or fatty foods. Kaphas have the tendency to move their bowels one time per day, whereas vatas and pittas move more often. On live foods, kaphas are helped and may find themselves moving twice a day. Kaphas have a moderate appetite and are the least thirsty of the three doshas. Excess water may throw them into imbalance. The best diets for kaphas include foods that are light, warm, and dry. Oily, fatty, fried, salty, sweet, cold, and heavy foods create a kapha imbalance, straining their already-slow digestion and increasing the tendency to gain weight. Therefore the all-American diet high in fat and sugar plus excess salt is the worst diet for kaphas. Fast foods are an absolute disaster for them, as are dairy products. The best foods are raw foods with an emphasis on bitter and astringent greens, with some heating and pungent herbs. The lighter the kaphas eat at each meal, the easier their digestion and the better their health. Kaphas generally do very well on live foods. The kapha-pitta types (people are often a combination of two or even three doshas) also have an easier time with raw foods because the pitta energy gives additional gastric fire for the winter. Raw foods can build the digestive power for the kapha and kapha-vata people, so they can do quite well all year long. Kaphas tend to have excess mucus, and raw foods are less mucus-producing than the same foods in cooked form. Because of their slow digestion, kaphas do well on two main meals a day that are separated by at least six hours. They do best avoiding snacking between meals.

Sweet, sour, and salty foods imbalance kaphas. Pungent, astringent, and bitter foods tend to balance them. Oily foods need to be eaten with care. For kaphas, vegetables are particularly balancing, especially leafy greens, because of their dry astringent qualities. Vegetables with a little bit of warm food (not cooked, but warmed) in combination with some pungent spices do very well for kaphas. By eating some astringent and bitter foods in the beginning of a meal, kaphas create a stimulant to digestion that helps the whole process. Having a salad first or some fresh raw ginger in warm water or in the salad dressing is really good for kaphas. Raw vegetables also supply fiber to stimulate the bowel function.

Sweet, sour, and watery vegetables may be neutral or aggravating, and must be eaten during an optimal season or time of day so that kaphas will be less likely to be aggravated. Cucumbers are neutral because they are watery, bitter, and astringent. Tomatoes are the least aggravating for kapha. Black and green olives, which are oily and salty, tend to aggravate kapha. Warmed, raw, leafy greens and vegetables are excellent for kaphas in general. Root vegetables are acceptable, but because they have more earthy qualities they may reinforce the inertia of a kapha person who is already too earthy and fixed. Good vegetables for kaphas are ones that are pungent and bitter, such as asparagus, broccoli, Brussels sprouts, cabbage, carrots, cauliflower, celery, eggplant, leafy greens, lettuce, parsley, peas, peppers, spinach, and all types of sprouts. Please remember that I am giving you Ayurvedic principles according to the Rainbow Green Live-Food Cuisine rather than classical Ayurveda. The best fruits for kapha are those that tend to be a little bit dry and astringent, such as pears, apples, and pomegranates. Nuts and seeds, because they are heavy and oily, are best eaten in minimal amounts. If they are soaked or sprouted they are better for kaphas. Pâtés in small amounts are acceptable. Generally, however, kaphas do not do well with large amounts of oil. The best seeds for kapha are sunflower, pumpkin, and flax. Stored grains, which are not a great food for anyone, are particularly not good for kapha because they are heavy and mucus-producing. Spices that are most beneficial for kaphas are ginger and garlic. Kaphas can be significantly aggravated by salt in the traditional sodium chloride form. There seems to be less aggravation if kaphas use Celtic salt, a sun-dried sea salt that contains approximately eighty-two minerals. In summary, kaphas do well with spicy, bitter, pungent, and astringent vegetables and a minimal amount of nuts and seeds, and use of astringent types of fruits.

The archetypal animal of the pitta person is the tiger, whereas for the kapha person it is the elephant, and for the vata person it is the dry, parched goat. Pitta people usually have a medium frame. They have a well-balanced physical body. They are very muscular. They are physically graceful and strong. The skin of a pitta person is lighter, coppery, and sensitive to the sun. They tend to have freckles. Pitta people tend to be very warm-bodied people and warm to the touch. They are the people you see running around in shorts in the middle of winter. Pitta people have a very strong digestive fire and good appetites and are least affected by poor food combining because they digest so well. They do become irritable if they don't eat when they are hungry, and eating tends to calm them down. They like cold drinks; their bowel function is regular and frequent. Because of their inner heat, pitta women bleed more heavily and for a longer time during their menstrual periods. Until they overheat, pitta people enjoy vigorous exercise.

The best diet for a pitta is a bland raw diet. They are the most sensitive of the three doshas to toxins in the air, food, and water, although vatas can be very sensitive as well. It is very important, as it is for everyone, but most important for pittas to eat only organic food and drink only filtered water. Sweet, bitter, and astringent-tasting foods, which are cool and heavy, are the most balancing. Spicy, oily, salty, and sour foods tend to imbalance pittas. Overeating is another big hazard to pittas, as one of their major tendencies is acid indigestion. A bland, organic, vegan, raw diet is best for the pittas. Flesh foods, eggs, alcohol, salt, caffeine, coffee, tobacco, mustard, garlic, onions, ginger, and other stimulants aggravate the emotional and physical heat and natural aggression of pittas. Foods that are sour, including citrus and dill pickles, also tend to aggravate pitta. Pittas in general are aggravated by sweet, salty, and sour foods. Lemon, however, which is sour, can be tolerated in small amounts because of its overall alkalinizing and liver-purifying effects. It is generally better that pittas avoid or minimize pungent foods and herbs such as cayenne, mustard, and excess ginger. Cold tastes, which are bitter and astringent, such as leafy greens, are balancing. Foods that are sweet-tasting are also balancing, except honey and molasses, which are very heating to pittas. Of course, in the Rainbow Green Live-Food Cuisine, honey and molasses are not recommended for anyone. High-protein foods, which increase the metabolic heat, should be kept to a moderate level. Foods such as carrots and beets, which purify and cleanse the liver, are balancing or at least neutral to pitta, even though they may be considered slightly heating. The balancing herbs for pitta are coriander, cinnamon, cardamom, fennel, cumin, and turmeric. Black pepper can be used occasionally.

Fruits and vegetables are the most balancing for pittas. Pittas also do best when they avoid salty, pungent, and sour tastes as well as hot, light, and dry foods. Because pittas have speedy metabolism they generally need to eat three main meals a day separated by at least four hours, but they may find themselves snacking. Vegetables, which are good for everybody, are particularly good for pitta. The exceptions to this are tomatoes, which are heating and pungent, and vegetables like radishes, onions, and hot peppers and garlic. Although beets, carrot, and daikon are slightly heating, they can be eaten, unless pitta is already aggravated. All of the vegetables in the brassica family are good for pittas, including cabbage and Brussels sprouts. Also good are asparagus, cilantro, cucumber, celery, fresh leafy greens, green beans, lettuce, okra, peas, parsley, and sprouts, as well as the squash family. Well-ripened sweet citrus fruits are acceptable for pitta because of the sweet taste. Avocados and persimmons (which are on the borderline) can be all right for pittas. Nuts and seeds, because they are hot and oily, should be used sparingly, but if they are soaked and sprouted they can be used in moderation. Coconut is very balancing for pitta. Sunflower and pumpkin seeds are also quite good.

Because this book cannot fully detail considerations for each dosha, I can only say that it is one of the overlapping systems of biochemical individuality that can be utilized to address your own diet. A few general Ayurvedic concepts will help convey the essence of the approach. Like the doshas, the seasons also play a role in balancing our diet. One of the key concepts in Ayurveda is that there is a constant interplay between the energy of the person, the energy of the food, and the energy of the environment. In the summer, it is better to eat more sweet, cool, bitter, astringent, raw, and high-water-content foods, such as vegetables, greens, and sprouts. In the spring, the diet is similar to that of summer, but we want to increase the raw foods, greens, sprouts, and vegetables and include a little bit more low-fat food. In the winter, we want to eat more pungent, bitter, astringent, warm, dry, and light foods including ginger and cayenne. In the fall, we want to eat more sweet, naturally salty, warm, heavy, and high-fiber foods, which include ginger, soaked nuts and seeds, and vegetables.

The stage of life that we are in also plays a role in selecting a diet. Everyone, no matter what their basic constitutional dosha, from birth to age twelve needs to eat a more kapha-balancing diet because children tend to have more of a kapha imbalance. This is a non-dairy diet (except for their mother's breastmilk) which is slightly spicy, warm, and dry. Dehydrated foods are the most balancing for kapha. Good spices for warmth and digestion are ginger, cumin, hing, cinnamon, and cardamom. For babies, which are in the kapha phase of life, the food should be blended and warmed to 105–110°F, and the diet should be slanted to a kapha-balancing diet. (See the section titled "Raising Rainbow Babies.") From age sixteen to midlife we need a pitta-balancing diet. Once the aging process begins to dominate, we need to have a more vata-balancing diet with an emphasis on increased hydration and a little bit more ginger and warming, oily, soupy foods. In some people the aging process begins at forty; in others at seventy or eighty; in some people not at all, depending on how well they take care of themselves.

When balancing the forces of food and one's own dynamic forces, the Ayurveda system can be useful. I recommend the in-depth exploration of this topic and the questionnaires presented in *Conscious Eating* as a way to first determine your dosha and then to begin incorporating Ayurvedic principles in your personalized diet. Remember that all suggestions about food and doshas are only tendencies, and you must find what works best for you.

## BLOOD TYPE AND DIET

Yet another piece in individualizing one's diet is the effect of blood type on our dietary choice. Unfortunately, certain people with very little research and with meat-eating biases have slanted and created, in a sense, a story of wild extrapolation as to what one should eat according to blood type. My experience has been that blood type plays a minimal role in dietary choices. For example, in the popular blood-type approach, if you are a type O, it is strongly recommended by blood-type proponents that you eat a high-protein flesh-food diet. In several conferences that were either vegan or live-food conferences, when I have asked people for a show of hands how many were type O (which includes myself, my friend David Wolfe, a leading live-food teacher, and Brian Clements, director of Hippocrates) over half the people were type O, yet they are successfully and healthfully eating a vegan diet and feeling really good. This points to a significant inconsistency and lack of understanding regarding the role that the blood type does play.

In *Conscious Eating,* I have printed a table of the world literature that scientifically discusses the actual research on one of the most important aspects of the blood type input, which is the lectins. Lectins are biological protein qualities of certain foods that react against your blood type. For example, excess sunflower seeds react with the blood cells and system of type O. Excess sesame seeds and soy react negatively with the blood and immune system of type B. (Please see *Conscious Eating* for an extensive list.)

There is very interesting book, *The Answer is in Your Blood Type,* written by medical doctor Steven Weissberg with Joseph Christiano, who is a fitness trainer and educator. In their research on blood type they studied five thousand people retrospectively. What they found was that if you are blood type A, and you do not eat a primarily vegetarian diet, you have a very high risk of dying at an early age (approximately sixty-one years) of heart disease or cancer. If you are blood type O, no matter what you eat, no matter how foolish you are in your dietary choices, how much beef you eat, alcohol you drink, or cigarettes you smoke, the average lifespan is eighty-six—according to this study. The point is that certain blood types tend to be healthier than others. The implication, from my perspective, is that all of the blood types would do better with a live-food, vegan diet; but it is highly recommended for a type A who wants to extend their life and minimize the chances of cancer and heart disease. All of the blood types benefit by eating organic and with some degree of wisdom. Type O's can get away with more dietary abuses such as fatty, fried foods and lots of flesh foods. The authors did theorize, without any hard scientific evidence, that type O's need more protein, but they did not insist it be flesh foods. Again, my experience with hundreds of vegans and live-foodists who are not necessarily on a high-protein diet, including myself, is that high protein is not essential. If you are a person who needs higher protein in your diet, we have very good vegan alternatives that can do the job. From the live-food vegan organic perspective, the choice of diet according to blood type is, to me, a minimum part of it. As long as you do not eat junk food, flesh, and dairy, and don't eat a lot of things that are generally unhealthy, as we talk about in the Rainbow Green Live-Food Cuisine, no matter what blood type you have, you are going to feel better. However, I do recommend that people pay attention to the lectins in the foods that may react negatively to your particular blood type.

Along with the lack of current science in the *Eat Right for Your Type* fad, there are some other major problems with the general hypothesis. Dr. Stephen Bailey, a nutritional anthropologist at Tufts University, points out that blood types existed before humans in animals and that there is NO anthropological evidence that all prehistoric people were type O. The clinical results from the Dean Ornish, M.D., vegetarian program, which has been shown to reverse heart disease in all blood types on a low-fat, essentially vegan diet, makes a strong statement against the *Eat Right for Your Type* hypothesis that type B and O "need" animal protein to be healthy. There is also no evidence in the medical literature that type O's have more hydrochloric acid or pepsin. These rationalizations have no scientific basis to support the speculative hypothesis that type O's do better with meat.

The theoretical foundation of the *Eat Right for Your Type* diet hypothesis is that the Cro-Magnons who lived 40,000 to 20,000 years ago were all type O and ate primarily meat. Along with the rest of the wild hypotheses in *Eat Right for Your Type,* this foundational position seems to be highly inaccurate. Paleontologist Robert Leakey, who is acknowledged worldwide as an authority on the evolution of the human diet, states that Cro-Magnons did not have canine teeth, and therefore would not have been able to use food sources that required canine teeth, such as large amounts of wild game. He thinks that the Cro-Magnon diet was probably similar to that of the chimpanzee, our closest genetic relative. Although chimpanzees did have canine teeth, they ate primarily a vegetarian diet. To sum it up, *The Food Revolution* by John Robbins quotes Fredrick

Stare, M.D., founder and former chairman of the Nutrition Department of the Harvard School of Public Health, as saying, "*Eat Right for Your Type* is not only one of the most preposterous books on the market, but also one of the most frightening."

## SUMMARY

At the Tree of Life Café, we have incorporated these exciting principles of how to personalize your diet into our everyday cuisine. This has taken much training and thoughtfulness on the part of our staff. We are now able to share this information through this book, through our Master of Arts in Vegan and Live-Food Nutrition program, our four-month Culinary Arts Chef Training program, our four-day Conscious Eating Live-Food Certification Program for the home chef, and our four-day Arizona Live! program.

As I look upon the dietary recommendations, a clear point is made: **the key to the healthy diet is organic and live.** The exact mix of carbohydrates, proteins, and fats depends on one's constitution.

I recommend the following percentages for the three basic dietary constitutional types: (1) Fast oxidizers and parasympathetics—50–55% protein foods, 25–35% carbohydrate foods, and 20% fat foods; (2) slow oxidizers and sympathetics—50–55% carbohydrate foods, 30% protein foods, and approximately 15% fat foods; (3) the mixed diet is about 40% protein foods, 40% carbohydrate foods, and 20% fat foods. In the Rainbow Green Live-Food Cuisine we combine these principles with Phases I, I.5, and II to make a complete healing and maintenance program.

Compared to diets such as the Zone Diet, one sees that for each phase we still include about 30% protein. This is important for stimulating glucagon production in Phase I and the good prostaglandins, which are anti-inflammatory, increase serotonin levels, and ameliorate depression. Contrary to information in the Zone Diet literature, however, a recent controlled study by Gene Spiller, Ph.D., showed that when individuals consumed protein-rich foods their insulin output was greater than when they consumed an equal amount of carbohydrate-rich foods. This directly challenges our simplistic myth that carbohydrates raise insulin and protein lowers it. My feeling is that both excess protein and carbohydrate in the wrong constitutional types may increase the insulin, but moderate amounts will not. Thirty to fifty percent of two thousand calories a day is 150–250 grams, which is excessive. Twenty to forty grams of protein for a non-pregnant person is appropriate for most constitutions. Protein in foods is not the same as protein in grams. I mention grams, which is exact amount of protein, to make the point more clear. Paavo Airola in his book *Are You Confused?* pointed out ten research papers showing that people did extremely well on just 20 grams of protein a day. The point that I want to make here is that we do not need excess amounts of protein in order to do well with the diet I am talking about. And for sure, we do not need meat or dairy protein. (As I pointed out before, these are also high in pathogenic microorganisms as compared to a vegan diet.) Recent research has shown that vegetarian protein more specifically decreases insulin resistance.

The quality of the raw vegan protein is very high because, eating raw, you get double the amount of protein for the same amount of calories. Research at the Max Planck Institute in Germany, for example, shows that when you cook your protein you lose 50% of it in its actual form. This means that 20 grams of live-food protein is equal to 40 grams of cooked protein. In addition, the point is not the amount of protein in grams but the amount of protein to best fill the metabolic production of cellular energy as ATP. And research has consistently shown that the less you eat, the healthier you are and the longer you live. That is the one proven fact about longevity. The average American diet has about twice as many calories as the diets of long-lived people such as the Vilcabamban Indians, the Maya Indians, and the Hunzas. A live-food, 30% or more protein diet gives half the calories, avoids the dangers of a diet high in animal products, and gives all the benefits of strength and endurance reported for those who are successful with Zone-type diets. The idea is that percentage refers to subjective ratio of concentrations. For example, for fast-oxidizer or parasympathetic types, it may actually only be 20–30 grams of protein per day, which can be as little as three tablespoons of chlorella/spirulina a day or three handfuls of nuts and seeds. The recommendation for 50% protein food refers to volume and concentration of food on your plate for that meal, not protein in grams.

Another important point in the Rainbow Green Live-Food Cuisine is that the word "carbohydrate" needs to be clarified. A cooked carbohydrate has a higher glycemic index because the starches are broken down into simple sugars. The Phase I diet that I recommend, in retrospect, is very similar to the Zone Diet in the use of carbohydrate. It's not about whether you have a high amount of carbohydrate or not. The real question is: Are you using low-glycemic carbohydrates? The problem with many vegetarian high-carbohydrate/low-protein diets is that they are either using high-glycemic fruits, vegetables, and starches, or they are cooking the carbohydrates, which turns them into high-glycemic foods. It is the high-glycemic foods that stimulate insulin, bad prostaglandins, and mycosis. Rainbow Green Live-Food Cuisine Phase I is very low-glycemic no matter what constitution. Phase II is moderate-glycemic in that, in terms of its effect, it stays away from the high-glycemic fruits and the complex carbohydrates (particularly if they are cooked) that are going to raise the blood glucose. One research project showed that giving pigs cooked potatoes made their blood glucose rise 50 points; the same amount of raw potatoes sent their blood glucose up 1 point. So we need to look clearly at the distinction between a cooked carbohydrate and a raw carbohydrate in terms of its glycemic effect. The point is that the diet we recommend optimizes the production of glucagon, which optimizes the good prostaglandins and stabilizes and lowers the production of insulin and therefore bad prostaglandins. The Rainbow Green Live-Food Cuisine diet sets up a very positive hormonal adjustment in your body.

The significance of this is straightforward: the production of good prostaglandins, PG1, is enhanced by the release of glucagon; glucagon is enhanced by eating a diet that's at least 30% protein. In all the diets I recommend, whatever the phase, that is the minimum percentage of protein. Both Phase I and Phase II have the potential to diminish the production of bad prostaglandins because they are low insulin-stimulating. Sweet carbohydrates

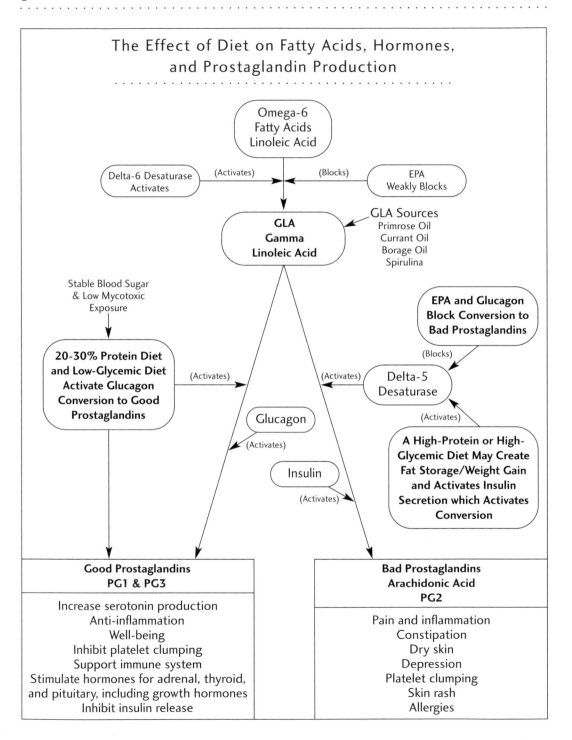

## The Effect of Diet on Fatty Acids, Hormones, and Prostaglandin Production

Omega-6
Fatty Acids
Linoleic Acid

Delta-6 Desaturase
Activates    (Activates)    (Blocks)    EPA
Weakly Blocks

**GLA
Gamma
Linoleic Acid**

GLA Sources
Primrose Oil
Currant Oil
Borage Oil
Spirulina

Stable Blood Sugar
& Low Mycotoxic
Exposure

**EPA and Glucagon
Block Conversion to
Bad Prostaglandins**

**20-30% Protein Diet
and Low-Glycemic Diet
Activate Glucagon
Conversion to Good
Prostaglandins**    (Activates)    (Activates)    **Delta-5
Desaturase**    (Blocks)

(Activates)

Glucagon

**A High-Protein or High-
Glycemic Diet May Create
Fat Storage/Weight Gain
and Activates Insulin
Secretion which Activates
Conversion**

(Activates)

Insulin

(Activates)

**Good Prostaglandins
PG1 & PG3**

Increase serotonin production
Anti-inflammation
Well-being
Inhibit platelet clumping
Support immune system
Stimulate hormones for adrenal, thyroid,
and pituitary, including growth hormones
Inhibit insulin release

**Bad Prostaglandins
Arachidonic Acid
PG2**

Pain and inflammation
Constipation
Dry skin
Depression
Platelet clumping
Skin rash
Allergies

and cooked complex carbohydrates produce higher amounts of bad prostaglandins, because they increase insulin production which accelerates the conversion of GLA to PG2 or "bad prostaglandins." Low-glycemic foods include moderately low-glycemic foods and moderately low-glycemic vegetables. Almost all vegetables are perfect carbohydrates eaten in the raw form because they are low- or moderate-glycemic foods.

Insulin directs the body to store fat and to burn carbohydrates as fuel. Low levels of insulin create a modest and stable blood sugar in the body and shift the metabolism to burn fat fuel. This shift creates more blood glucose going to the brain, which stabilizes the brain function. The typical American high-carbohydrate diet usually has lots of the high-glycemic foods and vegetables as well as complex carbohydrates and grains. I don't recommend this because it stimulates fungal growth production. As pointed out before, a high-protein diet may also increase insulin.

In other words, the Rainbow Green Live-Food Cuisine diet that I am recommending stimulates the body to burn fat. A fat-burning metabolism, according to some research, seems to give people more energy and stamina. It helps people to lose weight. It keeps the blood sugar stable while ensuring that the brain gets a consistent glucose fuel input. When the blood sugar is not going up and down, we do not have these consistent calls for more food, which turn into cravings for sweets. So this diet definitely helps us work toward stabilization of the blood sugar and therefore healing of hypoglycemia, as well as healing of the mycosis syndrome. It also seems to be a diet that, according to the Zone Diet research, enhances athletic performance and energy.

# AUTHENTIC FOODS

Authentic food is a concept that helps us absolutely optimize the idea of what quality food should be. The goal is to produce the most nutritious, high-energy food possible while protecting the soil for future generations. The farmers that are involved in this adventure each year probe deeper into the soil-plant-animal nutrition cycle and how to optimize it. Authentic foods stand in contrast to agribusiness giants who are beginning to take over the word "organic" and who do not understand the traditional small organic farmer's commitment to producing the highest-quality food. The authentic approach is a response to the transition of organic food production from small farms to large-scale agriculture.

Authentic farming does not discount organic farming; it is just one step further in the modern evolutionary process. Organic food production plays a very important role in healing our world. Its focus is getting toxic chemicals out of agriculture. Authentic food production focuses on enhancing the biological quality of food. So we are talking about a new set of concepts that do not dictate what one shouldn't do in order to be considered "organic." This involves what we can do to add energy to food and soil, by love and devotion in its production. This allows us to absorb the highest energy from our food, which is the main way that we derive energy from the planet. Authentic food lifts food to a new level of quality.

The term *authentic* has to do with farmers who are more concerned with quality than with mass production, even if it is organic. It identifies fresh, organic food produced by local growers who want to focus on what they are doing instead of what they are not doing. The concept of authentic goes right down to the fundamentals of how food was offered in the past. These principles are: (1) all food is produced by the growers who sell it; (2) fresh fruits and vegetables are produced within a 50- to 150-mile radius of the place of their final sale; (3) seed and storage crops are produced within a 300-mile radius of their final sale; (4) the growers' fields and greenhouses are open for inspection at any time, and the customers themselves can be the certifiers of their food; (5) all of the agricultural practices used on the farm selling "authentic" are chosen to produce food at the highest nutritional and vibrational qualities; (6) soils are nourished as they are in the natural world with farm-derived organic matter, minerals, and particles from ground rot; (7) green manures and cover crops are included with the broadly based crop rotations to maintain biodiversity; (8) pest-positive rather than pest-negative philosophy is involved, recognizing that pests appear when there is an imbalance and focusing on how to correct the cause of the problem rather than treating the symptoms. This is a holistic approach to farming. The goal, of course, is vigorous, healthy crops that are endowed with inherent powers to resist pests. (9) Any authentic farm or garden land would be a zone free of genetically modified organisms. The definition of authentic farming obviously stresses local, seller-grown, fresh, organic food—concepts that are not so easy for agribusiness to appropriate. This supports the health of the ecosystem, our bodies, and the local economy.

# ORGANIC FOODS

Organic foods are produced without using genetically modified organisms (GMOs) or toxic chemicals. Organic production methods, whether employed in conjunction with authentic farming or not, are vastly superior to commercial, chemical-based agriculture in producing foods with optimum nutrition. Foods produced by organic farming practices exhibit improved vitamin and mineral nutrition, as well as superior taste, shelf life, and phytochemical and anti-oxidant content.

Investigations are showing that wild-crafted foods (foods harvested from wild plants) have the highest nutritional content, with organic foods next and conventionally grown foods last. The USDA periodically publishes data on the nutritional content of food. Historically, since the 1940s, each publication of this data shows a decline in the average nutritional content of food. Wheat, for example, used to average a protein content of 19% in the 1940s, but today it averages about 12%. The same trend exists for fresh fruit and vegetables and other foods. So the nutrition content—even of whole, fresh foods—is declining, alongside additional losses from cooking and processing. There appears to be a strong correlation between the onset and trend of this decline in nutritional content of foods and the introduction of heavy reliance on chemical fertilizers, pesticides, deep tillage, gene manipulation, and other practices of conventional agriculture. These practices have been well-documented as leading to a decline in soil quality and loss of topsoil and fertility. Further evidence of this relationship between conventional practices and the decline in nutritional content of foods is the fact that, on a fresh-weight basis—which is the critical way to look at nutrition for consumers of raw food—organic foods have about twice the vitamin and mineral content as conventional foods. On a dry-weight basis, this difference in nutritional quality is less obvious, so scientists like to use the dry-weight comparison in order to claim that foods produced by chemical-based farming are not statistically different from organic. However, this obscures the fact that food is life-force energy, whereas food ash is not. Humans are biologically designed to consume food!

Organic farmers are performing an incredibly valuable service to society through their efforts to reform food production methods to better conform to nature and to protect the environment and human health.

## VEGAN NATURE FARMING

In *Spiritual Nutrition and the Rainbow Diet* and *Conscious Eating,* the theme is using the human diet as a tool to advance consciousness and evolution. This book, *Rainbow Green Live-Food Cuisine,* details how a raw-food, low-glycemic, organic, vegan diet is the best form of nutrition for humans to optimize health and longevity and to expand consciousness. At the Tree of Life Rejuvenation Center, our Vegan Nature Farming program is an outgrowth of this evolution.

On the continuum of organic farming and authentic farming, we have gone even one step further by developing a Vegan Nature Farming program. In this vegan farming method we employ Effective Microorganisms (EM) to energize the soil so that it delivers the highest amount of energy into our fruits and vegetables.

Vegan nature farming originated in 1935 when Mokichi Okada, a Japanese philosopher and spiritual teacher, began to develop a method of organic food production that he called "Nature Farming." At the time, chemicals were being introduced into agriculture in Japan. Okada recognized that these methods were contrary to the patterns of nature and created more problems than they solved. In particular, Okada believed that the use of toxic chemicals contaminated food and that chemical methods of farming produced foods that were inferior in nutrition to Nature Farming methods. He demonstrated the principles of Nature Farming to his followers, who took up the method and continued to spread it after he left his body in 1955.

Nature Farming is based on keenly observing natural ecosystems, such as forests and prairies, and then imitating and adapting the pattern of nature to the situation of human food production. Okada observed that in nature, "living soil" is the key to the health and stability of forests and prairies. He advocated that his followers imitate nature by seeking to create the conditions for living soil on their farms. Natural compost, composed principally or exclusively of plant materials, is the key input in Nature Farming. Mulching the soil with plant debris and patterning the farm layout based on the models of natural forests and prairies were additional techniques.

The Nature Farming method received a great boost in the late 1980s when Professor Teruo Higa, Ph.D., of the University of the Ryukyus in Okinawa, Japan, shared his amazing discovery of "Effective Microorganisms" (EM) with the proponents of Nature Farming. Dr. Higa began his research on microorganisms in the early 1960s, discovering that certain groups in combination were beneficial and "effective" in their ability to change the microbial characteristics of soil. By "effective" it is meant that these microorganisms were able to alter the dynamics of the microbial ecosystems of soil, water, plant surfaces, and other environments, and to enhance the growth and activities of the beneficial components, which led to the decline of activity of the detrimental components. Dr. Higa realized that this was a great tool that could have many uses in agriculture and the environment, where negative practices had created microbial imbalances. In the context of Nature Farming, EM proved to be the key to creating "living soil" in a reliable and predictable manner. EM also helped to solve many practical problems in transitioning farms to sustainable organic methods.

In 1998, Nature Farming and EM were introduced to me and the Tree of Life Rejuvenation Center by John Phillips, who had been working with Nature Farming since 1988, and with Dr. Higa since 1990. In December of 2001, John joined the staff of the Tree of Life Rejuvenation Center to work more closely with us in developing a model for a Vegan Nature Farming method using EM.

As mentioned, Nature Farming takes its model from nature itself. Natural ecosystems can have very high productivity of plant and animal life, yet they are self-sustaining. Indeed, one characteristic of such systems is that they are always naturally accumulating fertility. Also, they are naturally resistant to pests and diseases and can recover easily from fires, earth movements, windstorms, and other damaging events. This is in stark contrast to most farming systems, where productivity is continually threatened by loss of fertility, insects, diseases, weeds, and other pests, and where fire, wind damage, and other catastrophes can cause the system to fail totally.

The basis of Nature Farming is an appreciation for the power of "living soil," which is the key factor that makes the system sustainable and resilient. Living soil is created through the interaction of plants and the life of the soil, especially the microorganisms, earthworms, mites, and countless other creatures. In the forests and prairies, living soil is created by the accumulation of plant debris from season to season. Plants provide the food that serves as the primary production of these ecosystems, thereby supporting the extended food chains that develop there. Next to the plants, the microorganisms and other soil life are the most critical to the stability and productivity of the system. Microorganisms recycle the plant material and release nutrients to further promote plant growth. Microorganisms form symbiotic relationships with plant root systems and help provide nutrients, such as phosphorus, to plants in exchange for exudates from the plant root. Animals, from earthworms and mites on up, dwell and feed upon the soil-plant complex. This is the natural scheme of things, and humans evolved from this ecological base.

Indeed, E.B. Szekely, one of the earliest and greatest holistic physicians of the twentieth century, proposed that humans originally evolved from a subspecies he called *Homo sapiens sylvanus,* and the forests were our natural home. Szekely also proposed that the raw foods of the forests—the fruits, herbs, and vegetables—were our natural diet. When humans existed in harmony with the forest on their natural diet, life spans were much longer, and humans lived free of debilitating diseases. This is the true paradise lost!

Szekely suggested that we could return to this paradise by creating agrarian communities that are independent, co-operating, and involved in producing an abundance of plants that can be used in a raw-food vegan diet to promote health, longevity, and conscious evolution. This is what we are creating at the Tree of Life by developing Vegan Nature Farming and Rainbow Green Live-Food Cuisine.

To create a Vegan Nature Farming system to produce our live-food diet, we eliminated all use of organic fertilizers that contain animal by-products from the slaughter industry, such as bone meal, blood meal, feather meal, fish emulsion, and similar products. Essentially, this step has been the approach since the beginning, but we have learned that many blended organic fertilizers also contain some form of animal product as a source of nitrogen. So it is important to look at the ingredient lists more closely. Organic food *can* be produced without using animal wastes and by-products, and for some vegans, this is distinctly preferred. Vegan farming also provides protection from the possible problem of "mad cow disease."

Many plant materials used for composting are now suspect because of GMOs, so cottonseed meal, alfalfa meal, and soybean meal, for example, are less desirable sources of nutrients for organic production than they used to be, and must be sourced from organic producers who avoid GMOs. Even hay, so commonly used as mulch in organic farming, now must be sourced from organic producers not only because of GMOs, but because the latest herbicides being used in conventional farming are more resistant to natural breakdown in the environment and are causing herbicide damage to crops, even in cases where the hay is only used as an ingredient in making compost.

Composting kitchen waste from an organic, vegan kitchen recycles nutrients that can be used for vegan food production. At the Tree of Life we employ EM, Dr. Higa's special blend of beneficial microorganisms, to inoculate and energize compost and to make compost teas and vegan organic sprays for crops and soils.

Vegan farming does not necessarily exclude employing animals as companions and co-workers to help balance the agro-ecosystem. Ducks and geese may be used for weed control, and chickens and turkeys may be used to control harmful insects such as grasshoppers. Since these co-workers are willing to work for chicken feed and garden scraps, are kept compassionately in a natural environment, and are not used for human food, we see a mutual benefit in this arrangement. Earthworms also can be used to recycle wastes, and their castings make a fine compost and organic fertilizer.

We are especially interested in Nature Farming and the use of Effective

Microorganisms in developing our vegan organic gardens because there is evidence that foods produced by this method exceed normal organic foods and equal wild-crafted foods in terms of energetic and nutritional content. This may be because the synergy of Nature Farming with EM approximates nature's own system of growing.

Evaluation of this new system of Nature Farming with EM using a vegan ethic in producing authentic live foods is a work in progress at the Tree of Life Rejuvenation Center. Research into these methods is being conducted thanks to the assistance of the students in our "Spiritual Gardening & Sacred Landscaping" apprentice program. We are also planning to develop a Master's degree program, similar to our Master's program in Vegan and Live-food Nutrition, where we will further explore the growing and utilization of authentic live foods using a vegan approach to the Nature Farming with EM method. Participation in these programs is encouraged for all those who may be interested.

## PESTICIDE PESTILENCE

Although I see authentic food at the cutting edge beyond organic, I want to make it very clear that the organic movement plays an incredibly important role in the healing of the planet. I strongly urge everyone to go 100% organic. Presently more than 20% of the pesticides currently registered in the U.S. are linked to cancer, birth defects, developmental harm, or central nervous damage. I cannot even imagine how much this is involved with the current epidemic of hyperactivity and adult attention deficit disorder. Some research has shown that when children are put on an organic diet there is a 50% cure rate, without doing anything else. This is not surprising since most pesticides and herbicides are neurotoxins, and developing nervous systems are more vulnerable. That means that 50% of the eight to ten million children who are presently on Ritalin would no longer have to take the drug. The other 50%, given the natural ways of healing the brain that are available, probably could also be healed.

More than twelve thousand children in the U.S. are diagnosed with cancer every year. Cancer is now the second-leading cause, after suicide, of death for children under the age of fifteen. These high cancer rates in children were unheard of before the age of pesticides, herbicides, and genetically engineered food. More than half the food on our grocery shelves contains genetically engineered ingredients. These ingredients have not been adequately tested for their impact on human health. One of the most significant effects of an organic vegetarian diet is the tremendous health benefit of stopping the chronic poisoning from pesticide intake.

Let us understand, pesticides are designed to kill living creatures, and human beings are living creatures. The organic movement is one of the most important things we have to begin to rectify the destruction of our soils, the very high rate of cancer in children and adults, and the literal poisoning of the planet. The only people who benefit from this pollution are the corporations that profit directly from the sale of chemicals and indirectly from the suffering of others. I will point out again that farmers in countries that use heavy pesticides and herbicides have less ability to produce high-quality foods. In other words, their total agricultural output seems to be subtly dropping. One of their problems is that the pests are smarter than the corporations.

The poisoning of our global environment is a threat that has to be faced directly. If we are to stand up to corporate practices that threaten the health of farmers, rural communities, consumers, and ecosystems, we must vote with our mouths. By refusing to eat irradiated foods, commercial pesticided and herbicided foods, and genetically engineered food, we are making a very clear statement to the corporations and the governments that are typically influenced by corporate donations. We are saying that we, the public, will not buy your story or your food; we will not support the poisoning of the plants and all living creatures on this Earth. For this reason, I cannot stress strongly enough the importance of going 100% or close to 100% organic in our food choices. At the Tree of Life Café, we guarantee 100% organic live food.

The tide is turning. In May of 2001, ninety-one countries and the European community signed a treaty to phase out the persistent organic pollutants

(POPs), which include notorious pesticides such as DDT, PCBs, and dioxins that are wreaking havoc around the globe. More and more people are waking up to the fact that pesticides have been proven not only unsafe and counter-productive in the long run, but that the pesticide treadmill forces farmers to continually increase their use of poisonous substances to combat worsening pest outbreaks. An additional problem is that as these pests develop resistance, their natural predators are also being wiped out. Some of the corporations have gotten smarter about this. Not only have they created the pesticide-dependent farmer, but they are now promoting genetically engineered crops as "essential to feed a hungry world." This technology, which is being more seriously combated in Europe and other places than in the U.S., raises very serious concerns about biodiversity in the environment and about who controls the food supply.

In California from 1991 to 1999, the use of cancer-causing pesticides increased 121%, despite the common-sense principles and scientific evidence saying that the way to have healthy crops and to be healthy human beings is to reject the approach of "better living through chemistry" and instead seek better living through respecting the laws of nature. We face an obviously powerful and politically influential industry with a single goal, which clearly is not to feed and heal the planet, but to expand its multi-billion-dollar business.

In the United States alone in the 1990s, an average of 4.5 billion pounds of pesticides were used each year and another 700 million pounds exported. Unfortunately, pesticides do not recognize borders once they are dumped into the environment. Pesticides can travel thousands of miles through the atmosphere, waterways, and ocean currents, as well as in imported food and fiber. And so what we are seeing, even in the supposedly pristine polar habitats, is high levels of toxic pesticides, especially POPs. They are showing up in the tissues of native peoples, whales, penguins, and other animals. The same is true with genetically altered foods. Once they are released into the environment they have the serious potential of disrupting delicate ecosystems in devastating ways. By going organic we make a strong vote with the mouth to break this circle of poison.

Unless one eats organic fruits and vegetables, one is continually exposed to pesticides. One of the most important pathological effects of these toxins, besides initiating cancer, is the varying levels of neurotoxicity to the brain and the rest of the nervous system. These have more subtle symptoms such as reduced mental functioning, decreased mental clarity, poor concentration, and I believe hyperactivity and ADD. Some recent research has linked a higher rate of Parkinson's disease, which is a brain disease, to those people who have a history of higher pesticide use. So we do have some very suggestive evidence that the use of pesticides and herbicides really affects our mental function and brain physiology, including increasing the incidence of Parkinson's. This is not exactly a surprise when you realize that pesticides are designed as neurotoxins. Does it surprise us to think that we are biologically similar to the pests that we are trying to eliminate? Our nervous systems are more sophisticated and may take longer to poison, but it still happens.

The following excerpts are from a study titled "An Anthropological Approach to the Evaluation of Preschool Children Exposed to Pesticides in Mexico" by Elizabeth A. Guillette, Maria Mercedes Meza, Maria Guadalupe Aquilar, Alma Delia Soto, and Idalia Enedina Garcia, published in *Environmental Health Perspectives* (Vol. 106, No. 6, June 1998). It is the most stunning study I have read illustrating the powerful neurotoxic effects of pesticides and herbicides on our children. This shows why going organic is important at any age, but probably most important for children whose brains are developing.

"The children of the agrarian region were compared to children living in the foothills, where pesticide use is avoided. The RATPC [a physical, psychological, and mental assessment] measured varied aspects of physical growth and abilities to perform, or function in, normal childhood activities. No differences were found in growth patterns. Functionally, the exposed children demonstrated decreases in stamina, gross and fine eye-hand coordination, 30-minute memory, and the ability to draw a person. The RATPC also pointed out areas in which more in-depth research on the toxicology of pesticides would be valuable. . . .

"The 33 children exposed to elevated levels of pesticides, hereafter referred to as valley children, came from three towns and corresponding rural areas within the Yaqui Valley. The towns were Quetchehueca (n = 10), Bacum (n = 12), and Pueblo Yaqui (n = 11), all 10–30 feet above sea level. The criteria for town selection included a historical, continual use of pesticides since 1950, based on data from Hewitt de Alcanara, and a history of Yaqui Indian settlement. A previous study, which examined the village of Pueblo Yaqui, observed elevated levels of a number of pesticides or metabolites in 100% of the cord blood and mother's milk samples. Tesopaco, located in the foothills of the mountains (elevation 400 m), is a Yaqui settlement based on ranching. This town was used as the source of reference children (n = 17). All of the towns, regardless of location, were similar in infrastructure and the interfacing of tradition with modernization. . . .

"Pesticide use is widespread and continues throughout the year, with little governmental control. Contamination of the resident human population has been documented, with milk concentrations of lindane, heptachlor, benzene hexachloride, aldrin, and endrin all above limits of the Food and Agricultural Organization of the United Nations after 1 month of lactation. An initial site visit revealed that household bug sprays were usually applied each day throughout the year in the lowland homes. In contrast, the foothill residents maintained traditional intercropping for pest control in gardens and swatting of bugs in the home. These people cited their only exposure to pesticides as the governmental DDT spraying each spring for the control of malaria. (Identical DDT spraying also occurs in the agricultural areas and is repeated if a case of malaria occurs.) . . .

"A cursory look at the foothill and valley towns could easily lead one to the conclusion that no discernible differences were present in the Yaqui children. Heights varied between the tall and short for age, and weights ranged from the ultra thin to the obese. The lack of physical differences in growth patterns was borne out with anthropometric measurements.Anthropological participant observation indicated that the type of play was different in the two areas. Group play was observed more frequently in the foothills, with pretend parties for dolls and street games. Valley children appeared less creative in their play; they roamed the area aimlessly or swam in irrigation canals with minimal group interaction. Some valley children were observed hitting their siblings when they passed by, and they became easily upset or angry with a minor corrective comment by a parent. These aggressive behaviors were not noted in the foothills. Such clues indicated that additional aspects of development may be affected by environmental change, as opportunities and toys for play were available at both sites. In both areas, mothers were generally home on a full-time basis and showed interest in their children. . . .

"The rapid assessment tool did show that psychological and physiological differences in functional abilities exist between the valley and foothill children at 4 and 5 years of age. The jumping assessment, reflecting a decrease in stamina for valley children, could be an indicator of the presence of a physiologic modifier resulting in reduced intensity and/or frequency of play. In addition, playing ball or other activities involving gross or fine eye-hand coordination is less exciting or fulfilling when the child cannot perform the required skills. Of increased concern are the differences found with activities involving mental/neurological functioning. The inability to remember a meaningful statement after 30 min has implications for school performance and performance in social activity. The drawing of a person, often used as a nonverbal screening measure of cognitive ability, could also indicate a breakdown between visual sensory input and neuromuscular output, as found with brain dysfunction. The decreases in eye-hand coordination, as with catching the ball and dropping raisins into a circumscribed area, could also correlate with this type of brain dysfunction. This concept of breakdown between incoming sensory signals and neuromuscular output certainly deserves greater attention in future research. . . .

"Valley children had a significant decrease in their ability to catch a large ball ($P = 0.034$) at the distance of 3 m. This inability to catch a ball increased as the ball size decreased. Foothill children outperformed the valley children in catching the tennis ball at 1, 2, and 3 m ($p = 0.05$, $0.01$, and $0.003$, respectively). A stronger difference was found between the two groups in regard to fine eye-hand coordination; foothill children were better able to drop a raisin into a bottle cap (F = 7.3; df = 1, 44; p = 0.009). Interestingly, the location of the child's home (valley versus foothills) had a significant effect on these measurements, but the child's sex had no relationship to any of these outcomes.

"Children in both locations performed equally well in the immediate recall of numbers up to four digits. The valley children had more difficulty grasping the concept of repeating the numbers, although marked differences were found between towns. Children with such difficulty were encouraged to repeat one and then two vowel sounds made by the interviewer. Thus, the movement into repeating numbers became more comprehensible. Marked differences in recall were seen with 30-min memory (X2 = 14.3; P = 0.027). In recalling their gift, 59% of the 17 foothill children remembered both the object and its color, with all but one of the remaining children remembering just the balloon. In contrast, 27% of the 33 valley children recalled the balloon and color, 55% recalled the balloon only, and 18% could recall neither the object nor the color."

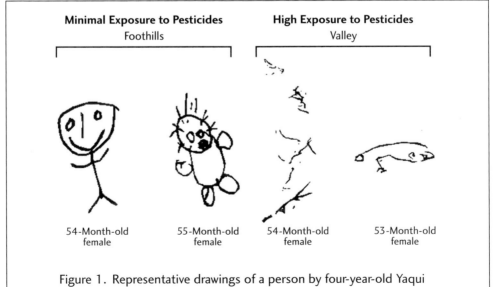

Figure 1. Representative drawings of a person by four-year-old Yaqui children from the valley and foothills of Sonora, Mexico.

An article in the *San Francisco Chronicle* dated February 3, 2003, titled "Polluted Bodies" is also quite revealing. It tells us that Michael Lerner, a twenty-year resident of seaside Bolinas, California, and the president and director of Commonweal, a health and environmental research group in Marin County, thought he was eating a healthy diet and avoiding exposure to industrial chemicals. Yet he found that his body was polluted with 101 industrial toxins as well as elevated levels of arsenic and mercury. Lerner was one of nine people in a collaborative study by the Mt. Sinai School of Medicine in New York City, the Environmental Working Group of Oakland and Washington, and Commonweal on the issue of body burden (the monotoxic chemicals in the body). On the average, each person studied had fifty or more chemicals in their bodies which have been linked to cancer in lab animals, are considered toxic to the brain and nervous system, or interfere with hormones and reproductive systems. Andrea Martin, Founder and former Executive Director of San Francisco Breast Cancer Fund, was found to have ninety-five toxins, fifty-five of which were carcinogens. For further info on this research visit www.ewg.org. The point is that no matter who we are, whether we are living on the ocean in Bolinas or in a large urban area, we are all in the same toxic neighborhood. To minimize the damage we need to eat all organic, have a regular detoxification program, and begin to clean up our planetary neighborhood.

One of the most significant effects of an organic vegetarian diet is the tremendous health benefit of stopping the chronic poisoning from pesticide intake. In 1985, the pesticide Temik in watermelon poisoned nearly one thousand people in the western United States and Canada. People had a variety of reactions, including grand mal seizures, cardiac irregularities, and even several stillbirths. Next, the dangers of alar in apples were exposed. In 1987, the National Academy of Sciences concluded that in our lifetime, pesticides in American food may cause more than one million additional cases of cancer in the United States. Laurie Mott and Karen Snyder of the Natural Resources Defense Council (NRDC) reported in the *Amicus Journal* that each year, 2.6 billion pounds of pesticides are used in the United States; and nearly all Americans have residues of the pesticides DDT, chlordane, heptachlor, aldrin, and dieldrin in their bodies. A 1987 Environmental Protection Agency report indicated that because of massive agricultural use, at least twenty pesticides, some of which are cancer-causing, have been found in the groundwater of twenty-four states. Between 1982 and 1985, the FDA detected pesticide residues in 48% of the most frequently consumed fresh vegetables and fruits. In 1975, the sixth annual report of the Council on Environment stated that dieldrin, which is five times more potent than the outlawed DDT, was found in 99.5% of the American people, 96% of all meat, fish, and poultry, and in 85% of all dairy products. Dieldrin is one of the most potent carcinogens known. It has caused cancer in laboratory animals at every dosage ever tested, no matter how infinitesimal. Low-level exposure in humans has been known to cause convulsions, liver damage, and destruction of the central nervous system. Fortunately, dieldrin was banned in 1974, but who knows how lethal the next new line of pesticides may be. Fooling around with pesticides is a form of American roulette. The drug companies are the only temporary winners.

Dioxin (2, 4, 5-T), an active component of Agent Orange, is considered by Dr. Diane Courtney, head of the Toxic Effects Branch of the EPA's National Environmental Research Center, to be the most toxic chemical known. According to *Diet for a New America,* millions of pounds of 2, 4, 5-T have been sprayed on American soil. The EPA has officially recognized that cattle grazing on land sprayed with dioxin accumulate it in their fat. According to pesticide industry authority Lewis Regenstein, those who eat beef get a dose of dioxin that has been concentrated as it moves up the food chain. Dioxin has been shown to produce cancer, birth defects, miscarriages, and death in lab animals in concentrations as low as one part per trillion. It is no wonder, according to David Steinman in *Diet for a Poisoned Planet,* that deaths from cancer in this country have risen from less than one percent in the beginning of the nineteenth century to one in four American men and one in five American women today. Although other factors, such as nuclear radiation and cigarette smoking, do play a role in increasing the incidence of cancer, I wonder how much the cancer rate would drop if we stopped actively putting all pesticides in our food chain. Even if their toxicity is acknowledged and they are banned, once they have been introduced into the environment, the chlorinated hydrocarbon pesticides are extremely stable compounds that do not break down for decades or longer.

I do not think scientists have discovered the full extent of the damage pesticides have already done to the nation's health. The types of cancers that are statistically emerging suggest that they are originating from the specific effects of certain pesticides. According to *Diet for a Poisoned Planet,* between 1950 and 1985, urinary bladder cancer increased by 51%; kidney and renal pelvis cancer increased by 82%. These types of cancers are directly associated with toxins in the drinking water. Testicular cancer, which occurs in significant proportion among farm workers and manufacturers of pesticides, has increased 81%. In 1985, non-Hodgkin's lymphoma, which is linked with pesticide exposure, increased by 123%. The Surgeon General's Report on Nutrition and Health in 1988 estimated that as many as 10,000 cancer deaths annually could be caused from the chemical additives in food. This estimate does not even include pesticides. It is extremely difficult to know the exact percentage of the cancer increase due to pesticides, additives, and other environmental factors in our food, water, and air, but most likely it is significant.

In addition to the single pesticide factor effect, which can be directly tested in the laboratory, there is often a more powerful synergistic effect from the multiple use of different toxins that react together in the environment. This synergistic effect is difficult to assess. The cumulative effect of widespread, chronic, low-level exposure to multiple pesticides is only partially understood. One National Cancer Institute study found that farmers exposed to herbicides and pesticides had a six times greater risk than nonfarmers of getting one specific type of cancer. Research at the University of Southern California discovered in 1987 that children living in homes where household and garden pesticides were used had a sevenfold greater chance of developing childhood leukemia. The *Amicus Journal* article entitled "Pesticide Alert" stated that in 1982, a congressional report estimated that 82–85% of pesticides registered for use had not been adequately tested for their ability to cause cancer. In addition, 60–70% of pesticides were not tested for creating birth defects, and 90–93% were not tested for the possibility of causing genetic mutations.

In the '90s, the tide of pesticide and herbicide use continued to increase rather than ebb. The following data come from a report in *Pesticide Action Network* published by Californians for Pesticide Reform (CPR). In California, which uses 25% of all the pesticides in the U.S., the trend is toward an increasing use and dependence on toxic pesticides and herbicides. California literally puts hundreds of millions of pounds of chemicals on our crops, soil, water, homes, schools, and work places each year. The environmental protection laws simply are not strong enough. Six and one-half pounds of pesticides per person are used in California, which is more than double the national average of 3.1 pounds per person.

Pesticide use in California increased 31% from 1991 to 1995, a jump from 161 to 212 million pounds per year. The increase occurred primarily in the intensity of pesticides per acre, as the number of agricultural acres stayed about the same. The use of cancer-causing pesticides rose 129% to more than twenty-three million pounds—what is now 11% of the total pesticide use in the state. Use of acutely toxic nerve poisons increased 52% to about nine million pounds. The use of restricted pesticides—those which regularly cause damage to people, crops, and the environment—increased 34% to forty-eight million pounds in 1995. The total volume of carcinogens, reproductive hazards, endocrine disrupters, category I acute systemic poisons, category II nerve toxins, and restricted-use toxins increased 32% between 1991 and 1995. This is approximately seventy-two million pounds, or 34% of the total reported pesticide use. Strawberries and grapes were the two most heavily pesticided crops. Strawberries received about three hundred pounds of active pesticides per acre, and grapes received a total of fifty-nine million pounds of pesticides in 1995.

A report by Californians for Pesticide Reform (CPR) shows that 87% of the forty-six California school districts surveyed used highly toxic pesticides in their routine building and lawn maintenance. These forty-six districts serve one and one-half million children. Seventy percent of these school districts used suspected carcinogens; 52% used pesticides that are known to cause birth defects or impair normal mental and physical development; 50% used pesticides suspected of disrupting the human hormonal system; and 54% used nerve toxins. This information was typically unavailable to parents, teachers, and the public. CPR had to use legal counsel to obtain these simple data.

According to the Environmental Working Group, every day one million U.S. children under the age of five consume unsafe levels of pesticides that are known to harm their developing brain and nervous system. An analysis of the federal information shows that most of the risk comes from four organophosphate insecticides: methyl parathion, dimethoate, pirimiphos methyl, and azinphos methyl. The foods most likely to contain toxic levels are peaches, apples, nectarines, popcorn, and pears. The baby foods most likely to have unsafe levels are pears, peaches, and apple juice. This study found that approximately one in four peaches and one in eight apples had levels of organophosphates that are unsafe for children. Can we afford not to protect our children by not buying organic produce?

If you think this increase in pesticides and herbicides is just a bunch of statistics and has no effect, think again. The incidence of childhood cancer increased 10.8% from 1973 through 1990, according to the EPA. (Cancer now kills more children under the age of fifteen than any other disease.) A child born today has a one in six hundred chance of developing cancer by the age of ten, according to the EPA. By a child's first birthday, the combined cancer risk of just eight pesticides on twenty foods they may have eaten exceeds the EPA's lifetime level of acceptable risk. Children eat more food and take in more water relative to their size than adults and thus have elevated exposures to pesticides and other contaminants. Industrial pollution is a form of national domestic violence. With these kinds of statistics, do you have any wonder why I so strongly stress the importance of feeding ourselves, pregnant mothers, and our children as close to 100% organic foods as possible?

The potential for health problems depends on the extent and type of pesticide exposure and the susceptibility of the individual. Children and the elderly are the most susceptible, the latter because their immune system and organ function decline with age. Children's bodies are smaller and they receive proportionally higher doses of toxins per body weight; their organs can be damaged more readily because they are not fully developed. Furthermore, many of the most frequently used pesticides affect the nervous system, and children are more susceptible to neurotoxins than adults.

Among the effects of pesticides, cancer is the most studied. Between 1969 and 1986, several types of cancer increased significantly among people ages 64 to 84 in six leading industrial countries. These cancer types are multiple myeloma (a cancer that starts in the bone marrow and spreads to other bones), melanoma of the skin, and cancer of the prostate, bladder, brain, lung, and breast. Although farmers' general lifestyle is healthier than city folks, with lower risks for most cancers and noncancer diseases, they were found to have specific cancers, including multiple myeloma, lymphomas, skin melanomas, leukemia, and cancer of the lip, stomach, prostate, and brain. Work-related exposures were theorized to be causing specific cancers among farmers.

Evidence has accumulated that many industrial chemicals (including many common plastics and pesticides) mimic estrogen hormones, thereby disrupting reproduction and development in humans, mammals, birds, and fish just like diethylstilbesterol (DES) did to mothers and fetuses who received the drug in the '60s. These estrogenic-like chemicals may be the cause for the increasing incidence of cancer of the breast, testicles, and prostate. These industrial chemicals have affected us in a variety of ways: (1) sperm counts in men worldwide average 50% of the average from fifty years ago; (2) the incidence of testicular cancer has tripled and prostate cancer has doubled in the past fifty years; (3) in 1960 the incidence of breast cancer was one in twenty, and in 1998 it was one in nine; and (4) young male alligators in pesticide-contaminated lakes in Florida have such small penises that they are unable to function sexually. Estrogen-mediated hormonal imbalances can create all these changes and more.

Estrogen is usually considered a female hormone, but males produce estrogen in small amounts. In the developing fetus, a specific ratio of androgens (male hormones) to estrogen must be maintained for proper sexual differentiation to occur. If the hormone balance is disturbed, the offspring may be born with two sets of sexual organs or a single set that is incompletely developed. Diminished sperm count and possible predisposition to cancer also may be set at this stage.

Examples of estrogen mimickers are DDT, DDE, dieldrin, dicofol, methoxychlor, some PCBs, alkyl phenols from penta- to nonylphenol, as well as bisphenol-A (the building block of polycarbonate plastics, used in many common detergents, toiletries, lubricants, and spermicides). Many of these estrogen mimickers resist breaking down in the environment and are highly soluble in fat; thus they accumulate in the bodies of fish, birds, mammals, and humans. Nonvegetarians obviously accumulate a higher amount. One study showed that the mothers' milk of vegetarians contained only 1% the amount of pesticides as the milk of meat-eating mothers. Many of these estrogen mimickers will cross the placenta barrier and pass into the developing fetus. This high estrogen exposure is one reason I recommend minimizing the use of soy, which is high in phytoestrogens. Soy milk is especially important to avoid for infants.

Even the conservative *Journal of the American Medical Association* has reported that estrogenic chemicals have an effect. Ana Soto, a researcher at Tufts University, combined ten estrogenic mimickers, each at one-tenth the dose necessary to produce a minimal response. She found that when all ten were combined, they were strong enough to produce an estrogenic response. This is significant because the U.S. government has been regulating based on its testing of individual chemical effects. They have almost no data on the synergistic effects of the many pesticides, herbicides, fungicides, plastics, PCBs, etc., working together.

There are at least nineteen major chemicals used on U.S. crops that are associated with disrupting the human hormone system. According to the Washington, DC-based Environmental Working Group, about 220 million pounds of these hormone disrupters are applied to sixty-eight different crops annually. In 1992, Frank Falck, M.D., Ph.D., Assistant Professor of Surgery at the University of Connecticut School of Medicine, examined the tissues from suspicious breast lumps in forty women and found that those tissues that were cancerous had higher levels of PCBs, DDT, and DDE (a DDT by-product) than the benign tissues. Dr. Wolff, Professor of Community Medicine at Mt. Sinai Medical Center in New York City, analyzed blood from more than 14,000 women and found that those who developed breast cancer had higher levels of DDE. He found that the women with the highest levels of DDE had four times the risk of breast cancer than those with the lower levels.

Since the 1960s, most researchers in the U.S. have expressed the opinion that the findings connecting the estrogenic pesticides with breast and other cancers are only preliminary, but the Israeli government has already acted on the evidence with exciting results. From 1976 to 1986, Israel was the only country among twenty-eight countries studied where the breast cancer death rate dropped. One explanation was that in 1978, Israel banned three estrogenic pesticides. Within two years after the ban, lindane levels in the tissues dropped by 90%, DDT by 43%, and BHC by 98%. By 1986, the death rate for breast cancer among Israeli women below the age of 44 had dropped by 30%.

Scientists can pretend to discern "safe" levels for an individual chemical, but they have no idea of any safe level for combining chemicals. In fact, there are no "safe" levels. Political decision-makers need to understand that we have to abandon the chemical-by-chemical regulation approach and regulate whole classes of chemicals. Furthermore, instead of setting standards according to pesticide effects on healthy adults, their effects on children should be used to set maximum exposure. Certain categories of dangerous chemicals, such as those that cause cancer and disrupt nervous system and hormone function, need to be immediately discontinued if we are to survive as a species.

In the *Journal of Food Science,* one of the few studies on the synergistic effect of pesticides reported that when three chemicals were each tested separately on rats, there was no obvious ill effect. When two of the three chemicals were added together, the health of the rats diminished. When all three were used synergistically, the rats all died within two weeks. This synergistic pesticide porridge of our food and water is probably creating the most overall damage to the health of all living forms in our environment. People who do not use purified water or organic food are exposing themselves significantly to this danger. The lack of available data on the health-destroying effects of pesticide use, both individually and synergistically, suggests that the EPA has to be regulating more out of ignorance than knowledge. More than 110 different pesticides were detected in all foods between 1982 and 1985. Of the twenty-five pesticides detected most frequently, nine are known to cause cancer. This is a serious situation.

The amazing observation is that pesticides do not even achieve their stated purpose, yet we still are willing to risk our lives to use them. Dr. David Pimentel of Cornell University, one of the world's leading agricultural experts, estimates that more than 500 species of insects are now resistant to pesticides. It is no accident that crops destroyed by insects have nearly doubled during the last forty years in spite of an almost tenfold increase in the amount and toxicity of insecticides. One study showed that recent pesticide usage by Filipino rice farmers costs the individual farmer more in medical bills than it generates in increased rice production. Even on a cost-benefit versus health approach, the use of pesticides comes out on the negative side of things. Aside from increased rates of certain cancers, farmers in the Philippines who were not organic growers suffered nearly double the kidney and respiratory problems compared to organic farmers and were five times more likely to experience eye problems. Farmers who used pesticides had considerably more skin complaints, gastrointestinal problems, neurological problems, and hematological problems.

In 1986, the Indonesian government sponsored a plan to decrease the use of pesticides. The rice production since then has increased by 10% and there is much less capital outlay for pesticides and their concomitant medical problems. In Bangladesh, farmers using integrated pest management spent 75% less money on pesticides and increased their crop harvest by 14% over those using high levels of pesticides.

In summary, pesticides can affect every living organism. Human beings are no exception. The more detrimental effects of pesticides, herbicides, and fungicides include cancer, nervous system disorders, birth defects, alterations of DNA; liver, kidney, lung, and reproductive problems; and an overall disruption of ecological cycles on the planet. According to Dr. David Pimentel, an entomologist and agricultural expert at Cornell University, pesticides cost the nation $8 billion annually in public health expenditures, groundwater decontamination, fish kills, bird kills, and domestic animal deaths. Pesticide usage is a major public health problem worldwide. It reflects a consciousness that is completely out of touch with the laws of nature.

Most genetically engineered plants are designed as pesticides in themselves or as plants that can withstand heavier applications of herbicides, such as Monsanto's "Round-Up" weed-killer. The result has been a three-fold increase in pesticide use in some places, because the plants can withstand them and, of course, this creates three times more toxic pollution. In this process of using genetically designed plants, corporations have taken control over seed supplies and the pesticides that they have designed to control them. The result is that this technology works against farmer-controlled, ecologically sensitive, sustainable, and organic methods. The organic methods are obviously reducing the amount of pesticides and helping to protect agricultural biodiversity.

The good news is that many people are listening. The total of organic products sold has grown about 20% per year in recent years, and many supermarkets now stock organic products. Please support this positive shift in the supermarkets, and buy organic foods. Yet, in the midst of consumers waking up, the large corporate use of pesticides continues. For example, in the year 2000, Monsanto sold more than 2.6 billion dollars' worth of Round-Up around the world. Monsanto's genetically engineered seeds are on more than 100 million acres.

What sort of consciousness does it take to continue to deliberately poison yourself and your family in order to get less effective crop outputs? What sort of consciousness does it take to manufacture these poisons and sell them (especially to sell poisonous chemicals banned in the U.S. to developing countries where the people do not understand how to minimally protect themselves because of ignorance and poverty)? Pesticide usage not only leads to disease, but directly destroys the life force of the soil. I do not understand how people can choose to spend money for something that not only does not work, but poisons humans and the environment.

## PROTECT YOURSELF AGAINST
## FOOD CHEMICALIZATION

We have the power to refuse to consume what is detrimental to our health and to the planet. This power of the marketplace is stronger than that of multinational corporations and Washington politics. Since there is very little real control and monitoring by the U.S. government or by the chemical companies, the responsibility for our health lies with us, as it always has. Let us put our money where our mouths are. Buy organic produce whenever possible. We have the power to restore the world to one that is aligned with the healing harmony of the universe. Let us do it.

Buying organic not only helps us avoid pesticide poisoning; it supports the organic farmers who are rebuilding the soil. The more organic farmers there are, the less the organic produce will cost. According to a study at Tufts University, organic produce has a nutrient content approximately 88% higher than commercially grown produce. This means that by buying organic produce we actually get more for our money and for our health.

Another way to oppose pesticide madness is to stay abreast of legislation that attempts to curb pesticide use. For example, we all need to support bills like the School Environment Protection Act. Presently, there is a movement to deregulate environmental protection on many levels, including pesticide regulation. Let the politicians know it is time they awoke and became more responsible to themselves and to their constituency.

According to the *Pesticide Monitoring Journal* published by the EPA, the major source of pesticide exposure comes from foods of animal origin. *Diet for a New America* points out that 95–99% of all the toxic chemical residues come from meat, fish, dairy, and eggs. One can substantially avoid this high toxic exposure by choosing to eat vegan foods such as fruits, vegetables, nuts, seeds, and grains, which are lower on the food chain and thus have less accumulation of these poisons.

As mentioned earlier, *The New England Journal of Medicine* published a finding that the breast milk of vegetarian women has only 1–2% of the pesticide contamination that is the national average for breast-feeding women on a flesh-centered diet. This is a significant indication of how much effect one can have on one's pesticide exposure by becoming vegetarian. It is possible to further decrease exposure by only eating organically grown vegetarian foods. Sometimes one is in places where it is not possible to obtain organic, vegetarian foods. It is still a safer choice to eat commercially grown fruits, vegetables, grains, nuts, and seeds rather than flesh foods. The body can detox a little pesticide exposure but becomes overwhelmed if the exposure is chronic or high.

David Steinman, in his book *Diet for a Poisoned Planet,* has done an enormous amount of work in studying exactly which fruits, vegetables, nuts, seeds, and grains have the lowest toxic residues. He analyzed foods for more than one hundred different industrial chemicals and pesticides, using laboratory detection limits that were five to ten times more sensitive than the normal FDA detection standards. He did this by taking his food samples from four different geographic regions, analyzing them exactly as they would be eaten, and repeating this for four years ending in 1986. This gave him a total of sixteen samples per food to analyze and average. Each of the foods was rated according to which toxins it contained and how much toxic residue was present. The combination of these two figures was factored into a cancer risk assessment. These findings were placed into three categories according to their safety. Safety was determined by the amount of pesticide residues and their cancer risk assessment. In *Conscious Eating,* there is a complete summary of his data. What I labeled as "relatively safe" are commercial foods that have minimal toxic effects. The next category, "marginally safe if eaten sparingly," is for foods to be avoided regularly. The third category is for commercial foods so potentially toxic that it is best to completely avoid them.

The best way to be safe, of course, is to avoid commercial foods. If enough people care about themselves and their children to buy only organic foods, the law of consumer demand on the market will force a shift that will increase the amount of organic farming and make more organic foods available at lower prices. Fortunately, a subtle shift toward organic farming and produce is happening in many parts of the U.S. and throughout Europe. Prince Charles in England is one of the outspoken leaders of this movement.

## GENETICALLY ENGINEERED FOODS: "IF IT'S NOT BROKEN, DON'T FIX IT"

Genetically engineered foods provide a more significant threat to our delicate worldwide ecosystems than even pesticides and herbicides. I want to quote John Hagelin, an award-winning quantum physicist and candidate who ran for president on the Natural Law Party ticket. He says, "When genetic engineers disregard the genetic boundaries set in place by natural law, they run the risk of destroying our genetic encyclopedia, compromising the richness of our biodiversity, creating a genetic soup. What this means for the future of our ecosystem, no one knows."

Dr. John Fagan, internationally recognized molecular biologist and former genetic engineer, says, "We are living today in a very delicate time, one that is reminiscent of the birth of the nuclear era, when mankind stood on the threshold of a new technology. No one knew that nuclear power would bring us to the brink of annihilation or fill our planet with highly toxic radioactive waste. We were so excited by the power of a new discovery that we leaped ahead blindly, and without caution. Today the situation with genetic engineering is perhaps even more grave because this technology acts on the very blueprint of life itself."

When you do not know what you are doing, and you insist on meddling, you have the potential to create a great deal of damage. There is an old saying: "If it's not broken, don't fix it."

The dangers of genetically engineered (GE) foods—also known as GMOs, genetically modified organisms—are multiple.

Once a gene is inserted into an organism, it can cause unanticipated side effects. Mutations and side effects can cause genetically engineered food to contain toxins and allergens and also to be reduced in nutritional value.

GE foods have potential to cause damage to the ecosystem, harm to wildlife, and alterations to the natural habitat. Our plant and animal species have evolved over millions of years, and introducing genetically engineered species upsets the delicate balance of the ecology.

Gene pollution can never be cleaned up.

The use of GE crops increases pesticide pollution of food and water supplies. Approximately 57% of the research done by biotechnology companies is focused on the development of plants that can tolerate larger amounts of herbicides.

GE foods may cause unpredictable, permanent changes in the nature of our food. The essential problem is that the genetic structures of our plants and animals have been nourishing the human race for thousands of years. Because genetic engineering is far from an exact science, the new genetic structure of a plant could give rise to unusual proteins that could really cause a problem for humans and our health. Examples of "leaky genes" or genetically engineered plants cross-pollinating with traditional varieties and passing on the genetically engineered trait have been reported in several places. In 2000, the National Institute of Agricultural Botany reported the first genetically modified super-weed in Britain. Pollen from a genetically engineered canola crossed with wild turnips. These turnips inherited the herbicide-resistant genes. In Mexico, cross-pollinating from genetically engineered corn has spread as far as sixty miles away. Reports in Canada that weeds are now able to tolerate herbicides designed for herbicide-resistant genetically modified crops have been showing up since 2000.

GE foods may be missing important elements or have changes in the nutrient ratios. Genetic engineering may accidentally or intentionally remove or inactivate substances in food that the engineers consider undesirable, but the new food or the missing substance may have particular qualities that we do not quite understand. For example, the nutrient chemistry in genetically engineered soy reveals 29% less choline, needed for nervous system development, and 27% more trypsin inhibitor, which inhibits protein digestion, and 200% more lectins, which are associated with greater food sensitivity.

The use of GE foods results in decreased effectiveness of antibiotics. It is now commonplace in genetic engineering to introduce antibiotics in genes as a marker to indicate that the organism has been successfully engineered. What we are looking at now may be foods with the potential to inactivate antibiotics.

GE foods can cause allergic reactions. One of the problems of these newly identified proteins is that the human body is simply not programmed to deal with them. One of the responses of the body to unnatural and toxic food is to have an allergic reaction. Reports of increased allergies to GE soy products are already coming out. Soy, which is now 70% GE in the U.S., has moved into the top ten allergic foods. It is now associated with significantly more severe allergies.

Harmful effects may not be discovered for years, in the sense that we do not have an idea of what can potentially happen as we introduce these new foods into our diet. As I point out in *Conscious Eating,* in my chapter on the biologically altered brain, there have been significant changes in quality of health as we have introduced refined, fried, fast, and junk food into our Western diet since the 1930s. What makes us possibly think that by further interfering with natural foods through genetic engineering that we are not going to cause more and more serious problems, and further alter the biologically altered brain? There are no long-term studies to prove the safety of genetically altered foods. I do not even want to wait to see these studies, because results will not be available until thirty years after the fact, and by that time, it will be too late.

GE organisms can have unanticipated negative ecological impact. There are some genetically engineered bacteria that looked like they were useful in one limited way, but independent researchers have discovered that they are capable of making the land infertile. One case to make this point is a bacterium called *Klebsiella planticola.* This soil bacterium has been genetically engineered to dispose of wood chips, corn stalks, and waste from lumber business and agriculture. As it turns out, it also produces ethanol in the process. When seeds were planted in soil that contained the waste products of this bacterium, they sprouted and died. The independent researchers found that the genetically engineered klebsiella is highly competitive with native soil microorganisms and strongly suppresses their activities. We need the more than 1,600 species of microorganisms found in a teaspoon of soil in order to have vital force in the soil. If it is not obvious, it should be—we cannot predict the effect of a new microorganism on the ecology and the environment. "If it's not broken, don't fix it."

GE foods may create newer and higher levels of toxins in the environment. Many plants produce a variety of compounds that are toxic to humans or alter the food quality. Generally speaking, as I point out in *Conscious Eating,* these toxic elements do not cause problems in the levels normally found in plants, unless we consume those plants in large quantities.

The practice of combining plant and animal species in engineered foods has the potential to create new and unpredictable levels of toxins. Even the FDA and the EPA now classify as insecticides certain corn and potato strains that are engineered to produce toxins that will kill insects. These plants are no longer even classified as vegetables! Insect-resistant crops make up about one-quarter of the acres of transgenic plants. One of the most serious ecological threats is crops carrying a gene from *Bacillus thuringiensis* (Bt). The Bt gene transferred into corn and cotton kills leaf-eating caterpillars. Every cell of these plants contains the Bt gene and produces Bt toxin. Bt is one of the world's most important biological pesticides. This is a direct threat to organic farmers. In 1999, the International Federation of Organic Agricultural Movements joined with the Center for Food Safety and Greenpeace in a lawsuit against the EPA, which approved genetically engineered Bt cotton, corn, and potatoes. Monsanto's Bt cotton harms a wider range of insects, including lacewings and ladybugs, and causes bees to be confused in their ability to distinguish the different smells of flowers. Monarch butterfly caterpillars, according to the journal *Nature,* were being killed by pollen from Bt corn. What potential damage might Bt toxin crops have on the flora that live in our own intestines?

How much proof do we need to see before we realize that genetic engineering can potentially create biological chaos? Genetic engineering companies try to make the claim that these genetically engineered foods are natural and equivalent to the original genetic strains. But that really is not the case. For example, although the industry has presented more than 1,400 examples of analyses demonstrating that Round-Up Ready soy is the "substantial" equivalent of natural soy, the manufacturer's own studies on cows suggest that when the herbicide Round-Up is sprayed on Round-Up Ready soy, the defensive response of the plant leads to increased plant estrogen levels. Therefore, it is possible that the sprayed soybeans contain a higher level of plant estrogen than the natural beans. The implications of this are obvious. We also know that a significant amount of people have become allergic to soy protein with stronger allergies than before, when exposed to genetically engineered soy.

Using bacteria to make genetically engineered tryptophan is another example of how toxins are created beyond our understanding. In 1989, there was an outbreak of a disease called eosinophilia-myalgia syndrome (EMS). A company selling tryptophan that was produced by genetically engineered bacteria was found to be the source of the problem. The tryptophan itself did not seem to be causing the EMS but rather the contaminants, which made up only .01% of the marketed product by weight. When the bacteria were genetically altered to produce these larger quantities of tryptophan, the increased concentration of tryptophan reached such high levels that unexpected chemical reactions produced new kinds of toxins which led to the EMS. However, this toxic tryptophan would have passed as a "substantial" equivalent and also passed the test for known toxin. The point is that we cannot test for toxins we do not even know about. The result of this genetically engineered tryptophan fiasco is that 37 people died, 1,500 people were partially paralyzed, and 5,000 were temporarily disabled.

One of the biggest problems with genetically engineered plants is their presumed ability to tolerate unlimited pesticides. In the '60s, the "green revolution" created higher crop yield at first, but then serious problems surfaced over time. With large-scale use of high-yield seed, higher levels of fertilizers and pesticides had to be used. Both of these inputs are costly, ecologically damaging, and damaging to the health of farm workers. The aggressive use of monoculture production destroyed the diversity of local ecologies, affected traditional crop varieties, and led to permanent loss of crop diversity. The need for increased irrigation used groundwater supplies faster than they were replenished, and a soil erosion problem developed. Then, after a few years, those "disease-resistant" crops began to become infected. Since the green revolution (over the last forty years), the use of pesticides in some places has undergone almost a ten-fold increase, and the crops destroyed by insects have nearly doubled. There are now more than five hundred species of insects that are pesticide-resistant.

These crops, because of the way they are commercially grown, are less nutritious. Some studies have found a reduction in IQ of up to ten points in the generation of children brought up on these "green revolution" foods. Genetically engineered crops—because they are so strongly tied to a monoculture approach, chemical fertilizer, herbicides, and pesticides—will probably cause an increase in all of the health and mental health problems associated with the "green revolution," and possibly on a grander and more serious scale, because the gene pool will have been disrupted. One clear example is the significantly increased use of Round-Up, the Monsanto herbicide that is sold along with the Round-Up Ready crops of soy, corn, and canola. According to the U.S. Fish and Wildlife Service, at least seventy-four plant species are endangered by Round-Up, and it kills fish at concentrations of 10 parts per million, impedes the growth of earthworms, and is toxic to soil microbes that help plants take up nutrients from the soil. The active ingredient in Round-Up is glycophosphate. In the 1990s, glycophosphate was listed as the third most common cause of all forms of pesticide-related illness in California. Studies have also linked exposure to glycophosphate with an increased risk of developing non-Hodgkin's lymphoma, the third-fastest-growing cancer in the U.S. Already, the Round-Up Ready crops are needing higher doses of

Round-Up to control the pests that commonly attack them. In the late '90s, the FDA tripled the amount of Round-Up active ingredient allowed to remain on crops, since the residue levels were exceeding the allowable legal limit set previously.

Nevertheless, because of economic incentives, the scourge of genetically engineered foods has increased. By the year 2000, two-thirds of the foods sold in U.S. supermarkets included genetically modified substances. In 1996 and 1997, there were nineteen genetically engineered products on the market. Now there are more than thirty. These include three varieties of soybeans, eleven varieties of corn (this does not include blue corn), four varieties of canola, papaya, two varieties of potatoes, five varieties of tomatoes, two varieties of yellow crooked-neck squash, five varieties of cotton, and dairy products. There are also products that originate from genetically engineered organisms, including candies, cookies, breads, cereals, corn syrup, oils, juices, detergents, dough conditioners, yeast, sugar, animal feeds, vitamins, and enzymes used in the processing of cheese. Genetically engineered soy is in soy flour, soy oil, lecithin, soy protein isolates, concentrates, vitamin E supplements, tofu dogs, cereals, veggie burgers, sausages, tamari, soy sauce, chips, ice cream, frozen yogurt, infant formula, sauces, margarine, soy cheeses, cookies, chocolates, cakes, fried foods, shampoos, bubble bath, cosmetics, and enriched flours and pastas.

Genetically engineered corn is in corn flour, cornstarch, corn sweeteners, corn oil, and many syrups. Products that may contain GE corn derivatives include vitamin C, tofu dogs, chips, candies, ice cream, infant formula, salad dressing, tomato sauce, breads, cookies, cereals, baking powder, alcohol, vanilla, margarine, soy sauce, tamari, sodas, fried foods, powdered sugar, and enriched flours and pastas.

Because genetically engineered canola is so prevalent, it is found in most canola oil products that contain canola derivatives. These include chips, salad dressings, cookies, margarines, soaps, detergents, soy cheese, and fried foods. Genetically engineered cotton is found in many fabrics and in cottonseed oil, as well as in products that contain fabrics or cottonseed oil, such as clothes, linens, chips, peanut butter, crackers, and cookies. With GE potatoes we are obviously looking at not only fresh potatoes, but potato chips, fries, mashed potatoes, baked potatoes, mixes, Passover products, vegetable products, and soups. With tomatoes, we are looking at sauces, purees, pizza, and lasagna. It appears that no plum or roma tomatoes have been genetically engineered and only one cherry tomato has been, but this may not even be true by the time this book is published. Most non-organic papayas grown in Hawaii are genetically engineered. Some crooked-neck squash and zucchini are genetically engineered.

Since 95% of the soymeal and approximately 90% of the corn grown in the U.S. are used as livestock feed, almost all non-organic meat, poultry, dairy, or egg products sold in the U.S. contain genetically engineered substances.

The possible dangers of eating genetically engineered foods and/or foods that contain genetically modified substances were highlighted by the research of Dr. Arpad Pasztai, a senior scientist at the Rowett Research Institute in Aberdeen, Scotland. He fed genetically engineered potatoes to rats. The rats developed smaller hearts, livers, and brains, and had weaker immune systems. Some rats showed significant brain shrinkage after only ten days of eating genetically modified potatoes. I consider this the most significant piece of data on the health dangers of GMOs and an ominous warning.

Public relations hacks for GE foods talk about their importance for "feeding the world's hungry." This is a cruel joke on the truth. The GE foods produce crops that are primarily intended as feed for livestock, not to provide nutrition to people. Contrary to GE food corporate public relations about producing more per acre, genetically modified soybean actually produces 4% less than conventional varieties, according to the research of Agronomy professor Ed Oplinger at the University of Wisconsin. His study covered soybean yields in twelve U.S. states. Other studies with Monsanto's transgenic soybeans showed 10% less productivity as compared to conventional varieties.

Part of the argument against genetically engineered food and for going organic is the importance of preserving heirloom seeds, which contain the original seed genetics. Heirloom seeds work on a deeper energetic soul level as well. Heirloom seeds contain the entire history of a people and of a land.

These seeds nourish our souls and strengthen our connection to the land. They are bred for nourishing people, not for making money. This shamanistic, Earth-based understanding is in sharp contrast to the intent of the genetic engineering corporations. This contrast is becoming clearer to many people throughout the world. For example, Vandana Shiva, an Indian scientist, determined after an international meeting in 1987 that the corporate chemical and food companies were attempting to control agriculture through patents, genetic engineering, and mergers. She believes that what the global-economy corporations call "growth" is really a form of theft from nature and from people. The globalized economy has legalized corporate growth, based on harvests stolen from nature and people. In response to this threat, she started Navadanya, a movement in India for seed-saving to protect biodiversity and to keep seed and agriculture free of corporate monopoly control. It is interesting that Navadanya's commitment to saving seeds means non-cooperation with patent laws that make the age-old practice of seed saving a crime. It is necessary to our survival that we follow her example by living and eating in a way that honors the natural and spiritual laws of the planet. Such a mass shift is a way that healing can take place.

So why does the corporate world push a technology that breeds ill health, is a danger to the world ecology, does not feed the world's poor and hungry, and is actually less economically productive per acre? Robert T. Frailey, Co-President of Monsanto's agricultural sector, puts it bluntly, "It's really a consolidation of the entire food chain." GE foods are created not because of health or productivity factors, but because they are patentable and give international corporations an opportunity to try to control the food chain and the world population that depends on it for sustenance.

## IRRADIATED FOODS—ANOTHER BIOHAZARD

Irradiated food is a biohazard. Irradiating food completely disorganizes the energetic field. This is also true of microwaved food. There is an appearance that irradiation kills all the infecting bacteria, but even *E. coli,* the bacterium most often cited when arguing for the use of food irradiation, has evolved new forms that are radiation-resistant. There have been several situations in which food companies have taken rotting food and irradiated it to get rid of the bacteria. This does not, however, get rid of the toxins that the bacteria produce. Botulism is one of those cases where the toxin produced is worse than the bacteria itself. The focus in this book is not on the whole issue of food irradiation, except to say that it significantly decreases the quality and energy of food. A substantial number of studies show that irradiated food, when given to certain animals, caused increased incidence of tumors. In one study in India, researchers fed irradiated wheat to children, and after about a month, the children began to develop leukemia-like changes in their chromosomes and white blood cells. When researchers stopped giving the irradiated wheat, the children's blood picture went back to normal. Again, we do not understand the implications of using this technology. If it's not broken, don't fix it. The choice to "fix it or make it better" only applies to the corporations for which "making it better" is translated as more profit and control. The implication for a solution again and again is to go back to basics and respect the natural laws. With this approach, we can have a healthy diet, which will sustain our lives and the quality of our own DNA.

By eating authentic, organic, whole foods the way nature has given them to us, we have a sound way of eating that begins to bring us back to health as a nation and a world. Unfortunately, this obvious natural path is not so easy for people to follow in a world dominated by corporate greed, rather than an economy organized around improving the quality of health for all people and the world. The once publicly defeated issue of food irradiation has re-emerged after Hudson Foods' recall of 25 million pounds of beef due to *E. coli* contamination. For reasons that are typical of American corporate thinking, the press came out with some pro-food-irradiation articles arguing that since the food supply is contaminated, food irradiation is a quick and easy way to fix the problem. Of course, the deeper issues are not addressed. How did the food supply become so contaminated? What are the ramifications of building hundreds of nuclear irradiation plants? What are the damaging effects of nuclear irradiation on the food and the people who end up eating it?

The real reason that the food supply has become contaminated is because of inhumane, hygienically filthy, and fecally contaminated animal processing facilities. The focus on rapid slaughtering rates—in many facilities up to three hundred cows per hour—almost guarantees filth and contamination by pathogen-containing fecal matter, especially in beef and chicken. Cheap industrial food has the least chance of being safe or humane. In my world, killing animals for food could never be humane, but mass-produced animals for slaughter remains vastly different from the respect and prayer a Native American would go through before killing a buffalo. Food irradiation does not solve the problem, it only gives the illusion of helping. It actually makes the situation worse because it makes possible the conditions for lowering the hygiene standards even further.

Who are we kidding? Food irradiation is not 100% effective. It is already known that food irradiation does not eliminate all the *E. coli* and salmonella. Food irradiation has become a source of mutant bacteria and perhaps viruses that are radiation-resistant. It is the old antibiotic-resistant story with a new twist. In addition, food irradiation plants are unsafe. Radioactive accidents have already happened at the few food irradiation plants that exist in this country and worldwide. Since 1974, the Nuclear Regulatory Commission has recorded 54 accidents at 132 irradiation facilities around the world. In New Jersey, which has the highest concentration of irradiation plants, almost every plant has a record of environmental contamination, worker over-exposure, or regulatory failures.

Food irradiation plant accidents can be extremely dangerous to surrounding communities and to workers at the plant. In 1991, a worker in Maryland suffered critical injuries when exposed to ionizing radiation from an electron beam accelerator. In 1988, Radiation Sterilizers, Inc., in Decatur, Georgia, had a leak of cesium-137 capsules into the water, which endangered the workers and contaminated the facility. It is unclear how much got into the community, but clean-up costs were greater than $30 million. In 1986, Radiation Technology in New Jersey had its license revoked for thirty-two worker safety violations and for throwing radioactive garbage out with the trash. In 1974, Isomedix in New Jersey flushed radioactive water down toilets and contaminated pipes leading to sewers. To irradiate all flesh food alone, hundreds of facilities would be needed. The only radioactive isotope available for this level of usage is cesium-137, which is not only deadly today, but remains dangerous for approximately six hundred years.

There is no solid evidence to show that eating irradiated food is safe, but there is some evidence to show that it has specific dangers. Food is irradiated with gamma rays, which break up the molecular structure of the food and create free radicals. The free radicals react with the food to form new chemical substances called "radiolytic products." Some of these include formaldehyde, benzene, formic acid, and quinones, which are known to be harmful to human health. In one experiment, for example, levels of benzene, a known carcinogen, were seven times higher in irradiated beef than in non-irradiated beef. Some of these radiolytic products are unique to the irradiation process and have not been adequately identified or tested for toxicity.

Irradiating food destroys somewhere between 20 and 80% of the vitamins, including A, $B_1$, $B_3$, $B_6$, $B_{12}$, folic acid, C, E, and K. Amino acids and essential fatty acids are also destroyed. Enzymes, of course, are destroyed, as are the bio-photons.

A significant number of studies show some dangers of eating irradiated food for animals and humans. Raltech Scientific Services, Inc., after a series of twelve studies on feeding irradiated chicken to different animal species, found the possibility of chromosome damage, immunotoxicity, greater incidence of kidney disease, cardiac thrombus, and fibroplasia. According to *Food & Water Journal,* from which I received much of this information, USDA researcher Donald Thayer concluded, "A collective assessment of study results argues against a definitive conclusion that the gamma-irradiated test material (irradiated chicken) was free of toxic properties." Rats who received irradiated food showed a statistically significant increase in testicular tumors and possible kidney and testicular damage.

In attempting to determine what to do about food irradiation, the FDA reviewed 441 toxicity studies. The chairperson in charge of new food additives at the FDA, Dr. Marcia van Gemert, testified that all 441 of the studies were flawed. The FDA, however, determined that at least five studies were acceptable under 1980 toxicological standards. The Department of Preventive Medicine and Community Health of the New Jersey Medical School found that two of these studies were methodologically flawed. In the third of the five studies, animals eating a diet of irradiated food experienced weight loss and increased miscarriages, possibly due to radiation-induced vitamin E deficiency. The remaining two of the five studies used food irradiated at levels below the FDA-approved 100,000 rads and thus cannot be used to scientifically justify food irradiation at a higher level. Nevertheless, with none of the five studies supporting the use of food irradiation, the FDA has approved the use of food irradiation in our food supply. This includes vegetables and fruits as well as spices, and a variety of flesh foods.

## GO ORGANIC

For those interested in health, what we are looking at is an unsavory situation. We are faced with commercially grown foods, irradiated foods, genetically engineered foods, and government authorities who are choosing, in essence, to make it very difficult to discern whether something has been irradiated or genetically modified. It presents a complex problem. There is, however, a very simple solution: **go organic, authentic, or grow your own.** That takes us back to the idea of authentic food that flies under the radar of government control and big business operations. That is what we are doing at the Tree of Life. Our Rainbow Green Live-Food Cuisine is 100% organic and authentic as possible. This simple yet powerful solution is what we are recommending as a way of addressing the problem.

There are many positive steps to take in addition to the Rainbow Green Live-Food Cuisine, such as checking where you buy groceries to make sure the buyers are committed to not marketing irradiated or genetically engineered foods.

The good news is that the growing tide of GE junk foods directly encourages us to move toward health and a higher quality of life, and greater awareness of how we want to live. I want to take what appears to be negative and turn it around by saying that this is a very positive inducement to lead our lives as authentic, full, healthy human beings. The Rainbow Green Live-Food Cuisine is specifically about helping us to achieve these goals.

If we follow the guideline to eat only whole, organic, high-energy, authentic foods, the irresponsible tampering with our food supply will have little effect on us personally. If these issues pain your heart and conscience to help others, then there are many positive steps to take. One of the most active organizations dealing with the world issues of food is Food First: Institute for Food and Development Policy (see Resources Directory).

There is no shortcut to health and happiness except by following the natural and spiritual laws of life to the best of one's ability and present knowledge. Humanity and all sentient beings are sustained by the same radiating light of the universe within and without us. If we are to be in harmony with this light as it comes to us through the natural interplay of earth, water, air, and fire via the vegetable kingdom, then it is essential to choose to eat organic, authentic agricultural products that are grown in the fullness of this light. We should be very cautious when we attempt to tamper with nature.

*Chapter*

# HEALTH SECRETS
# OF LIVE FOODS

## BENEFITS OF
## CALORIE RESTRICTION

The secret of properly eaten live foods is that they restore health and promote longevity. The interesting question is: how do they do this? Let's start with some of the basic information that has been known for centuries about longevity, as well as the more recent research starting back in the 1930s. Dr. Kenneth Pelletier, as part of his longevity research, studied cultures that had the highest longevity and created the healthiest people, such as in the Vilcabamban region in Ecuador (particularly the Vilcabamban Indians), the Hunzas of West Pakistan, the Tarahumara Indians of Mexico, and the Russian people of the Abkhasian region. He found that they ate significantly less total calories, about 50% less than the typical American diet.

Back in the 1930s, Dr. Clive McCay of Cornell University found that he was able to double the life span of rats when their food intake was halved. Professor Huxley studied the life span of worms, and he found that by periodically underfeeding them, he extended their life span by nineteen times. Research in the last fifty years has also shown that undereating increases the life span in fruit flies, water fleas, and trout. (Of course, what we are most interested in is the research about mammals, because mammals most closely mimic our health status.) Please note that Dr. McCay published his study with rats in the *Journal of Nutrition,* and he found that the calorie-restricted rats were not only considerably longer-lived, but more healthy and youthful as compared to the control rats. The control rats became weak and feeble, and when they neared the end of their natural life span, which is approximately 32 months of age (equal to 95 years in human terms), all of the control rats were dead. However, the calorie-restricted rats were still alive, youthful and vigorous, and the oldest lived 1,456 days, approximately 150 years in human terms. Later, in the 1960s, calorie-restricted rats at the Morris H. Ross Institute were able to live up to 1,800 days, or approximately 180 years in human terms. In the 1970s, the doctors Roy Walford and Richard Weindruch at UCLA Medical Center showed that even gradual restriction of calorie intake in *middle-age mice* could extend the life span up to 60%.

In a review of all the research, one finds that some of the increases in life span were 50%, other research shows 65%, and even as high as 83% extension of life span. In other words, food restriction or calorie restriction is a sound and experimentally proven way to extend life span. *Calorie restriction is the only thing we know that is able to consistently slow aging in all varieties of animals, including the various mammalian species.* Calorie restriction results in extended life span and lower blood pressure, reduces destructive antibodies that attack the brain, reduces the loss of certain brain cells, strengthens the immune system, slows the aging process, lowers cholesterol and heart disease risk, reduces muscle oxygen loss and improves muscle function, reduces free radical damage to the body's tissues, helps stabilize the blood sugar in adult-onset diabetes, and helps the body run at peak metabolic efficiency.

The good news about this research, particularly that of Walford and Wein-druch, is that it showed that middle-age mice on calorie restriction can get very significant anti-aging results. Caloric restriction has passed every test as a treatment for aging. It has also been shown to postpone degenerative diseases of aging such as cancer, arthritis, and atherosclerosis. It improves insulin and glucose levels, cholesterol levels, blood pressure, physical strength and stamina, immune function, and cardiovascular function. In fact, it seems to help every measure of health that we check for longevity.

Many therapies, antioxidant treatments, and so forth that prevent or treat many of the main chronic diseases can extend what we call mean life span. But maximum life span is a measure of who lives longest in any species. In other words, it is the extreme outer limit of life-span potential, and in that case, we are really talking about prevention or reversal of aging, rather than simply achieving a normal life span.

As we summarize the profound calorie-restriction research, it is clear that not only has caloric restriction in mice, rats, and other mammals shown that they live longer, but the caloric-restricted animals are much more youthful, vigorous, and energetic as compared to the normals who eat whatever and how often they want. Of course, being more youthful, vigorous, and energetic is what everybody would like. And not only are the caloric-restricted animals more youthful, but they show virtually no chronic degenerative diseases. It is important that aging control and life extension can be achieved in a variety of the mammal species. It certainly suggests that positive results from calorie restriction can be achieved in humans. In fact, there is not a single instance that I am aware of in the history of medicine that such powerful evidence for animals could not be used to achieve similar success in humans.

Although doing double-blind research on humans is difficult, there are many historical cases of health and longevity benefits from undereating. This is not a new finding. For example, Saint Paul the Anchorite lived to be 113 eating only fresh dates and water. Thomas Cairn, born in London in 1588 and who lived to be 207, was another famous undereater. A Mr. Jenkins, born in Yorkshire, England, who lived from 1500 to 1670, ate no breakfast, like Thomas Cairn, and had either raw milk or butter with honey and fruit for lunch and dinner. The French also understood this. The Countess Desmond Catherine lived to be 145 eating only fruit. This information is taken from the work of Dr. Edmond Bordeaux Szekely.

One of the most famous undereaters of all time is Luigi Cornaro, who lived from 1464 to 1566. Luigi was a Venetian nobleman, in the Ministry of the Bishop of Padua. By the time he was 40, he had nearly eaten himself to death. He was attended by Doctor Father Benedict, who schooled him in the art of natural living and undereating. Father Benedict had been taught by an Essene from Africa called Constantine, who was teaching the Essene natural ways at the Solano School of Medicine, where Doctor Father Benedict was trained. Luigi survived his overeating and lived to be 102. Once he learned the simple techniques, he simplified his diet to twelve ounces of food and fourteen ounces of fluid per day. He had two simple statements about longevity, which incidentally, he taught to the Pope. They were, "The less I ate, the better I felt," and "Not to satiate oneself with food is the science of health." So, this new research that we are looking at is not quite as new as we think it is.

The next breakthrough in anti-aging work, relevant to the importance of live foods, began in the 1990s with Dr. Weindruch and Dr. Tomas Prolla. At the University of Wisconsin, with the use of micro-array gene chips—which can measure the expression of thousands of genes at the same time—they were able to study gene expression rapidly and effectively in mice, rats, monkeys, and humans. Drs. Weindruch and Prolla studied the gene profiles of muscles in normal and calorie-restricted mice and found major changes in gene expression between the two groups. Their findings were published in the esteemed journal *Science*. For the first time in history, scientists could study the gene expression, in other words, the underlying RNA and DNA causes of aging. These two doctors saw that gene expression was significantly altered by caloric restriction in a way that seemed to slow the aging process. Weindruch and Prolla compared normally fed and calorie-restricted five- and thirty-month-old mice. Their experiment with the thirty-month-old mice showed a significant difference in age-related gene expression with the caloric restriction. They showed that long-term calorie restriction did slow the aging gene expression.

The next major breakthrough was made by Dr. Stephen R. Spindler, Professor of Biochemistry at the University of California at Riverside. He made a remarkable discovery using gene chips to study the expression of 11,000 genes in the livers of young and old normally fed and calorie-restricted mice. Spindler found that 60% of the age-related changes in gene expression from calorie-restricted mice occurred just a few weeks after they started the calorie-restricted diet. This is quite a significant finding, because it indicates that even if it takes years for the full effects of caloric restriction to become expressed, the genetic profile for anti-aging develops quite quickly when you restrict the diet. Dr. Spindler found that caloric restriction specifically produces a genetic anti-aging profile and can reverse the majority of the deleterious age-related changes in gene expression. He found a four-fold change in short-term calorie restriction and a 2.5-fold change with long-term calorie restriction with 95% reproducibility. Dr. Spindler noted that caloric restriction does not prevent deterioration or genetic changes in a gradual way, over the life span of the animal, but instead *reverses most of these aging changes in a short period of time.* In fact, his research lasted only 30 days in these mice. In another set of research, he found that the rapid changeover from a genetic aging profile to an anti-aging profile occurred in older animals, as well as young and middle-aged ones. This is a very important finding, because it makes it clear that no matter what age you are, it is not too late to slow down or reverse the aging process. His findings do suggest (it is too soon to prove) that caloric restriction could potentially reverse aging and improve and extend life span in old animals, and therefore humans as well. Dr. Spindler's research is quite exciting. There had been no previous suggestion in the literature, to the best of my knowledge, that caloric restriction could reverse age-related changes in gene expression. The earlier research measured the physiological changes that could be reversed by caloric restriction, but not the genetic changes.

An exciting aspect of Dr. Spindler's research results is that short-term caloric restriction, although it does not necessarily produce the total number of anti-aging changes at the genetic level, causes most of the important changes. His impression, in a recent interview in *Life Extension* magazine, is that even if people lose ten pounds, regardless of what their weight is before they start the diet, then many of the physiological parameters of health will improve. He states what many people already know—that weight loss improves your glucose sensitivity, lowers your blood glucose, lowers your blood insulin levels, improves your heart rate, and improves your blood pressure. So, even losing weight for a short period of time has beneficial effects.

One of the beneficial effects of eating live food and detoxifying the system is the anti-cancer effect. It is well established that caloric restriction is "pro-apoptotic," meaning it promotes cell suicide of damaged or cancerous-type cells. Stephen Spindler and others think that the pro-apoptotic effect results because calorie restriction lowers what are called chaperone levels. Chaperones are a particular class of proteins that help reorganize the correct folding of proteins. They also are involved in helping cells make the decision on whether or not to commit suicide. Chaperones are part of the biological mechanism for regulating gene expression. High chaperone levels tend to decrease the amount of toxic cell and cancerous cell suicides. Caloric restriction encourages a lower level of chaperones, and therefore more apoptosis and more anti-cancer effect. If you have a high chaperone level, which occurs with age, the cells are less apt to commit suicide, even though they are damaged severely or may be secreting harmful substances to the tissues around them, or even converting to cancer.

Dr. Spindler also found some association, particularly in older animals, of an expression of the genes that seems to indicate that the animal is undergoing inflammatory stress and other kinds of physiological stress. This stress grows with age. And, in his reported study, the majority of these inflammatory gene expressions and stress gene expressions diminished dramatically with caloric restriction. Now that even the general medical community is noticing that chronic inflammation plays a more important role in chronic disease than we originally thought (particularly heart disease), this is another important benefit of calorie restriction.

To summarize Dr. Spindler's results, which were published in the *Proceedings of the National Academy of Sciences:* (1) No matter what age you have attained, you still get an anti-aging effect with caloric restriction. (2) The anti-aging effect can happen as quickly as one month on a low-calorie diet. (3) The caloric restriction of only four weeks also seemed to partially restore the liver's ability for metabolizing drugs and for detoxification. (4) Calorie restriction seemed to quickly decrease the amount of inflammation and stress, even in older animals.

Dr. Stewart Berger in his book *Forever Young* speaks clearly about working with this anti-aging principle. All of this research shows that a reduction in daily caloric intake, down to about 60% of "the normal American diet," seemed to create an anti-aging effect. When the different test animals underwent a 40% drop in normal calorie intake, they lived approximately 83% longer. This is approximately 137 years in human terms. Dr. Berger clarified what a 60% level of calories means. For women, who normally need 2,000 calories per day, it is about 1,300. For men, who run around 2,700 calories, it is about 1,650. Dr. Berger extrapolated that if your weight is approximately 20% less than the normal insurance scale weights, you are achieving that caloric restriction effect and, ideally, optimal longevity and well-being.

## LIVE FOODS—A NATURAL WAY OF CALORIE RESTRICTION

From a live-food point of view, research such as that discussed above is extremely exciting and validating. Eating live foods is the simplest and most powerful way to achieve this healthful caloric effect, without even having to diet. This is because cooking foods usually results in destroying 50% of the protein, according to the Max Planck Institute, and approximately 60–70% of assimilable vitamins and minerals, up to 96% of the $B_{12}$, and 100% of enzymes and phytonutrients. In other words, one need only eat approximately half the amount of food and calories on a live-food diet as on a cooked-food diet to get an equivalent amount of vitamins, minerals, protein, and phytonutrients. **On a healthy live-food regime one automatically gets the anti-aging calorie-restriction effect without having to diet.** On live foods, one normally achieves what I consider a healthy weight. This is the optimum weight for life extension and protection against chronic disease. Using myself as an example, my weight has ranged somewhere between 148 and 152 since 1983. I have no special diet. I do not do anything but eat live food. And I reached what Dr. Berger considers the optimal weight. It happened totally naturally on live foods long before I read Dr. Berger's work.

Periodic fasting, as we have known for centuries, is one of the most powerful ways to extend life and minimize chronic disease. Fasting is an accelerated form of calorie restriction, and its effects go right along with Dr. Spindler's caloric restriction research findings. The Tree of Life Rejuvenation Center is one of the leading (if not the top) spiritual fasting retreat centers in the world. Because we lead group fasting retreats, Shanti (my partner) and I are fasting a total of one month per year on green juices.

These two simple health measures, eating live foods and periodic fasting, create optimal conditions for extending life, avoiding and/or minimizing chronic disease, and optimizing quality of life. This is really a subtle secret of live foods. In retrospect, we can also now begin to understand Dr. Pelletier's research showing that the longest-lived people in the world, just like those mice that the scientists worked with, ate approximately 50–60% of the total calories of the American diet. And certainly, the exceptional historical anecdotal cases of health and longevity benefits of undereating, as shown by St. Paul, Thomas Cairn, Mr. Jenkins and Countess Desmond Catherine, all point out the same thing. **Undereating creates extended life span. However, with live foods it is not experienced as undereating.** It is joyous and comfortable eating with the Rainbow Green Live-Food Cuisine.

## COOKED VS. RAW FOODS

Why is it that live food gives us the best effect in terms of cutting down our caloric intake and maximizing the quality of our food intake? One of the keys to this is pointed out by Viktoras Kulvinskas in his book, *Survival into the 21st Century*. Viktoras, who is considered one of the founders of the modern live-food movement, estimates that the overall nutrient destruction when you cook food is 80%. Although there is some variation in the research findings, most agree that at least 50% of the B vitamins are destroyed by cooking. $B_1$ and $B_{12}$ losses have been recorded up to 96%, folic acid losses up to 97%, and biotin losses up to 72%. Vitamin C losses are approximately 70–80%. The well-known Max Planck Institute for Nutritional Research in Germany found only 50% bioavailability in proteins that have been overcooked. This study found that cooking alters proteins into substances that disrupt cellular function and speed up the aging and disease process.

In general, I contend that cooking coagulates the bioactive mineral and protein complexes and therefore disrupts mineral absorption, including calcium absorption. Cooking also disrupts RNA and DNA structure, which minimizes the amount of complex protein that our bodies are able to take in. It destroys most of the nutritive fats and creates carcinogenic and mutagenic (producing changes in gene pattern) structures in the fats, as well as producing free radicals.

According to Dr. William Neusome of Canada's Department of Health and Welfare, Food Research Division, cooking may transform certain fungicides into cancer-causing compounds. It has not been proven yet, but it is not unreasonable to assume that with all of the potent pesticides, herbicides, and additives that go into our food, cooking has the potential to transform a certain percentage of these into more carcinogenic or mutagenic compounds. Research done at Stockholm University, in cooperation with Sweden's Natural Food Association, showed that the heating of carbohydrate-rich foods, such as potatoes, rice, and cereals, creates acrylamide, a probable human carcinogen. The researchers found that a bag of potato chips may contain up to 500 times more acrylamide than allowed in the drinking water by the World Health Organization (WHO). French fries sold at McDonald's and Burger King in Sweden showed 100 times the level permitted by WHO in the drinking water. Acrylamide has been found to cause benign and malignant stomach tumors and to also cause damage to the central and peripheral nervous systems. Acrylamide occurs in baked potatoes, French fries, biscuits, and bread, as well as other high-carbohydrate foods.

When about to cook a meal, the cook often declares, "I'm going to fix dinner (or lunch or breakfast) now." There is no need to *fix* raw food: "If it's not broken, don't fix it." "Fixing" it by cooking is actually destroying the nutritional components.

**It becomes rather obvious that by eating live foods, we are able to get complete nutrition with eating 50–80% less food.** This is why, when we become sensitive to what we are eating, people on a live-food diet naturally reach an optimum diet and weight. This is one reason a live-food diet is optimal for extending life, preventing chronic degenerative disease, and increasing vitality, energy, and youthfulness.

It is my belief that the wholeness of raw foods is not only health-producing but non-reproducible by a science that tends to fragment things. Cooking, or other forms of processing such as microwaving, destroys qualities and components of our food for which the significance is not yet and perhaps will never be known in its totality. Cooking is not only a risky business but significantly diminishes the amount of nutrients—vitamins and minerals, protein, fats, and other lesser-known phytonutrients, such as bioflavonoids (like rutin, hesperin, vitamin P, flavones, flavanols) and methoxylated bioflavonoids, including nobelatin and tangeritine. These latter two have more cortisone activity per weight than injectable cortisone. They also act to remove heavy metals, drugs, and hydrocarbons from our body and decrease red blood cell clumping. Many of these phytonutrients supply another basis for understanding the Rainbow Green Live-Food Cuisine.

## PHYTONUTRIENTS

It is useful to think about the multi-colored rainbow diet from a phytonutrient point of view. In my book *Spiritual Nutrition and the Rainbow Diet,* I correlate these colors with the chakras, beginning with red and the root chakra. Some of the phytonutrients that are associated with the red color are reservatrol, ellagic acid, and quercitin. These are found in tomatoes, watermelon, pink grapefruit, and cherries. For the color orange, we have the carotenes.

## Rainbow Phytonutrients

| COLORS | PHYTONUTRIENTS | FOODS |
|---|---|---|
| Reds | reservatrol, ellagic acid, quercitin | tomatoes, strawberries, cherries, raspberries, grapes, pink grapefruit, watermelon |
| Oranges | carotenes | carrots, peppers, squash, sweet potatoes, yams, pumpkins, apricots, cantaloupe, mangoes |
| Yellows | limonene | lemons, grapefruit, oranges, other citrus |
| Greens | indole-3-carbinol, thio-cyanates, zeaxanthins, sulforaphane, isothiocyanates, lutein | arugula, cabbage, beet greens, collard greens, broccoli, Brussels sprouts, kale, mustard greens, watercress |
| Blues | bilberry | blueberries, bilberry |
| Purples/Indigo | lycopene, terpines | raspberries, grapes, strawberries |
| Whites | allylsulfides, quercitin | apples, cauliflower, radishes, chives, leeks, scallions, garlic, onions |

They are found in mangoes, carrots, apricots, cantaloupe, peppers, squash, sweet potatoes, yams, and pumpkins. Yellow is limonene, found in lemons and other citrus fruits. And then comes green, which has the phytonutrients indole-3-carbinol (very important for preventing breast and prostate cancer), thio-cyanates, zeaxanthin, sulforaphane, isothiocyanates, and lutein. Some of these, like zeaxanthin, are famous for protecting the eyes, and particularly for protecting against macular degeneration. The key food sources of these greens are arugula, cabbage, beet greens, collard greens, broccoli, Brussels sprouts, kale, mustard greens, and watercress. The next is blue—blue is the throat chakra—and the associated phytonutrients are found in blueberries and bilberry. And then we have the third eye, which is more a combination of the purples and indigo, and includes the phytonutrient lycopene and the terpines. Foods containing these phytonutrients are grapes, strawberries, raspberries, and foods with a mixture of colors in between. And finally, the crown chakra is white, and the associated phytonutrients are the allylsulfides and quercitin. These are found in chives, leeks, scallions, garlic, onions, apples, cauliflower, and radishes. This list gives a more complete understanding of the Rainbow Green Live-Food Cuisine.

There are more phytonutrients than we really understand. And when we cook food, we are destroying all of these. Following this logic, you can see that with cooked foods, we naturally double our calorie intake. This often creates a level of weight that is the opposite direction of what we need for optimal health and longevity. Cooking also dehydrates the food and disorders and de-energizes the normal biological water present in all live foods, and this creates a problem of dehydration and decreased biological water.

## ENZYMES

The next question beyond calorie restriction is: why does live food create the best anti-aging effect, life extension effect, anti-chronic degenerative disease effect, and the highest amount of vitality of any type of food? Part of the answer to this comes from the fact that when you cook food, you also destroy the enzymes. (Cooking at a boiling point for three minutes kills all enzymes present.) Enzymes contain the power of life itself. Eating a live-food diet helps to maintain the quality and quantity of our enzyme pool, and therefore our health and longevity. Enzymes are not simply catalysts that make digestion and all other metabolic processes work; they are living proteins that direct the life force into our basic biochemical and metabolic processes. Enzymes even help repair our DNA and RNA.

Enzymes help transform and store energy; they make active hormones; participate in their own production cycle; dissolve fiber and prevent clotting; they have anti-inflammatory, anti-edema, and even analgesic effects. Other research, which I discuss in depth in *Conscious Eating,* shows that these enzymes can help balance and enhance the immune system; help to heal cancer, multiple sclerosis, rheumatoid disease, and arthritis; and minimize the effect of athletic injuries by decreasing recovery time. Enzymes are an aid to digestion, too. Enzymes work within the cellular structure, and the cell nucleus and the cell mitochondria, which are the energy factories in the body. Some enzymes move freely within the body, such as in digestion or in the serum of our blood. Many of the free enzymes, particularly the proteases, are bound to transfer proteins in the serum. These binding proteins, alphaglobulins, transport enzymes and other molecules to various parts of the body to regulate all of the body processes.

With age, under stress, and after illness, the amount of enzymes in our bodies decreases. This is because the enzymes are critical for our health and are used up in those situations. As our enzyme pool diminishes with age, our ability to perform the tasks that keep the body healthy also diminishes. Aging happens when enzymes decrease in concentration in the body. Therefore, some enzyme researchers—like Dr. Edward Howell, the progenitor of enzyme research, and live-food teachers like Ann Wigmore—believe that enzyme preservation is a secret to longevity. One very clear way to preserve the body's store of enzymes is to eat living or raw foods, because foods in their natural state are loaded with digestive and other enzymes, which we then take into our body to actually build up our enzyme reserve. The enzymes in live food help with digestion, and therefore minimize the use of our own enzymes and thus preserve the enzyme pool.

## EXTRA ENERGY IN LIVE FOODS

Live food is a gift of nature that begins at birth, when we suckle our mother's breast, and continues as we draw our life force from the all-giving breast of Mother Nature. Live foods, because of their high energetic structural integrity, give the healthiest food-source nutrients on the physical plane. Raw foods contribute the most energy to our subtle organizing energy fields. This is a theory I introduced in 1987, in my book *Spiritual Nutrition and the Rainbow Diet,* which explains that the matrix of the human condition and all life's condition depends on a subtle energetic matrix that precedes the physical. When this matrix is energized, it becomes more coherent and serves as a better energetic pattern for the different levels of the physical formation. When the energetic matrix is dispersed and weakened, as through entropy, we have an aging effect, we have less effective replication on the RNA and DNA level, the cellular level is less organized, and the whole body functions less effectively. The result is an accelerated aging process. Live foods or raw foods contribute the most energy to our subtle organizing energy fields, as compared to cooked and other forms of processed foods, and therefore have the greatest anti-aging effect. Processed foods and junk foods actually decrease and often disrupt our subtle organizing energy fields.

## LIVE-FOOD HISTORY AND MODERN RESEARCH

The history of live foods goes back before we had these fancy theories. We can trace it thousands of years to the Pelegasians, ancient Greeks reported by the father of history, Herodotus, to have lived to an average age of 200 years. They ate mostly fruit, vegetables, nuts, and seeds. Another long-lived group that reportedly preferred live foods was the Essenes. According to his biography, Pythagoras, in approximately 500–600 B.C., studied with the Essenes on Mount Carmel. Not only did he become enlightened, but he learned about live foods and then took that knowledge back to Greece with him. This knowledge was passed on to Plato and Socrates.

In the U.S., as early as the 1820s, there was a live-food awareness. The Mormons, including Joseph Smith and twenty-five of his core group, ate primarily live foods because they were aware that it enhanced spiritual sensitivity and development. So, amazing as it may seem, the live-food movement for spiritual purposes actually began in the 1820s. The biggest breakthrough in live foods that affected the modern world, however, was at the Bircher-Benner

Clinic in 1897, when Dr. Max Bircher-Benner discovered the writings of Pythagoras about the virtues of live foods and began using this information in his clinic. He himself benefited from live foods when he found that they healed his jaundice and his inability to eat. In summing up the whole essence of the healing and disease process, Bircher-Benner wrote that the tremendous increase in disease experienced in Europe was not inevitable. He wrote, "We are pressed by an overwhelming burden of incurable disease which hangs over our lives like a dark cloud. It is a burden that will not disappear until men [and women] become aware of the basic laws of life." From my perspective, one of the basic laws of life is to eat our foods whole, organic, and in their natural, raw state.

In the early part of the twentieth century, another great physician, Max Gerson, discovered the healing power of live foods, first for his own migraines, and then for the healing of lupus, which was considered incurable at that time. He applied his approach to every sort of medical disease, from clogged arteries to mental disorders, and he began to believe that live food and a live juice diet is more than just a specific cure for certain diseases. Dr. Gerson taught that consuming raw foods is a way of eating that restores the diseased body and mind's ability to heal itself. He saw that live foods are a way to rebuild the vital regenerative force of the total organism. In 1928, he was able to cure Albert Schweitzer's wife of T.B. and later healed Albert Schweitzer of insulin-dependent diabetes. He also found a live-food diet extremely effective for the treatment of cancer and in 1958 published a book called *A Cancer Therapy—Results of 50 Cases.* All of these cases were healed with live foods. As part of Gerson's legacy there are live-food clinics throughout Europe today, as well as fasting clinics using juices that help people heal according to these principles.

One of the more recent leaders in the live-food movement is Dr. Norman Walker, who lived to the age of 116 and ate primarily raw foods and juices. Dr. Szekely saw more than 123,600 people at his clinic in Mexico over a period of thirty-three years, from 1937 to 1970 (approximately 17% of them came with diagnoses of "incurable"), with a better than 90% success rate using live foods.

Dr. Szekely discussed four categories of food, which I believe is a helpful way to begin to understand the issues. He did not categorize them according to their biochemistry but according to their energetic effect. He categorized foods that have a high degree of life force as biogenic. This means having the ability to enhance the human life force, or energize the subtle organizing energy fields. Biogenic foods help us to reverse entropy and the aging process. They are just-picked, high-enzyme raw foods, namely sprouts and baby greens, that have the capacity to revitalize and regenerate the human organism. The second category of foods he called bioactive. These are foods capable of sustaining and enhancing an already healthy life force. They add to our subtle organizing energy fields. These bioactive foods include fresh, raw fruits and vegetables. Because they are not as young and vital and just off the vine, they have a little bit less enzymes and life force, but are still extremely beneficial to the system. The third category is biostatic food, which basically includes fresh organic foods that have been cooked. These foods are marginally life-sustaining in the short term, but are gradually life-force-depleting in the long term. The fourth category is called biocidic foods. These are life-destroying foods, foods that without question disrupt and deplete the subtle organizing energy fields. The biocidic foods are highly processed commercial foods, full of additives, preservatives, pesticides, herbicides or hormones, that often have been microwaved, irradiated, and/or genetically engineered. They are the plastic, convenient junk foods. They also include all cooked flesh, because cooked flesh so rapidly putrefies.

We actually have a wide variety of food choices. The ideal, of course, is to choose foods that add so much energy to our system that they reverse the effects of entropy, and therefore reverse the aging process and enhance health. These, of course, are the organic, whole, raw, biogenic and bioactive foods.

There are many advantages to biogenic and bioactive foods. One of these is increasing immunity. Specific immunity-supporting factors in raw foods are the gibberellins and abscisic acid, which are found in avocadoes, lemons, cabbage, and potatoes. The other way that raw food helps to boost the immune system is that it keeps us healthy by its detoxification properties, anti-free-radical enzymes, cleansing properties, and the physical and energetic enhancement of our total organism. In other words, when we are healthy, the immune system naturally follows suit.

Another subtle point to this is based on research by Dr. Paul Kouchakoff, medical doctor in the 1930s, who found that when we eat cooked foods, we get an increase in the white blood cells in our system, as if the cooked food is a foreign body. This does not happen when we eat live foods. Therefore, we can conclude that cooked food, in essence, is a stress on the immune system.

One of the most important aspects of live foods is that they are live wires. The bioelectricity of live foods is not normally considered when we think about qualities of food and its effect. In Russia, Dr. Israel Brekhman did a simple experiment. Mice were fed cooked food and live food at different times. Then he measured the amount of energy and endurance that the mice had. When the same mice were eating only the live food, they had three times more energy and endurance than when they were eating cooked food. Theoretically, if it were simply a matter of calories, there should not be a difference in endurance. However, there is. This is because food is not simply calories. It is all the subtle nutrients, general nutrients, and electrical energies of the food. The electrical potential of our tissues and cells is a direct result of the aliveness of our cells. Live foods enhance the electrical potential in cells, between cells, and at the interface of cells with the microcapillary electrical charge. When cells have the proper microelectrical potential, they have the power to rid themselves of toxins and maintain their selective capacity to bring in appropriate nutrients and oxygen supply.

Professor Hans Eppinger, who was the chief medical director at the first medical clinic at the University of Vienna, found that a live-food diet specifically raised the microelectrical potential throughout the body. He discovered that a raw-food diet increases selective capacity of the cells by increasing the electrical potential between the tissue cells and the capillary cells. He saw that raw foods significantly improved the intra- and extra-cellular excretion of toxins, as well as absorption of nutrients. He and his co-workers concluded that live foods were the only type of food that could restore microelectrical potential of the tissues, once their electrical potential and ensuing subtle cellular degeneration had begun to occur. In essence, you can say that by restoring the electrical potential of the cells, raw foods rejuvenate the life force and health of the organism. Therefore, a live-food cuisine is a powerful natural healing force, which gradually restores the microelectrical potential and overall functioning of every cell in our body.

Kirlian photography has been a useful way to validate our understanding of the bioelectrical effects of live foods. Different researchers have found an electroluminescent field (natural radiation fields) surrounding living organisms that takes the form of a coronal discharge that we can see with Kirlian photography. The Kirlian photography clearly shows that live foods have a much stronger auric or luminescent field than cooked food. Some research even shows that the same person eating junk or cooked food has a much smaller field than when they change their diet and eat whole, natural food. This leads us back to the original point, which is that all living organisms are made up of patterns of resonant energy or subtle organizing energy fields. This energy is reflected in the functioning of each cell, and the electrical fields of the cells maintain the integrity of the biological system.

The electroluminescence that we see with Kirlian photography can be said to be a measure of life force in the cell. And, the stronger the life force of each cell, the stronger the electroluminescence in the Kirlian photography. In essence, it is the sum of the electrical potential of each cell. The more healthy our electrical potential of each cell, and that of tissues, the more healthy we are.

Considering the importance of the electrical potential takes us to a statement made by Nobel laureate Szent-Gyorgyi, who described the essential life process as a little electrical current, sent to us by the sunshine. He is referring to highly charged single electrons, which are involved in transferring their energy to our own submolecular patterns, without changing our molecular structure.

Dr. Joanna Budwig, who has degrees in medicine, physics, pharmacy, and biochemistry, is one of the first researchers to combine an in-depth knowledge of quantum mechanics and physics with an in-depth knowledge of human biochemistry and physiology. She has concluded that not only do electron-rich live foods act as high-power electron donors, but electron-rich foods also act as a solar-resonant field in the body to attract, store, and conduct the sun's energy in our bodies. She theorizes that the photons of the sunlight, which she calls "sun electrons," are attracted by sun-like electrons resonating in our own biological systems, especially in the double-bonded electron clouds found in our lipid systems. These sun-like electrons are also called "pi electrons." And these pi electrons have the ability within our molecular structure to attract and activate the sun photons. Dr. Johanna Budwig believes that the energy we absorb from these solar photons acts as an anti-entropy factor or anti-aging factor. As a result of her theory, she believes that live-food—and particularly flax seed, which is three highly active electron clouds and their double bonds—helps bring a tremendous amount of pi electrons into the system. On the other hand, people who eat refined, cooked, highly processed food diminish the amount of solar electrons energizing the system and reduce the energy down from the amount necessary to create a high-electron solar resonance field. In fact, according to Dr. Budwig, processed foods may even act as insulators to the healthy flow of electricity. In other words, the more we take in solar electrons as a result of our dietary intake of live foods, the better we are able to resonate, attract, and absorb solar electrons, in direct resonance from the sun and other solar systems.

Our health and consciousness depend on our ability to attract, store, and conduct electron energy, which is essential for the energizing and regulation of all life forces. The greater our store of light energy, the greater the power of our overall electromagnetic field and, consequently, the more energy available for healing and maintenance of optimal health. Metaphorically, a strong solar resonance field promotes the evolution of humanity to reach our full potential as human (sun) beings. Light supports evolution, and a lack of pi electrons in our bodies hinders it.

Biophotons, discovered by German researcher Dr. F.A. Popp in 1984, represent another level of energy. Dr. Popp wrote a paper titled "Biophoton Emission: New Evidence for Coherence in DNA" pointing out the existence of the biophotons, which are the energetic phenomenon of ultra-weak photon emission from living systems. Dr. Popp showed that the DNA is an important source of photon emission, and he was able to measure this emission with a device he created called the "biophoton meter." He found 97% of the DNA associated with biophoton transmission, and only 3% filled with genetic information. These ultra-weak photon emissions from the living cells in organisms are different from the phenomenon of bioluminescence.

Basically, what Dr. Popp found is that the healthiest people have the highest amount of biophoton emission, and people who are the sickest have the lowest amount. The existence of biophoton emission is a critical aspect of understanding why it is important to have an abundance of live food in one's diet, because biophoton emissions are given off by DNA, RNA, and other forms of macromolecules, including enzymes, chlorophyll, and hemoglobin. Dr. Popp found that wild, organic foods gave off twice as much biophoton energy as cultivated organic crops. He found that cultivated organic foods gave off five times as much biophoton energy as commercially grown food, and that cooked and irradiated foods gave off almost no biophoton energy. The scientific and health message here is obvious.

People have been eating live foods for thousands of years. Those who continue to eat live foods, in this tradition, seem to have an extended life span, higher quality of health, abundant vitality and even joy, and significantly less chronic disease. Recent research into calorie restriction has supplied some evidence as to why those who are on a high percentage of live food seem to have such superior health and longevity. In my clinical experience, the minimum percentage of live food in the diet to have this healing and energetic effect is 80%. As we go deeper into the physics of it, we begin to understand that live food has the highest amount of quality nutrient concentrates, the highest amount of phytonutrients, vitamins and minerals, the highest amount of bioelectrical energy, the highest amount of biologically active water, the highest amount of pi electrons, the highest amount of biophotons, and the highest amount of subtle organizing energy field energy. In other words, from the physical to the electrical to the subtle organizing energy field level, live foods are superior for our health and well-being than any other type of food.

When we nourish ourselves with live foods, and in particular the Rainbow Green Live-Food Cuisine, we have the most potent diet for maintaining health and well-being that is available on the planet. The wonder and delight of this is that the Rainbow Green Live-Food Cuisine is absolutely delicious. As you will see in this book, with our more than 375 delightful recipes, eating primarily raw foods is a gentle, tasty, nature-oriented, and gradual way to restore health, diminish and heal from chronic degenerative disease, and extend quality of life and longevity. On a live-food (80–100% intake) diet, one can have a low-protein, low-fat, high-carbohydrate diet, or a high-protein, moderate-fat, low-carbohydrate diet, or somewhere in between, according to one's biological individuality. There is no limitation. As I point out in detail in *Conscious Eating,* from an Ayurvedic approach you can completely balance a person of any dosha, including one with a vata constitution, once you understand the principles.

As we probe deeper into the understanding of live foods, as I explain in more detail in my books *Conscious Eating* and *Spiritual Nutrition and the Rainbow Diet,* live foods can help to turn us into superconductors of not only the electrical energy, but of the cosmic energy. In this way, they help us enhance our sensitivity to the Divine. In my experience with thousands of people in many, many groups who have turned toward live foods, the overwhelming natural response is to be open and to move toward a more spiritual life, whatever one's particular religious tradition may be. Live foods serve as one of the building blocks for spiritual development and ultimately what I call full person awakening on every level.

## SUMMARY

In summary, the Rainbow Green Live-Food Cuisine is the optimum diet for longevity, quality of health, hormone balance, and for your individual constitution. Not only is this diet low-glycemic, but it is extremely high in minerals. David Wolfe, an internationally recognized live-food expert who has surveyed the world literature on the topic of mineralization, points out that high-mineral foods are often low-glycemic, and that high mineral intake is essential for optimal organ, endocrine, and mental functioning and expansion of consciousness. This diet also supplies the minimum of 30% protein foods, what research shows is needed to have the glucagon effect that produces the good prostaglandins. In a personal observation of this diet, in my sixtieth year I was able to do 601 consecutive push-ups. Although we haven't done any extended clinical research, I consistently observe that people who follow this diet have the highest energy, clarity of mind, endorphins and neurotransmitter production, and optimal joy in life.

The individualizing of the constitutions, as we adjust the protein and carbohydrate input, gives us an optimal situation to turn off the compost button, enhance neurotransmitters, enhance prostaglandins, and enhance optimal physiology. In this way we enhance our quality of life.

In addition, by being organic, this diet supports the healing of the global ecology, as well as our personal ecology. In avoiding pesticides, herbicides, and genetically engineered food, we decrease the amount of neurotoxins and carcinogens that we take into our system.

By eating live food, you naturally get all the benefits of the longevity produced by a low-calorie diet. You can eat half as much food to get the same amount of nutrients, including protein. The result is that you naturally go to an optimal weight for longevity as well as an optimal protein-carbohydrate-fat mix according to your constitution for your neuro-hormonal balance, neurotransmitter production, endorphin production, and a stabilization of blood sugar and therefore the mind. We have the optimal diet that matches your constitution and brings you to optimal qualities of health for self and the planet.

Optimal health simply requires the appropriate adjustment of your natural fruits and vegetables, nuts and seeds, algaes and sea vegetables, in the raw form (the way they were meant to be eaten, like every other living organism on the planet eats them). This takes us to optimal health—physically, emotionally, mentally, and spiritually.

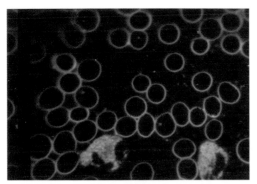

**Normal Blood**
(Dark-Field Microscope)

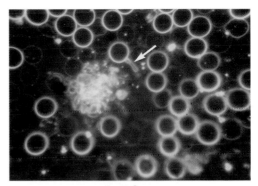

**Ascit form**

An ascit is a virulent bacteria, transitioning into a pre-fungal form, that has pleomorphed from healthy protits on its way to becoming a more toxic fungal and eventually a mold form.
(Dark-Field Microscope)

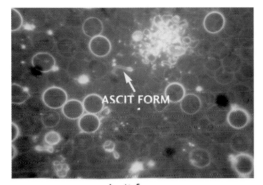

**Ascit form**

Note (1) ascites and (2) the endobiotic yeast load in the plasma.
(Dark-Field Microscope)

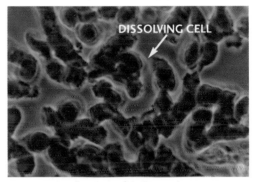

**Destruction of Cell Membrane**

With fungal infection, the red blood cells lose their negative charge and stick together. As the infection continues, they lose their cell membrane and literally melt into each other, losing both form and function. (Dark-Field Microscope)

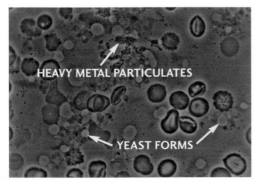

**Yeast Fungal Infection with
Heavy-Metal Particulates**
(Phase-Contrast Microscope)

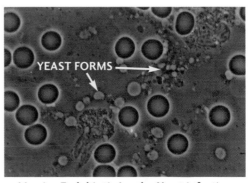

**Massive Endobiotic Load—Yeast Infection
in Live Blood**

The round forms are the endobiotic yeast forms in the infected blood. (Phase-Contrast Microscope)

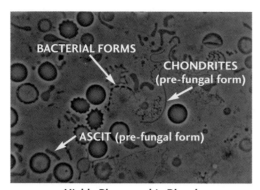

**Highly Pleomorphic Blood**
This slide shows many levels of fungal forms. The lines are: (1) The first stages of yeast. (2) Bumps on cells are fungal colonies on cell walls. (3) Free endobiotic yeast forms. (4) Ascite or higher fungal forms. (5) Bacterial pleomorphic forms. (Phase-Contrast Microscope)

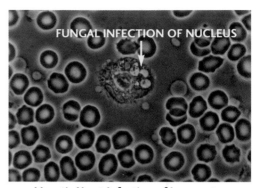

**Mycotic Yeast Infection of Leucocytes**
Fungally infected white blood cell. (Phase-Contrast Microscope)

**Lymphatic Cancer**
Dry-field slide showing a highly mycotic area in the lymph zone.
(Dry-Field Microscope)

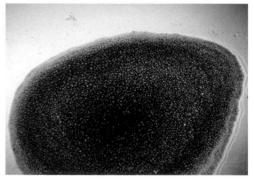

**Post-Lymphatic Cancer**
After 3 months on Phase I Rainbow Green Live-Food Cuisine, the fungal forms are gone and the lymphatic cancer has faded away.
(Dry-Field Microscope)

**Mycotoxic Disturbance of Breast Tissue**
White areas in breast region suggest fungal infection in breast tissue.
(Dry-Field Microscope)

**Normal Breast Tissue**
Normal tissue returned after 3 months on Phase I Rainbow Green
Live-Food Cuisine. (Dry-Field Microscope)

# Vegetable Medley

*See Page 203*

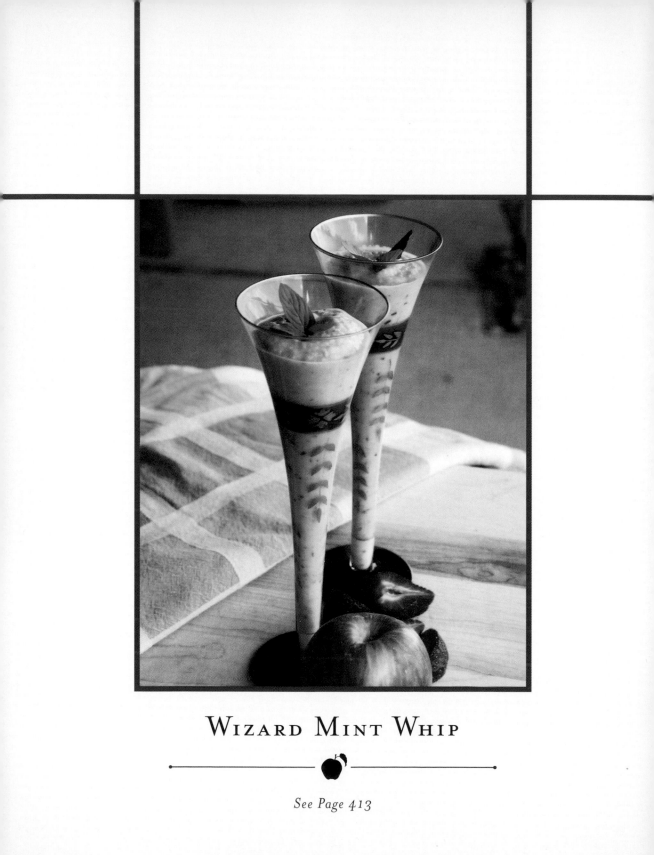

# WIZARD MINT WHIP

*See Page 413*

# Spontaneous Salad & Miso Orange Dressing

*See Pages 245 & 260*

# DANDELION CREAM SALAD

See Page 233

# CURRIED CARROT AVOCADO SOUP

*See Page 293*

# Apple Cinnamon Bread & Buckwheaties with Almond Mylk

*See Pages 318, 371, & 386*

Rainbow Green Live-Food Cuisine

# Recipes

## KEY TO RECIPES
. . . . . . . . . . . . . . . . . . . . . . . . . . . . . . . . . . . . . . . . . . . . . . .

Phase I

Phase I.5

Phase II

# Table of Contents

## SALAD DRESSINGS

## CHUTNEYS, SALSA, SAUCES, AND SPREADS

## SOUPS

### Jams, "Sweet" Sauces, and "Sweet" Spreads

### Porridge and Breakfast Dishes

# The Secrets of
# Rainbow Green Live-Food
# Cuisine Preparation

**P**reparing Rainbow Green Live-Food Cuisine is a true culinary adventure into a joyful world of health, vitality, and sumptuous tastes. If you are embarking upon the journey of live-food preparation for the first time, a wonderful treasury of new skills, equipment, ingredients, and helpful tips awaits you. This chapter is a map offering the "how to" and the help that you will need on your journey. The Mystery awaits you!

## TASTE BALANCING

One of the main ways that we are able to help create balance for people is through a balance of flavors. The concept of taste balancing, shared with the Tree of Life Café by our former master chef, Chad Sarno, has been incorporated into our program for making gourmet, cultural, raw food. Taste balancing is a major key to preparing delicious food. It supports holistic food preparation that celebrates the balance of flavors and the balance of feeding each body, from the emotional body to the spiritual body, with intention. When we feed people's physical, emotional, and spiritual bodies with comforting food, it creates balance in a variety of ways.

In each of our foods, we like to have a taste base. That base, a balance in each dish of a sweet, salt, acid, and fat taste, gives us a foundation for making almost any ethnic dish. Again, the base components, which you will find in the majority of the recipes in this book, all have the four elements: sweet, acid, salt, and fat. For example, in a pâté, you may want to use pine nuts as a fat, carrot for sweet, a little lemon juice as the acid, and Celtic sea salt for salt. Together those elements make up your base for the pâté.

## Taste Balancing Table

| Sweet | Salt | Acid | Fat |
|---|---|---|---|
| low-glycemic fruits | Celtic sea salt | lemon | oils |
| cherry tomatoes | olives | lime | nuts & seeds |
| bell peppers | miso | grapefruit | nut butters |
| carrots | sea veggies | apple cider vinegar | avocado |
| beets | especially dulse | sauerkraut | coconut pulp |
| orange juice | | | olives |
| white miso | | | |
| coconut water | | | |

For the fat taste, we can use all sorts of oils: cold-pressed oils, olive oil, flax, hemp, sunflower, sesame, soaked nuts and seeds, unsoaked nuts and seeds, nut butters, avocado, coconut, or olives. For acid taste, we use citrus (including lemon, lime, grapefruit, and orange), apple cider vinegar, and sauerkraut. For salt, we use Celtic salt, which contains eighty-two minerals. It is an uncooked, live salt. We consider miso a live food because when it is fermented, it is activated with enzymes. Miso creates a very nice salt taste, and barley miso can be used as a bouillon substitute. Olives are good for a fat and salt taste, and they are the most mineralized fruit. For sweets, we do not use a lot of dried fruits, because they are too mycogenic; instead, we tend to use the sweeter vegetables, and some of the lower-glycemic fruits. We will occasionally use soaked raisins, soaked dried apricots, apples or pears, and occasionally a little orange juice. We also use coconut water and the sweeter vegetables like cherry tomatoes, bell peppers, carrots, and beets. Sweet white miso is very good for a sweet and a salt.

Each culture has characteristic flavors that are achieved through the usage of specific herbs and spices. For example, in Italian and Sicilian cuisine, the key flavors are garlic, basil, oregano, and olive oil. For Thai and Balinese, the more fundamental flavors are basil, lemon grass, tamarind, galangal root, curry, cumin, and coriander. For Mexican and Spanish, use cilantro, cumin, garlic, olive oil, jalapeño, and other chiles. Moroccan and African cuisines emphasize cilantro, cinnamon, ginger, and cumin. Japanese and Chinese cuisines use ginger, garlic, and sesame. Middle Eastern cuisine features garlic, mint, oregano, cinnamon, parsley, sesame, and fenugreek. For Indian cuisine, one should use garlic, ginger, cardamom, curry mixtures, cumin, and the general masala taste, as well as sesame, saffron, cinnamon, fenugreek, turmeric, and fennel. For American cuisine, use garlic, oregano, dill, cinnamon, and chiles.

Each culture also emphasizes different foods. For example, in Italian and Sicilian cuisine, lemon, olives, tomato, and spinach are used. Thai and Balinese emphasize lime and coconut. Mexican and Spanish use lime, tomato, and avocado. Moroccan and African use olives, orange, lemon, tomato, and eggplant. Japanese and Chinese use lime, mung bean sprouts, bok choy, assorted veggies, snow peas, and cucumber. Middle Eastern and Greek cuisines use lemon, eggplant, tomato, and cucumber. Indian cuisine uses cauliflower, spinach, peas, and lemon. American cuisine features peas, carrots, lemon, and tomato.

When examining which foods, herbs, and spices work well together, especially when used to achieve certain cultural flavors, one notices a bioregional influence: plants that grow among one another often combine synergistically in the kitchen. It is, in a sense, a part of the divine blueprint of how humans are best suited by eating locally. For example, tomatoes and basil can be companion-planted and are complementary ingredients in cuisine.

So, if one wants to make an Italian salad, for example, use Italian produce like tomatoes, olives, and spinach, along with a little olive oil and lemon, which are common there, and then salt. Next, add the herbs that are particular to the Italian culture. If desiring a Thai dish, coconut pulp and sesame are certainly going to be used. One can use coconut with a little bit of lime, and then add the spices that are appropriate to Thai culture. To accompany these basic flavors, include peas, carrots, and cauliflower for Thai cuisine.

It is important to understand how the amounts of salt, acid, fat, and sweet complement each other and the ethnic herbs to make a complete taste. For instance, there are certain components that emphasize certain herbs. So, if you have cilantro in a dish, then you want to add less lemon. This is because the acid in the lemon emphasizes the cilantro and brings its flavor out more. If you were going to use basil instead of cilantro, you would add more lemon. Also, think about oil as a vehicle for flavor. If you just have lemon and salt and herbs, those flavors will go right to the taste buds, that acid taste or the taste of salt. But the oil smooths the flavors over the palate and brings them into balance. That is why the fat component is important.

The art of this culinary approach is balance. We achieve this by using fresh, seasonal ingredients that satisfy the four taste components, balancing the herbs, and finding our own unique style of putting the ingredients together into a sensational dish. In this endeavor, start with a recipe base, and then play with the elements. When you look at any of these recipes, you can see the base in them, the four tastes, and the vegetables, herbs, and spices that give the recipe a specific cultural flair. So, when creating your own Rainbow Green Live-Food Cuisine recipes from scratch, create a recipe base, add the four tastes, and then play with the herbs and spices for the particular cultural cuisine that you choose.

If you wish to further explore this taste balance idea and the culinary science behind cultural cuisine, read Chad Sarno's book, *Vital Creations* (see Resources Directory).

The Rainbow Green Live-Food Cuisine is not only the healthiest cleansing (Phase I and I.5) and maintenance (Phase II) evolutionary diet for individual health, the health of the planet, and the awakening of consciousness, but it is also is a joyful exploration of culinary artistry and delightful tastes.

## KNOW YOUR INGREDIENTS

This section focuses on the foods and ingredients used in our recipes at the Tree of Life Café. We emphasize foods that are nutrient-dense and low in sugar. Many of these items are available from the Health Store on the Tree of Life website: www.treeoflife.nu.

### GREEN LEAFY VEGETABLES

Among the most nutrient-dense of all plant foods are the dark green, leafy vegetables, especially kale, dandelion, spinach, chard, collards, arugula, parsley, and green cabbage. These vegetables are high in alkaline minerals, protein, and chlorophyll. As such, they are regenerative and purifying.

### BUYING/STORING NUTS AND SEEDS

It is recommended that organic nuts and seeds be purchased direct by mail order from specialty suppliers (see the Resources section). The nuts and seeds obtained from health food stores or conventional markets are susceptible to rancidity, as they may have been stored on the shelf, possibly for long periods of time. Ideally nuts and seeds should be stored in the freezer or refrigerator to prevent the oils from going rancid. If this is not possible, store them in a cool, dark, and dry place. Be especially careful with high-oil-content nuts and seeds like Brazil nuts, macadamias, and pine/pignoli nuts. If they look yellow, it is likely that they are rancid.

## Buying Oils

Conventional cooking oils should be avoided, as they have been highly processed. Even "cold-pressed oils" could have been influenced by heat at some stage of processing. Recommended oils include:

- Stone-pressed olive oil.
- Cold-pressed flax seed oil (which should be used within three weeks from date of pressing, as it is highly susceptible to rancidity).
- Hemp seed oil (which should be used within six weeks from date of pressing, as it is highly susceptible to rancidity).
- Cold-pressed sesame, coconut, sunflower, and almond oils.

See the Resources Directory for recommended sources of these products.

## Herbs & Spices

Where possible, fresh herbs and whole spices are used at the Tree of Life Café, as their flavors are so much richer and delightful than their dried counterparts. Spices such as fennel, dill, cumin, clove, cinnamon, and cardamom can be bought in whole form and easily ground in a spice mill or coffee grinder.

## Stevia

Stevia is a sweet herb native to North and South America. Only one species, *rebaudiana,* tastes sweet enough to be called "sweet leaf" in Brazil and Paraguay, where it grows wild. Stevia is a great sweetener alternative. Recent research indicates that it does not raise blood sugar levels. Whole stevia leaf can be bought at health food stores or by mail order, or you can grow your own. Grind the whole leaf into a powder and add to food and teas for a sweet taste. You can also buy water-extracted stevia in liquid form from your local health food store in the supplements section. Avoid alcohol-extracted and refined forms of stevia. Unrefined stevia is dark green in color.

## Goji Berries

Clinical analysis shows that this unusual berry is a powerful antioxidant that contains eighteen kinds of amino acids (six times higher than bee pollen), more beta carotene than carrots, and five hundred times the amount of vitamin C by weight than oranges. It is loaded with vitamins $B_1$, $B_2$, $B_6$, and E. It has been found effective in increasing white blood cells, protecting liver function, lowering cholesterol, relieving hyper-tension, and helping strengthen the immune system while building muscle tissue and burning body fat. Goji berries are known for enhancing longevity.

The Tibetan goji berries offered by The Tree of Life Rejuvenation Center have been grown in protected valleys in wild and cultivated areas of Inner Mongolia in million-year-old soil where pesticides have never been used. They have been dried and are packaged in a vacuum-sealed bag. The berries may be eaten alone in their dried state as a snack, or they can be soaked and incorporated into recipes.

## Flax Seed

Golden flax seed is packed with nutrition and is an essential daily addition to a healthful diet. Golden flax seed has greater nutritional value than the more common brown flax seed. It contains fiber, lignans, and omega-3 fatty acids, as well as both soluble and insoluble fiber, helping to clean your intestinal tract and promote regularity. Lignans provide a powerful support to the immune system and cellular health. Omega-3 fatty acids are essential for balanced brain chemistry. Flax seed is one of the few sources of omega-3 for vegetarians. We recommend 2–4 tablespoons for slow oxidizers and 3–6 tablespoons for fast oxidizers each day.

The seeds can be ground in a spice mill or coffee grinder and used in many recipes, or they can simply be sprinkled on top of other foods, such as salads or granola or even fruit. When flax seed is soaked, the soaking water becomes thick and jelly-like, providing a versatile thickening and binding ingredient for many recipes.

## Celtic Sea Salt

Light-grey Celtic sea salt consists primarily of sodium and chloride (33% sodium and 51% chloride). Due to a unique method of harvesting from ocean water (on the northwestern coast of France), along with gathering the naturally evaporated salt using wooden tools, it also contains many trace minerals not found in other sea salts.

Common table salt lacks minerals and trace elements because it is purified and refined, leaving only sodium and chloride. After refining, common table salt is mixed with iodine, bleaching agents, and anti-caking agents, which creates a pure white, free-flowing product. Even many salts labeled "sea salt" are washed or boiled, which removes minerals and trace elements, rendering them highly toxic to the human body. Celtic sea salt is the most energetic and complete salt we have found. Research indicates that sea salt is used by the body for mineralization, hydration, and to restore a healthy sodium-potassium balance.

## ALMOND BUTTER AND SESAME TAHINI

Almond butter is made from raw, unsoaked almonds that have been ground. Likewise, tahini is the succulent butter ground from raw sesame seeds. Many commercial tahinis and almond butters involve exposure to intense heat in the grinding process. As such, their labels, which identify them as "raw," are very misleading. High-quality, commercially prepared almond butter and sesame tahini that have *not* been exposed to extreme heat are available from the Tree of Life Health Store (see the Resources section).

Both almond butter and sesame tahini are versatile ingredients for many types of recipes, particularly soups and salad dressings. Tahini is especially enhancing with its creamy, dairy-like texture and rich flavor. These butters make a great snack straight out of the jar, as a dip for crudités or apple slices, or as a spread for raw bread or crackers.

## MESQUITE MEAL

Milled from the mesquite tree bean and pod (a species native to the beautiful Sonoran Desert, home of the Tree of Life), mesquite meal is a high-quality source of soluble fiber, omega-3 fatty acids, and many minerals and amino acids. It is an excellent addition to nut porridges, granolas, nut/seed mylks, desserts, and sweet treats. The Tree of Life's low-glycemic mix is suitable for Phase II of the cuisine.

## HEMP SEED

The tiny shelled seed of the amazing hemp plant has a pleasant nutty flavor, similar to sunflower seeds. The seeds are packed with nutrients—they are an excellent source of the essential fatty acids (EFAs), and they deliver these EFAs in a balanced 3.75:1 ratio. Hemp seed contains the rare fatty acid gamma-linolenic acid (GLA). Hemp seed is a source of complete protein, containing all the essential amino acids.

Most hemp seeds are irradiated upon import; however, the Tree of Life is able to supply truly live, organic hemp seeds (see Resources Directory), which we call hemp nuts.

Hemp seed is great with granola, sprinkled on salads, and is especially tasty in tomato-based sauces. Hemp seed is a delicious substitute for other nuts and seeds in most any recipe.

## OLIVES

Olives should be water-cured or cured in Celtic sea salt only. Olives are rich in monounsaturated fat, with high proportions of essential amino acids, vitamins E and A, beta-carotene, calcium, and magnesium. They also provide a good meat substitute because of their nutrient density.

## MISO

Miso (pronounced mee-so) is a delicious, all-purpose, high-protein seasoning that has played a major role in Japanese culture and cuisine for centuries. It is traditionally used as a seasoning for soup, with its fermented, sour taste. Because it is fermented, its use is restricted to Phase 1.5 and Phase II recipes.

Unpasteurized miso is a "living food" containing natural digestive enzymes, lactobacillus, and other microorganisms that aid digestion and have been shown to ward off and destroy harmful microorganisms, helping to create a healthy digestive tract.

The Tree of Life Café recommends barley and chickpea miso made by the South River Miso Company, which is cultured with sea salt by a unique fermentation process.

## Coconut

Young coconuts are not just delicious—they are highly nutritious and easy to digest. All the recipes with coconut in the book are referring to this variety.

The water/milk of young coconuts is very sweet (unless you are using Hawaiian or Mexican coconuts) and therefore using and drinking coconut water is only recommended for Phase II and I.5 when diluted. Young coconuts are generally available from Asian markets. Also known as Jelly, Shaved, Green, Thai, or Asian coconuts, this type of coconut is cylindrical with a pyramid-shaped top and white in color, having been shaved down from their original green outer shell. As the young coconut matures, its water turns into hard pulp. These "mature" coconuts are the ones generally found in the market. The pulp of a mature coconut is more fibrous and has a much higher oil content.

Mature coconuts are used in the creation of health-enhancing coconut oil that is mostly solid at room temperature, so it is often referred to as coconut butter. Raw, unprocessed coconut oil smells fragrant like fresh coconuts, while most commercial coconut oils—including the brands commonly found in health food stores—are often deodorized and heat-processed, and therefore are not recommended. Cold-pressed coconut oil is available from the Health Store on the Tree of Life website.

The saturated fats in coconut oil are medium-chain fats (triglycerides, or MCTs) and therefore unlike most other sources of saturated fats (long-chain triglycerides), which are stored in the body as fat reserves. The high MCTs found in coconut oil are easy to digest, even for people who typically have trouble digesting fats. In fact, MCTs actually assist the body in metabolizing fat efficiently. As such, coconut oil provides a readily available fuel source. Saturated fats are also an important building block for all the cells of the human body.

Coconut oil has a high (50% +) lauric fatty acid and caprylic acid content, from which it derives its anti-parasitical, anti-viral, and anti-fungal properties. Those with intestinal problems such as candida or other systemic infections can therefore benefit from the daily inclusion of coconut oil in their diet.

Coconut oil can be added to nut mylks, dressings, desserts (acting as a thickener when chilled), and even soups. Coconut oil also makes an excellent skin lotion and massage oil.

Detailed instructions on how to open young coconuts are available on the Tree of Life website: www.treeoflife.nu. Follow the links to the Tree of Life Café recipe section.

## Minimize Garlic and Onions

Garlic and onions are well known for their powerful cleansing and regenerative properties (because they contain high amounts of organic sulfur). However, their use at the Tree of Life Café is minimized because they tend to disrupt the balance between the left and right sides of the brain. This disturbance leads to an agitated mind-state that hinders the practice of meditation. On occasion, minimal quantities may be used to balance the flavors in a recipe. Hing (asafetida) is recommended as a garlic/onion replacement.

## A Note About Nama Shoyu and Bragg's Amino Acids

These raw, soy-based condiments are a popular flavoring agent for many raw-food chefs. These products are not used, however, in the Rainbow Green Live-Food Cuisine. This is because soy is difficult for the body to process and it is likely to be contaminated by GMO crops. It has also been shown that during processing there is a formation of naturally occurring MSG. Dark miso makes a good substitute for these products.

## Wild Rice

Wild rice has long been thought to be a raw food product in the live-food movement because of its said ability to sprout. Apparently this information is incorrect. Industry processing of wild rice to remove bacteria and the husks involves high heat treatment. Growers and processors in the wild rice industry inform us that the seed is subject to 300°F temperatures for about one hour forty-five minutes. Unprocessed wild rice is amber-colored and turns the familiar dark brown color only after this high heat processing.

Soaking wild rice causes splitting, which has been incorrectly identified as sprouting. This splitting is not the same as sprouting, which produces a long thin shoot and eventually leaves in unprocessed wild rice used for planting. There is potential for wild rice to be a raw food product with low temperature dehydration, but to our knowledge there are no such suppliers. Therefore the Tree of Life Café no longer uses wild rice in its cuisine.

# FOOD PREPARATION EQUIPMENT

High-quality food preparation equipment is essential for optimizing the health-giving properties of the recipes in this book. The purchase of quality equipment for the living foods kitchen requires a small investment, but the durability and the results are well worth the initial cost. Most of the items listed here are available from the Health Store on the Tree of Life website: www.treeoflife.nu.

## Selecting a Chef's Knife

A good chef's knife is your most important tool in the kitchen. Purchase the best-quality knife you can afford. High-carbon steel blade is recommended, as it is the most durable material. Try it out in the store if possible, noticing how it feels in your hand. A good knife should have balance—like an extension of your arm.

Ceramic knives are an excellent alternative to steel because they do not lead to browning in fruits and vegetables due to oxidation caused by the metal, nor is there any subtle metallic taste imparted to the food. They will also last months/years without sharpening. Ceramic is a very hard material; this, however, makes these knives liable to breakage if care is not taken in their use and handling.

For mincing fresh herbs, a cleaver with a slightly rounded blade is essential. Use a rocking motion, moving back and forth across the herbs, finely chopping them.

*The Professional Chef's Knife Kit* by the Culinary Institute of America is an excellent reference book for information on the care and sharpening of knives, as well as instruction in a variety of professional cutting techniques.

## BLENDERS

A high-speed blender is essential in the living foods kitchen. Household blenders are unable to adequately process or achieve the desired smoothness when blending hard nuts and seeds—the motors will quickly burn out with this type of use. The following brands are recommended:

- Vitamix (probably the most versatile and durable blender available).
- K-Tec Blender.
- Juiceman Smoothies (a good choice for those with a tight budget).
- Tribest Blender (great for traveling).

## JUICERS

The selection of a juicer for your living-foods kitchen should be carefully considered. Most home juicers are of the centrifugal type. The quality of the juice extracted from this type of juicer is less than ideal because as the centrifugal mechanism spins at high speed, it shreds the produce, which therefore oxidizes more rapidly. Centrifugal juicers also tend to waste produce because they are unable to fully break down the cell wall and extract all the juices.

The best type of juicer is one that masticates the produce at low speeds and therefore preserves the health-giving qualities of the juice. Masticating juicers produce a very dry pulp, as the juices are completely extracted, thus providing a greater return on your investment. The juicer of the brand name "Green Star" is perhaps the best masticating juicer currently available. The Green Star is capable of juicing all types of produce, including green leafy vegetables (even grasses); it can also effectively homogenize nuts and seeds for pâtés.

We also recommend the Champion Juicer for its ability to homogenize ingredients and juice carrots (for which the Green Star is less capable). If you are in the market for a juicer, we recommend the Green Star as it is more efficient for juicing greens and homogenizes ingredients.

## FOOD PROCESSORS

A high-quality food processor enables you to process vegetables in a variety of forms; it will also allow the processing of nuts and seeds to a variety of consistencies. Look for one with 8- to 10-cup capacity. Cuisinart is a time-honored favorite brand, although there are many good food processors on the market today.

## DEHYDRATORS

When looking for a dehydrator it is important to choose one that is fan-operated, which provides even drying temperatures throughout. It should also allow for temperature selection and control. Many home models lack quality temperature controllers.

The Tree of Life Café recommends the Excalibur dehydrator because of its efficient fan-operated system, accurate temperature control, and ease of use and cleaning. The Excalibur has up to nine trays that slide in and out of the dehydrator without disturbing other levels, as would be the case with the common circular stacking models. See below for more information on dehydration.

## COFFEE GRINDER OR SPICE MILL

A coffee grinder can be used to grind whole spices, and it works perfectly for grinding your daily flax seed. A quality spice mill may be more effective for grinding hard spices to a fine powder and will simultaneously provide air-tight storage for your whole spices. In this case, purchase a spice mill for each type of whole spice you use, such as black and white peppercorns, nutmeg, coriander, cardamom, cinnamon, cumin, caraway, and anise.

## SPIRAL SLICER (A.K.A. SALADACCO)

A spiral slicer is essential for creating pasta-like "noodles" from a variety of vegetables such as zucchini, carrot, squash, and root vegetables. It is easy to make both flat ribbon "noodles" and super-thin angel hair "pasta" with this clever tool.

## MANDOLINE

A most versatile kitchen tool, the mandoline is simple to use and will perfectly slice veggies and fruits thick or thin. With the switch of a blade, you can instantly julienne, grate, or shred. Essential for making vegetable "pasta" for live-food lasagna and or other wide "noodle" dishes.

# MISCELLANEOUS HINTS AND TIPS

## AMERICAN/ENGLISH TRANSLATIONS

Zucchini — Courgette

Eggplant — Aubergine

Cilantro — Coriander

Arugula — Rocket

## CONVERTING PHASE II TO PHASE I DISHES

Often it is simple to convert a recipe from Phase I.5 or Phase II to Phase I by substituting ingredients. However, if a higher-glycemic food is a vital ingredient, this may not be possible. Stevia can be used to impart a sweet flavor in some recipes. Other types of substitutions include using lime or lemon in place of apple cider vinegar. To substitute miso, try adding more salt to the recipe, although this will not compensate for the fermented flavor of the miso.

## DEHYDRATION

Low-temperature food dehydration is a technique that warms and dries food yet will not destroy enzymes. It has been suggested by Edward Howell in his book *Food Enzymes for Health and Longevity* that food enzymes are destroyed when the food temperature reaches 115–120°F. However, recent research by The Excalibur Dehydrator Company suggests that it is actually better to begin the dehydration process at 145°F for the initial stage of the drying process. The reasoning is that as the food is dehydrating, it literally "sweats out" the moisture it contains. This moisture inside the dehydrator reduces the food temperature, as much as 20–25 degrees.

This information changes how we think about the entire process of food dehydration. It means that the safest way to dehydrate is to begin drying at 145°F for a maximum of three hours for foods with a high water content. After this the temperature is set in the "normal" range of 110–115°F through the completion of the drying process. By doing this we are inhibiting bacterial growth by reducing the time the food spends in the dehydrator. The longer that a food is in the dehydrator, the more potential exists for the enzymes to be destroyed, even at lower temperatures. Low-temperature dehydration for sustained time, as practiced for years by the live-food community, may not be safe because sustained low-temperature dehydration encourages bacterial growth and fermentation. At the Tree of Life we feel that the new approach is both safer and more efficient. Through research from our Master's Degree Program in Vegan Live-Food Nutrition, we hope to have more exact temperatures and times regarding this technique, but for now we only have estimates. Join the free Tree of Life Newsletter at www.treeoflife.nu for updates on this important information.

This technique of dehydration is only recommended for the Excalibur Dehydrator because of the way that it dries food. First the Excalibur has the Parallexx™ Horizontal-Airflow Drying System, which evenly distributes air, eliminating "hot" spots. Also, a thermostat controls the temperature in the Excalibur; therefore when it reaches the set temperature the heating element shuts off. The advantage to this is that when the temperature is higher, moisture is evaporated from the food (instead of being trapped inside by hardening of the outer surface). Then as the temperature goes down, moisture is able to pass from the inside to the outside of the food as the outer moisture is evaporated. In this way the food dries much more quickly and evenly so there is less chance of bacterial growth.

The Excalibur dehydrator comes equipped with Teflex sheets. These non-stick sheets are used whenever the food to be dehydrated is of a more liquid-like consistency that could spill through the plastic net sheet that is normally used on the dehydrator tray.

SALTING AND MASSAGE

The technique of salting, as indicated in many recipes, helps to soften hard vegetables such as cabbage, kale, broccoli, etc. Salt causes the vegetables to release moisture as it breaks down the cell walls. Digestion is made easier when these fibers are broken down. Foods that are high in cellulose will wilt slightly, creating a texture similar to cooked food. Green leafy vegetables can be "massaged" by using the hands directly to rub the salt into the greens. This effect is further enhanced by adding a small amount of an acid, such as lemon juice or apple cider vinegar. It is recommended that only Celtic sea salt be used for all food preparation.

SOAKING AND SPROUTING

Many nuts, seeds, and grains must be soaked or sprouted before they can be used in live-food cuisine. Soaking the seeds and nuts removes the enzyme inhibitors they contain, thereby activating a food's full nutritional potential. Below is a chart to guide you in this process.

## Soaking and Sprouting Guidelines

| Seed Type | Dry Measure | Soaking Time | Sprouting Time | Yield | Length@ Harvest | Tips |
|---|---|---|---|---|---|---|
| **NUTS** | | | | | | |
| Almonds | 1 cup | 12 hours | | | None | Store in water in refrigerator. |
| Pecans | 1 cup | 1–2 hours | | | | |
| Walnut | 1 cup | 1–2 hours | | | | |
| Macadamia | | Do not soak | | | | Yellow seeds indicate rancidity. |
| Pine nuts | | Do not soak | | | | Yellow seeds indicate rancidity. |
| In-shell Pistachio | | Do not soak | | | | |

| Seed Type | Dry Measure | Soaking Time | Sprouting Time | Yield | Length@ Harvest | Tips |
|---|---|---|---|---|---|---|
| **SEEDS** | | | | | | |
| Hulled Pumpkin | 1 cup | 4 hours | 24 hours | 2 cups | ⅛ inch | |
| Hulled Sunflower | 1 cup | 4 hours | 24 hours | 2.5 cups | ¼–½ inch | Can spoil if not used promptly. |
| Hulled Buckwheat (careful, soaking/ sprouting too long will cause fermentation) | 1 cup | 15 minutes | 24 hours | 2 cups | ⅛ inch | Use only raw groats. |
| White Hulled Sesame | 1 cup | 4 hours | | | | |
| Black Sesame | 1 cup | 4 hours | | | | |
| Hemp Seeds | 1 cup | Do not soak | | | | |
| Golden/ Brown Flax Seeds | 1 cup seed, 1 cup water | 8 hours | | | | |
| Golden/ Brown Flax Seeds (for grinding) | 1 cup | Do not soak, just grind and eat dry | | | | |
| **GRAINS** | | | | | | |
| Rye | 1 cup | 6 hours | 5–7 days | 3 cups | 4 inches | |
| Spelt | 1 cup | 6 hours | 5–7 days | 3 cups | 4 inches | Spelt is a primitive wheat. |
| Wheat | 1 cup | 6 hours | 5–7 days | 3 cups | 4 inches | |
| Kamut | 1 cup | 6 hours | 5–7 days | 3 cups | 4 inches | |
| Barley | 1 cup | 6 hours | 5–7 days | 3 cups | 4 inches | |
| Amaranth | 1 cup | 3 hours | 24 hours | 3 cups | ⅛ inch | |
| Millet | 1 cup | 3 hours | 12 hours | 3 cups | 0–⅛ inch | |
| Quinoa | 1 cup | 3 hours | 24 hours | 3 cups | ¼ inch | |

| Seed Type | Dry Measure | Soaking Time | Sprouting Time | Yield | Length@ Harvest | Tips |
|---|---|---|---|---|---|---|
| **GREEN SPROUTS** | | | | | | |
| Buckwheat | 1 cup | 6 hours | 5–7 days | 3 inches | | |
| Sunflower | 1 cup | 7 hours | 5–7 days | 3 inches | | |
| **SMALL VEGETABLE** | | | | | | |
| Alfalfa | 3 tablespoons | 5 hours | 5 days | 4 cups | 2 inches | |
| Clover | 3 tablespoons | 5 hours | 5 days | 4 cups | 2 inches | |
| Fenugreek | ¼ cup | 6 hours | 5 days | 4 cups | 2 inches | Good to dissolve mucus |
| Kale | ¼ cup | 5 hours | 5 days | 4 cups | 1 inch | |
| Mustard | 3 tablespoons | 5 hours | 5 days | 4 cups | 1.5 inches | Spicy |
| Radish | 3 tablespoons | 6 hours | 5 days | 4 cups | 2 inches | Spicy |
| **MISCELLANEOUS** | | | | | | |
| Sun-dried Tomato | 1 cup | 3–4 hours | | | | Warm water speeds up the soaking process. |
| Raisins | 1 cup | 3 hours | | | | Warm water speeds up the soaking process. |
| Dulse Sea Vegetable | 1 cup | 2 minutes | | | | Massage in water and drain immediately to retain minerals. |
| Wakame | 1 cup | 2 hours | | | | Quite chewy, chop well. |
| Sea Palm | 1 cup | 15 minutes | | | | |

Data resourced from: *http://www.supersprouts.com*

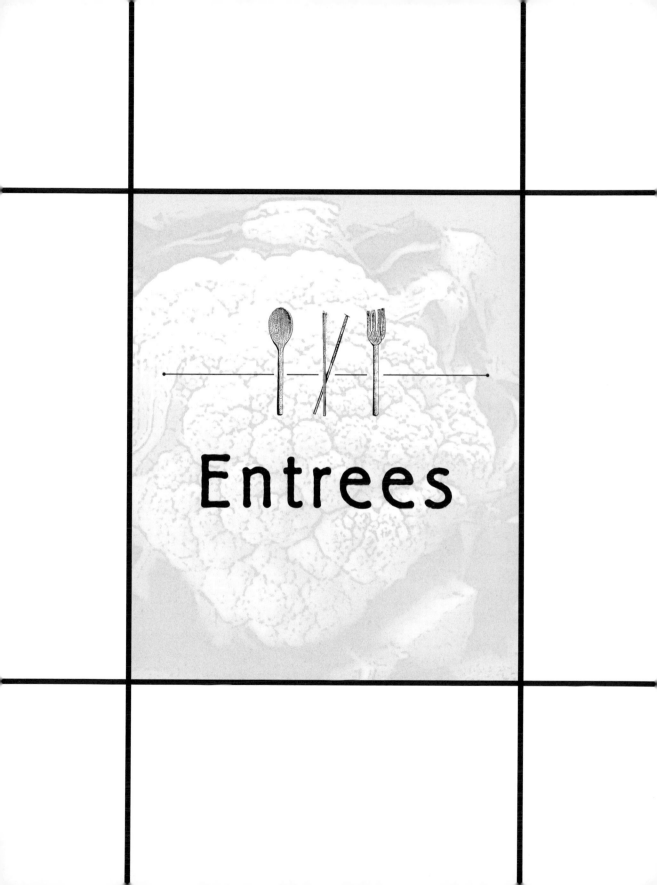

# Entrees

# ALMOND VEGGIE STIR (UN)FRY

1 head cauliflower, chopped
1 yam, chopped
1 C broccoli, chopped
1 C almonds, soaked
½ C macadamia nuts, unsoaked
1 C coconut water
1 T lemon juice
1 T ginger
3 T kefir lime leaves (chopped)
1½ t Celtic salt

Homogenize nuts and stir in lemon juice, ginger, kefir lime leaves, and salt. Add coconut water until creamy and smooth. Cover veggies with mixture. Spread onto dehydrator sheet and dehydrate for 1–2 hours at 145°F. Garnish with chopped almonds and lime leaves.

# ALOO PALEEK

2 C spinach leaves
2 C walnuts, soaked
¼ C lemon juice
¼ C coconut water
Pulp of 1 coconut
2 t Celtic salt
2 t cumin
¼ t hing

Chop spinach into thin strips and set aside. Blend remaining ingredients to a thin, creamy sauce, adding water when necessary to achieve desired consistency. Adjust spices. In a mixing bowl, stir spinach into sauce and serve. The sauce is yogurt-like in taste. Traditionally, this is a very saucy dish and makes for great comfort food.

# Autumnal Chili

2 C avocado

1½ C sun-dried tomatoes, soaked

1 C almonds

1 C carrots, diced

½ C fresh cilantro, de-stemmed

½ C lime juice

2½ T Celtic salt

3 T chili spice

2 T dried cilantro

1 T cumin

1 T cayenne

1 T paprika

Combine almonds, avocado, lime juice, tomatoes, and tomato soak water in blender and mix on high until smooth. Add remaining ingredients except carrots and mix for additional minute. Stir in carrots and serve immediately.

# Bok Choy Paneer

3 C bok choy, shredded
(spinach can be substituted)

½ C red bell pepper, diced

2 T fresh basil, finely chopped

½ C pine nuts, unsoaked

1 C walnuts, soaked

1½ T lemon juice

1 T ginger juice

1 T garam masala

½ T Celtic salt

½ T garlic, minced

¼ T fresh ground black pepper

Combine bok choy, red bell pepper, and basil in a mixing bowl and set aside. Process remaining ingredients in a food processor with the "S" blade until smooth; combine and mix well. Marinate for 1–2 hours. Serves 4–6.

# Chennai Curry

5 tomatoes

3 C coconut pulp

¼ C cilantro

¼ C lemon juice

¼ C parsley

2 t Celtic salt

1 t cumin

¼ t hing

¼ t turmeric

¼ t mustard seed

¼ t fresh ground black pepper

⅛ t cayenne

Chop three of the tomatoes in small chunks and set aside with the fresh herbs. In the blender, combine the remaining ingredients and adjust seasoning to taste. In a mixing bowl, stir the chopped tomatoes together with the blended sauce.

# Chili

4 tomatoes

2 avocados

½ C sun-dried tomatoes

1 T fresh ginger

2 t Celtic salt

2 T chili powder

2 t ground cumin

1–2 t cayenne

2 carrots

2 celery stalks

1 red pepper

½ C chopped leeks

¼ C olive oil

1 t Celtic salt

Blend tomatoes, avocado, and sun-dried tomatoes in the food processor with ginger, 2 t salt, chili powder, cumin, and cayenne (to desired spiciness). Chop all veggies into small cubes and marinate in olive oil and 1 t salt. Place in the dehydrator at 145° for 1 hour. Mix all ingredients together. If your dehydrator is big enough, place the entire bowl in the dehydrator at 145°F for about an hour and serve warm with *Sour Cream*.

## CLASSIC NEATBALLS

1½ C pecans
3 stalks celery
½ C cauliflower
⅓ C fresh parsley
2 T dried ground fennel
½ t Celtic salt
1 t fresh ground black pepper
2 T olive oil
2 T fresh lemon juice
⅓ C golden flax seeds, ground

Process all ingredients except flax in food processor with the "S" blade until smooth, adding more water as needed. Transfer to a mixing bowl and stir in ground flax until the mixture is firm enough to shape into balls. Place on a dehydrator tray and dehydrate at 145° for 1–2 hours. Serve with your favorite sauce.

# CREAMY YAM MASH

2 yams
2 T coconut butter
I t Celtic salt

*Variation:*
Add cinnamon to taste

Blend yams in a food processor with the "S" blade until relatively smooth. Place in a glass bowl and cover with coconut mylk or water. Place bowl in dehydrator for about 3 hours at 145° and then at 115° for 3 hours. Remove from dehydrator when the liquid has mostly evaporated. Blend in a high-power blender, adding remaining ingredients. (Only a high-power blender will make it very creamy.)

# CURRIED VEGETABLES

### CURRIED COCONUT SAUCE:

Pulp of 4 coconuts
7 carrots
2 C coconut water
I½ T curry
I t coriander
2 t thyme

2 t marjoram
¾ t cayenne
I½ t cumin
I t Celtic salt
½ t fresh ground black pepper

In a blender, process all ingredients until smooth and creamy. Add more coconut mylk if necessary. Pour mixture over a medley of chopped (bite size) vegetables.

# Eggplant Casserole

3 small eggplants
2 t Celtic salt

### Sauce:
½ C olive oil
2 T fresh thyme, minced
½ t Celtic salt

### Garnish:
½ C sun-dried tomatoes, soaked and diced
½ C parsley, finely chopped

Peel and slice eggplant into ½" rounds and cover with water. Add salt and soak for 8 hours. Drain and combine with sauce and massage the eggplant 3–5 minutes. Spread the mixture on a dehydrator tray with a Teflex sheet and dehydrate at 145°F for 1–2 hours. Combine in a mixing bowl with sun-dried tomatoes and parsley and mix well. Serve warm. Serves 4–6.

# FALAFEL

1 C almonds, soaked
1 C walnuts, soaked
½ C sesame seeds, ground
¼ C parsley, minced
¼ C cilantro, minced
1 T garlic, minced
1 T fresh sage, minced
2 T fresh oregano, minced
½ t black pepper
1½ t Celtic salt
2 T olive oil

Process almonds and walnuts in a Champion Juicer with the solid plate, or process in a food processor with the "S" blade. Combine all ingredients in a large bowl and mix well. Form into patties and dehydrate at 145°F for 2 hours and then at 115°F for 2–3 hours, or until desired moisture is obtained. Serve with *Lemon Tahini Sauce.*

# GARAM MASALA GOBI

1 head of cauliflower
½ pound macadamia nuts, unsoaked
¼ C olive oil
Juice of one lemon
1 T Celtic salt
3 T garam masala
Cayenne pepper to taste
1 bunch of cilantro to garnish

Break apart cauliflower into florets and set aside. Blend macadamia nuts in high-power blender with just enough olive oil to reach a creamy consistency. Add juice of about one lemon and Celtic salt and cayenne pepper to taste, along with garam masala. Blend until thoroughly mixed. You may want to add more garam masala. Pour sauce over florets and massage into the cauliflower, making sure all are evenly coated. Place in casserole dish and dehydrate for approximately 1–2 hours at 145°F. Chop cilantro and sprinkle on top to garnish before serving.

## GARDEN NEATBALLS

1 C almonds, soaked
½ C walnuts, soaked
1 C olive oil
¼ C leeks
2 celery stalks
1 T sage
1 T marjoram
1 T thyme
2 t Celtic salt

Homogenize nuts with oil. Finely chop and stir in leeks, celery, herbs, and salt. Roll into 1½" balls and dehydrate for 2–3 hours at 145°F. Serve with *Marinara Sauce.*

## GREEN DRAGON BROCCOLI

2 C broccoli, chopped
1 bunch kale, finely chopped

½ bunch dandelion leaves, remove stems and chop

### SAUCE:

½ C fresh mint, minced

¼ C raisins

2 jalapeño peppers, seeded and finely chopped

2 T fresh lemon grass, minced

1 T lime leaf, minced

1 T coconut butter

2 t Celtic salt

1 t tarragon

Water for consistency

In a blender, process all sauce ingredients until smooth.

Place broccoli into a glass rectangular dish and pour sauce over broccoli. Massage the sauce into the broccoli for 30 seconds. Strain the excess marinade and set aside. Place mixture on a dehydrator tray and dehydrate for 1 hour at 145°F. Remove from dehydrator and toss kale, dandelion greens, and wilted broccoli with the marinade.

# KEBOBS

### MARINATED VEGGIES:

2 heads broccoli, florets

1 head cauliflower, florets

2 pints cherry tomatoes

3 zucchini, mandoline lengthwise

1 C almond butter

1 bunch of mint

1 handful cilantro

1 T ginger

Celtic salt to taste

Pepper

Cayenne to taste

Place broccoli and cauliflower florets in dehydrator to soften for one hour. In a blender combine almond butter, mint, cilantro, ginger, salt, pepper, and cayenne. Massage mixture onto all the vegetables.

*Variation:*

Add ¼ C soaked raisins to the sauce for Phase II.

### KEBOB NEATBALLS:

2 C pumpkin seeds, soaked
2 C sunflower seeds, soaked
4 carrots, shredded (omit for
    Phase I)
½ fennel bulb
2 T curry to taste

In a food processor with the "S" blade, blend all ingredients. Form into balls and dehydrate at 145°F for 2 hours.

On bamboo kebob spears, place marinated vegetables and neatballs. Place entire kebob back in dehydrator for another hour at 145°F. Serve warm.

# LASAGNA

### ZUCCHINI PASTA:

3 medium-sized zucchini
¼ t Celtic salt

Cut zucchini into thin slices using a mandoline, or a large vegetable peeler. Sprinkle slices with Celtic salt and let sit to soften.

### CHEEZE:

2 C almonds, soaked
1 C hulled sesame seeds, soaked
2 T lemon juice
1 t Celtic salt
¾ C water

Process in a food processor with the "S" blade until smooth and creamy; add additional water if necessary.

## TOMATO SAUCE:

4 large tomatoes
2 red or yellow bell peppers
1½ C sun-dried tomatoes, soaked
1 C sun-dried tomato soak water
½ C olive oil
1 T fresh basil
1 t Celtic salt
¾ t fresh oregano
¾ t fresh thyme
½ t fresh ground black pepper

In a blender, process all ingredients until smooth. Add more sun-dried tomatoes for a thicker sauce or more water for a thinner sauce.

## ZUCCHINI CHEEZE FILLING:

3 medium-sized zucchini
¼ t Celtic salt
½ C cheeze mixture

Grate zucchini into a large bowl and sprinkle with Celtic salt. This will help to draw out moisture. Let sit for 5 minutes. Drain liquid and hand-squeeze zucchini to remove excess moisture. Stir cheeze mixture into drained zucchini and mix well.

## SPINACH FILLING:

3 C spinach, finely chopped
½ C cheeze mixture

Place chopped spinach in a large bowl and stir in cheeze mixture.

## TO ASSEMBLE:

Alternate layers of zucchini pasta, tomato sauce, cheeze, zucchini cheeze filling, and spinach filling in a 9 × 13 glass dish.

*Optional:*
Dehydrate for ½ hour at 145°F to warm the lasagna.

# MAGIC WANDS

1½ C pine nuts, unsoaked
1 C walnuts, soaked
¾ C water
¼ C olive oil
3 T lemon juice
2 T Celtic salt
2 t ground ginger
1 t cumin
1 t cayenne
1 t coriander
1 t white pepper
15 nori sheets

Lay out nori sheets on dehydrator trays. Combine all ingredients in high-power blender and mix until creamy. Spread 2–3 T of mixture onto each sheet of nori and allow to dehydrate for 1.5 hours at 145°F. Next, roll each sheet of nori up and continue to dehydrate for another 2 hours. These wands may be served warm or, if desired as travel food, fully dehydrated and stored in sealed baggies for a convenient snack.

# MALAI KOFTA

### WALNUT BALLS:

1 C walnuts, soaked
2 C winter squash, peeled
3 stalks celery, minced
2 T fresh lemon juice
1 t fresh ginger, grated
2 t Celtic sea salt

1 t cumin
¼ t turmeric
⅛ t coriander
⅛ t mustard seed
¼ t hing

Process walnuts, squash, and minced celery through the Champion Juicer with a solid plate. Combine with remaining ingredients in a mixing bowl and knead by hand to ensure a thorough mixing. Form the dough into golf ball-sized pieces and dehydrate on mesh trays at 145°F for 1–2 hours.

SAUCE:

2 C walnuts, soaked
¼ C coconut pulp
¼ C coconut water (substitute with water for Phase I)
¼ C lemon juice
2 t Celtic salt

Blend all ingredients to form a creamy yogurt sauce. Serve the walnut balls on a platter surrounded by this sauce.

# MASHED TATERS

1 C cauliflower
1 C pine nuts, unsoaked
½ C macadamia nuts, unsoaked
3 T olive oil
1½ T Italian seasoning
½ T garlic, minced
½ t Celtic salt
Fresh ground black pepper to taste

Process in a food processor with the "S" blade until all ingredients are smooth. Add a little water if needed to achieve consistency. Serves 4–6.

# Mediterranean Patties

2 C pecans, soaked

5 carrots

2 zucchini

2 C broccoli, chopped

1 C sun-dried tomatoes, soaked

½ C cilantro, chopped

2 cloves garlic

4 T lemon juice

½ C parsley, finely chopped

2 t marjoram

3 t Italian seasoning

2 t mint

1½ t Celtic salt

1 t fresh ground black pepper

½ t cayenne

½ t cinnamon

¼ t allspice

½ to ¾ C golden flax seeds, ground

Process all ingredients (except flax seeds) in a food processor with the "S" blade until a fine mixture. Place in large bowl and mix in ground flax seeds until the mixture no longer sticks to your hand but is still very moist. Form into small patties 3" in diameter and ¼" thick. Place on a dehydrator tray and dehydrate at 145° for 2–3 hours and then at 115°F for 1–2 more hours or until desired moisture is obtained. They should be crispy on the outside but still a little moist on the inside.

# Mexican Burritos

## Tortillas:

1 C golden flax seeds, soaked
½ ripe avocado
Celtic salt to taste
Water for consistency

*Variations:*
Add different spices and vegetable pulp for a completely different taste.

Blend ingredients in a high-power blender, adding water to create a smooth batter. Spread ½ C batter evenly on Teflex sheets to a thickness of about ¼" and 6" in diameter. The thinner your batter, the less time it will take to dehydrate. Dehydrate at 145°F for 1–2 hours, flip the tortilla over and remove the Teflex sheet, and continue dehydrating at 115°F for 2–3 hours until the tortillas are soft and flexible. Remove the tortillas from the dehydrator before they are crisp. Makes ten 6" tortillas.

## Tastes Like Refried Beans Pâté:

2 C sunflower seeds, soaked
1 C sun-dried tomatoes, soaked
2 T or to taste Mexican seasoning
1 T red raw miso (omit for Phase I)
1 t cayenne
1 t Celtic salt

Process all ingredients in a food processor with the "S" blade until smooth and creamy; add a little water for consistency.

## GUACAMOLE!:

2 ripe avocados
1 tomato, diced
¼ C fresh cilantro, finely chopped
2 T lemon juice
½ t cumin
½ t hing
½ t Celtic salt

Blend all ingredients, except tomatoes, which should be mixed in by hand.

## TOMATO SALSA #1:

4 ripe tomatoes, diced
½ C cilantro, finely chopped
1 t cayenne
1 t hing
2 T lemon juice
Celtic salt to taste

Mix and serve.

*Optional:*

1 clove garlic, minced

## SOUR CREAM:

1 C macadamia nuts, unsoaked
½ C sunflower seeds, soaked
1 T lemon juice
1 t Celtic salt

Blend in a high-speed blender until smooth.

## ASSEMBLY:

Lay tortilla flat and layer ingredients on one half, adding shredded lettuce on top. Roll tortilla into a burrito. Enjoy!

# NORI ROLLS

Nori sheets, dried not toasted.

## FILLING:

5 C sunflower seeds or almonds,
  soaked

⅓ C lemon juice

1½ C carrots, grated
  (remove for Phase I)

½–1 t ginger juice

¼ t hing

1½ t Celtic salt

½ C water

Process all ingredients in blender. Use filling as is or divide mixture into three parts to create three different fillings by adding one of the following to each mixture:

3 T ume plum vinegar
  (use only for Phase II)

1 T miso paste
  (use only for Phase II)

1 T ginger juice

Spread filling to desired thickness in rectangle covering the bottom third of the long side of an un-roasted nori sheet. If you will be eating the nori roll a while after creating it, place dry lettuce leaves on nori prior to spreading filling. Using lettuce as a moisture barrier, lay another lettuce leaf over ALL the fillings (veggies included) so that they do not come into contact with the nori sheet. Along the center line of this rectangle, lay fillings of choice in lengthwise strips. Some possibilities include:

Carrots

Celery

Daikon radish

Avocado

Cucumber

Sweet red or yellow bell peppers

Sprouts

Chopped nuts

Sesame seeds

Cut fillings as desired—grate or slice into thin julienne-style strips. Do not fill nori too full or you may struggle to roll it. Tightly roll nori starting from the filled end. When you come to the end of the nori sheet, wet your finger and run it along the loose end and then press this end into the roll. This should help to keep your roll closed. To slice nori roll, use a sharp serrated knife and cut slowly, exerting only enough pressure to cut while being careful not to squash the roll. Keep your knife clean for easier cutting! Serve with *Wasabi Sauce* and *Pickled Ginger*.

# Noritos

4 sheets nori

2 large avocados

1 tomato

8 leaves romaine lettuce leaves, washed and dried well

¼ C pitted olives

1½ C sprouts, all types

2 T olive oil

1½ t Celtic salt

Mix avocado, salt, lemon, and oil together by hand in bowl (mixture should be chunky). Stir in olives, tomatoes, and sprouts. Place nori sheets on flat surface and top with whole romaine leaves so that entire surface area is covered (moisture causes nori to disintegrate). Spoon avocado mixture onto leaves and roll as if making a burrito. Store in sealed container for up to 4 hours. Great to make for air travel or even in the car outside the health food store.

# OCEAN ROLLS

1½ C sweet potato pulp
½ C carrot pulp
⅓ C olive oil
⅓ C fresh dill, minced
⅓ C fresh basil, minced
1 T Celtic salt
1 T galangal, minced
1 t hing
Dash of cayenne

Process sweet potatoes and carrots through a Champion Juicer or Green Star with the solid plate. Combine remaining ingredients in a large mixing bowl and mix well.

8 nori sheets
12 lettuce leaves
1 cucumber, sliced thin and lengthwise
1 avocado, sliced thin and lengthwise
1 C sprouts, clover, sunflower, buckwheat, etc.

Lay out one sheet of nori on a Japanese rolling mat. Place lettuce leaves on nori before spooning two tablespoons of mixture. Add avocado, cucumber, and sprouts. Roll tightly and serve immediately with *Wasabi Sauce.*

# PAD THAI

### PAD THAI NOODLES:

There are many options here! Some of our favorite noodles are made from the following:

Butternut squash
Green or red cabbage
Carrots
Turnips
Zucchini
Young coconut pulp

Using a vegetable spiralizer or another slicer you will be able to make beautiful spaghetti-style noodles. If you do not have either of these tools, finely sliced cabbage makes nice pasta, too. If your pasta is too hard, sprinkle it with a little Celtic salt and let it sit for a few minutes or until it reaches desired softness.

### PAD THAI SAUCE:

1 C coconut pulp
½ C coconut water
½ C macadamia nuts, unsoaked
¼ C filtered water
1 clove garlic
⅛ C lime juice
1 t apple cider vinegar
    (omit for Phase I)
½ t Celtic salt
½ t ginger
¼ t cayenne
¼ t black pepper

Process all ingredients in a blender until smooth. Mix with noodles. Garnish with coarsely chopped vegetables. Some nice ones include: sugar snap peas, sweet peppers, carrot, cauliflower, broccoli, cilantro, and sesame seeds.

# Pasta with Red Pepper Marinara

2 C red bell peppers, chopped

1 C tomatoes, chopped

½ C sun-dried tomatoes, chopped

½ C apple, chopped (omit for Phase I)

2 T olive oil

1 T garlic, minced

Dash of cayenne

1 t Celtic salt

2 T fresh basil, chopped

2 T fresh chives, chopped

1 T fresh thyme, chopped

In a blender, process red bell peppers, tomatoes, apple, olive oil, garlic, cayenne, and salt until smooth. Add basil, chives, and thyme and pulse until the herbs are small pieces. Serve over pasta. Pasta can be made from zucchini or butternut squash. Process the pasta using a Vegetable Spiralizer.

# Pizza

### Pizza Crust # 1 (see recipe below)

### Almond Pizza Cheeze:

2 C almonds, soaked

2 T lemon juice

1 clove of garlic

1 t cumin

1 t Italian seasoning

½ t oregano

Water for consistency

Process all ingredients in blender with ½ cup water and lemon juice. Blend until consistency is thick and smooth, adding more water as necessary to create a smooth cheeze.

## TOMATO PIZZA SAUCE:

4 large tomatoes, squeeze out
    liquid if you prefer a thick
    sauce
1½ C sun-dried tomatoes, soaked
½ C olive oil
1 T Italian seasoning
1 T basil
¾ t oregano
1 t Celtic salt
½ t fresh ground black pepper
½ t cayenne

Process all ingredients in a blender until smooth.

*Optional:*

1–3 sweet red or yellow peppers

## PIZZA TOPPINGS:

The sky is the limit! Here are some ideas.

- Olives
- Shredded lettuce
- Thinly sliced tomatoes
- Marinated mixed vegetables
- Marinated sun-dried tomatoes (cut in thin strips, toss with olive oil, Celtic salt, and Italian seasonings)
- Cilantro
- Red bell pepper
- Basil
- Parsley
- Avocado
- Dulse, soaked and drained

Assemble pizza layer by layer and enjoy.

# Pizza Deluxe

### Crust:

1 recipe *Basic Cracker,*
   dehydrated

### Herbed Cheeze:

1½ C pine nuts, unsoaked
  3 T lemon juice
  3 T olive oil
  2 T water
1½ T Celtic salt
  1 T chickpea miso (omit for
     Phase I, substitute more salt)
  1 T fresh dill, minced
  1 T fresh basil, minced

Combine all ingredients in blender until creamy-smooth.

### Sauce:

1½ C sun-dried tomatoes, soaked
 ½ C fresh tomatoes, chunked
 ½ C olive oil
  2 T fresh basil, minced
  1 T oregano, minced
  2 t Celtic salt
  1 t dried basil
  1 t cracked black peppercorns,
    freshly ground
  1 t cayenne pepper
 ½ t fresh ginger, minced

Combine all ingredients, including ¾ C tomato soak water, in blender and mix on high for one minute.

TOPPINGS:

1 C black olives, pitted and
    chopped
1 C manzanilla olives, pitted and
    chopped
1 C sun-dried tomatoes, soaked,
    chopped, and drizzled with
    olive oil

1 C zucchini, cut into thin
    half-circles
1 C fresh cherry tomatoes, cubed
½ C fresh basil, cut into thin
    strips
½ C fresh oregano, minced

ASSEMBLY:

Each cracker should be a rectangle, about 4" × 3". Spread ½ to 1 T *Herbed Cheeze* onto each cracker. Pour 2 T sauce over cheeze and cover with toppings of choice. Dehydrate about 2–3 hours at 145°F so that cracker is soft and slightly chewy, sauce appears dry, and cheeze is warm. Delicious as an appetizer or main course.

# PIZZA CRUST #1

4 C buckwheat, sprouted
2 C nuts/seeds of choice:
    sunflower, pumpkin, and
    almond
1 C sun-dried tomatoes, soaked
  2 medium-sized tomatoes
1 T olive oil
1 t cayenne
1 T Italian spices
1 t thyme
1 t Celtic salt

Process buckwheat in a food processor with the "S" blade with ½ cup of water until smooth. Place in large mixing bowl. Process nuts/seeds with ¼ C water until smooth (also in the food processor). Combine with buckwheat and add the remaining ingredients and mix well. Batter should be relatively thick. Spread batter onto Teflex sheets to a thickness of ¼", shaping as desired (mini rounds, squares, triangles!). Dehydrate at 145° for 2–3 hours then flip over and remove Teflex sheets and continue dehydrating for 4 hours at 115°F. Prepare pizza toppings just prior to serving.

# Pizza Crust #2

———————————————

4 C buckwheat, sprouted
4 C sunflower seeds, soaked
1 C fresh cilantro, finely chopped
1 C fresh basil, finely chopped
3 T oregano
2 t basil, dried
1 t oregano, dried
½ t crushed bay leaf
½ t parsley, dried
1 T Celtic salt
½ t hing

Process all ingredients in a Champion Juicer with the solid plate, or a food processor with the "S" blade. Spread batter onto Teflex sheets to a thickness of ¼", shaping as desired (mini rounds, squares, triangles!). Dehydrate at 145° for 2–3 hours, then flip over and remove Teflex sheets and continue dehydrating for 4 hours at 115°F. Prepare pizza toppings just prior to serving.

# PIZZA PARLOR CRUST

———————◆———————

2 C sunflower seeds
½ C fresh cilantro, finely chopped
1 T olive oil
1 t Celtic salt

Process sunflower seeds and cilantro in a Champion Juicer with the solid plate. In a mixing bowl knead salt into the dough and slowly add the olive oil to increase pliancy. Form dough into your favorite pizza crust shape approximately ¼" thick, place on a dehydrator tray, and dehydrate at 105° for 3–4 hours or until the desired moisture is obtained.

# POPEYE'S SPINACH PIE

———————◆———————

### CRUST:

1½ C walnuts, soaked
6 sun-dried tomatoes, soaked
1 C Moroccan olives, pitted
1 t marjoram
1 t sage
1 t thyme
1 t Celtic salt

Blend all of the above, *except* olives, in a food processor and press the mixture evenly into a pie crust. Dehydrate at 145°F for 1–2 hours, and then press chopped olives into the bottom of the crust.

### FILLING:

2 avocados

4 C spinach

1 T basil

1 T thyme

1 T oregano

1½ t jalapeño

1½ t Celtic salt

Blend all of the above in a food processor until smooth. Chill for 2 hours, and then spoon into the crust.

### PIE TOPPING:

2 zucchinis

¼ C olive oil

1 T rosemary

Slice zucchini as thinly as possible and marinate in olive oil and rosemary. Dehydrate at 145°F for 1–2 hours, and then layer on top of the pie. Serve with *Sour Cream.*

# RAWTWURST WRAPS

1½ C almonds, soaked

½ C pumpkin seeds, soaked

½ C pine nuts, soaked

¾ C water

2 avocados

1½ t fresh ginger, chopped

1½ t cayenne powder

1½ t Celtic salt

1 large carrot, grated

1 bulb fennel, finely chopped

¼ C parsley, chopped

3 T whole caraway seeds

1 head romaine lettuce

Homogenize nuts and seeds and then blend with water, avocado, ginger, cayenne, and salt. By hand, mix in the grated carrot, fennel, parsley, and caraway seeds. Form dough into sausage-like shapes and place on dehydrator sheets. Dehydrate for 2 hours at 145°F and serve in whole lettuce leaves with live *Sauerkraut, Alive Mustard,* or *Living Catsup.*

# RAW-VIOLI

3 eggplant, thinly sliced into long strips, and 10 sheets of nori

Soak eggplant in salt water overnight.

FILLING:

1 C almonds, soaked
1 C pine nuts, unsoaked
2 T olive oil
2 T lemon juice
1½ T Italian seasoning
1 T garlic, minced
½ t Celtic salt
½ t black pepper
½ t cayenne
¼ C water

Process all ingredients in a food processor with the "S" blade until a smooth paste.

*Hand-mix in:*
1 T fresh thyme, minced
2 T fresh basil, minced

To assemble, after soaking thinly sliced eggplant in salt water overnight, strain off water. On half of each eggplant slice, put 1–2 T filling and fold over to form raw-violi. Place on dehydrator sheet. Cut nori into 3–5 squares and on half put 1–2 T filling. Fold over to form raw-violi and place on dehydrator sheet. Dehydrate for 1–2 hours at 145° or until eggplant is slightly dried out. Serve with *Cilantro Pesto* or *Yellow Bell Pepper Curry Sauce* (Phase II).

# SAVORY SAGE CROQUETTES

2 C almonds, soaked
2 C Brazil nuts, unsoaked
1 C pine nuts, unsoaked
¾ C ground golden flax seeds
½ C olive oil
¼ C lemon juice
4 T Celtic salt
4 T fresh sage, minced
2 T fresh oregano, minced
1 T dried ground sage
1 T leeks, minced
2 t cracked black peppercorns

Begin by homogenizing the almonds, Brazil nuts, and pine nuts using a blank plate with a Green Star or Champion Juicer. Conversely, you may achieve similar results by placing the nuts in a food processor and mixing them for several minutes with the olive oil and enough water (about ¼ cup) to get mixture to turn over. Transfer nut mixture to medium mixing bowl and stir in all remaining ingredients except the ground flax seeds. After mixture has been well stirred, form it into several palm-sized, circular patties (or try heart shapes for fun). Roll each croquette in flax meal for a "breaded" effect. Place croquettes onto a mesh dehydrator tray and dehydrate for 2 hours at 145°F and then 115°F for 3 hours. Croquettes should be served warm. May be stored in refrigerator for up to 3 days.

# Savory Spring Rolls

2 heads of white cabbage

1 C walnuts, soaked

1 C almonds, soaked

½ C pine nuts

1 large carrot, finely chopped

1 bell pepper, finely chopped

½ C olive oil

½ C water

1 t cayenne

1 T marjoram

1 T sage

1 T thyme

1 t fresh ginger, finely chopped

1½ t Celtic salt

Cut the base off the cabbage heads and soak them in a sink filled with warm water. Homogenize walnuts, almonds, and pine nuts. Mix remaining ingredients together and knead into the nut mixture. Carefully peel the leaves off the soaking heads of cabbage. Spoon the nut mixture and any additional shredded veggies you have on hand into the cabbage leaves. Carefully tuck the ends and roll it up like a spring roll. Use a toothpick through the center to help keep it together. Serve with *Alive Mustard,* a salad dressing, or your favorite dipping sauce.

# SOUTHWESTERN STUFFING

3 C walnuts, soaked
2 C almonds, soaked
3 C red bell peppers, diced
¾ C olive oil
2 t fresh sage, minced
2 t fresh thyme, minced
1 t fresh marjoram, minced
1 t fresh rosemary, minced
2 t poultry seasoning
2 t Celtic salt
2 t black pepper

Combine nuts and oil in food processor and mix until ingredients are well chopped. Pour mixture into a large mixing bowl. Stir in bell peppers, herbs, salt, and pepper. Form mixture into 1" × 4" loaves on Teflex sheets on dehydrator trays. Dehydrate for 2 hours at 145°F and then 115°F for 4 hours. Stuffing should be served soft, moist, and slightly warm.

# SPICY BROCCOLI

2 large heads of broccoli, cut into florets
½ C almond butter
½ C sesame oil
¼ C soaked raisins (Phase II only)
8 kefir lime leaves, finely chopped
1 T ginger, peeled and chopped
Serrano or cayenne pepper to taste
Sesame seeds
Purple cabbage for garnish

Blend ingredients and massage into broccoli, making sure all florets are covered. Place into casserole dish and dehydrate for 1–2 hours at 145°F. Garnish with sesame seeds and finely chopped purple cabbage.

# Spinach Cream Curry

3 cups spinach, chopped in
   fine strips
1 cauliflower, cut into small
   florets

### Sauce:

¼ C olive oil

1 t Celtic salt

2 cardamoms, crushed

1½ t ginger, grated

1 large tomato, chopped

1¼ t coriander

1¼ t cumin

¼ t turmeric

½ t cayenne

½ t garam masala

1½ C coconut water

3–4 t chopped coriander leaves

⅛ t paprika

   Pinch of cumin seeds

Blend sauce and combine with
vegetables.

# SPINACH TOSTADAS

### TOSTADA SHELLS:

2 C almonds, soaked
1 C pumpkin seeds, soaked
½ C sun-dried tomatoes, soaked
½ C water
1 t cayenne
1 t Celtic salt
Poppy seeds

In a food processor, homogenize nuts and seeds, then blend with sun-dried tomatoes, water, and spices. Cover a counter top with plastic wrap and place dough on it. Cover dough with another layer of plastic wrap and use a rolling pin to roll dough into a ¼" sheet. Sprinkle with poppy seeds and use a circular cookie cutter 4" in diameter (or the lid of a large jar) to cut out "tostada shells." Place shells in the dehydrator at 145°F for 1–2 hours.

### TOPPING:

4 avocados
4 C spinach
¼ C fresh cilantro
2 t lime juice
1 t jalapeño, chopped
1 t cumin
1 t Celtic salt

Blend all of the above until smooth. When shells have finished dehydrating, place them on the counter (poppy seed side down), and spread a ½" layer of the mixture over each one.

GARNISH:

2 tomatoes, seeded

I head lettuce (any kind)

I bell pepper (red, yellow, or
orange)

¼ C fresh cilantro

Dice the above veggies and sprinkle over the tostadas. Serve as is or with a fresh salsa.

# STIR RAW VEGETABLES

I head of broccoli, finely
chopped

2 zucchini, cut into thin
rounds

2 yellow squash, cut into thin
rounds

SAUCE:

I C cilantro, finely chopped

½ C olive oil

I½ T turmeric

I½ T ginger juice

½ T Celtic salt

2 t cinnamon

2 t allspice

¼ t cayenne

Combine sauce in a large mixing bowl and add vegetables. Massage the sauce into the vegetables for 2–3 minutes. Serves 4–6.

*Optional:*

Place on a dehydrator tray with a Teflex sheet and dehydrate for I–2 hours at 145°F. Serve warm.

# STIR RAW VEGETABLES WITH PANG-PANG SAUCE

4 carrots, cut into thin rounds

3 zucchini, cut into thin rounds

3 stalks celery, finely chopped

1 head broccoli, finely chopped

### PANG-PANG SAUCE:

2 C fresh basil, chopped

1½ C coconut water

½ C almond butter

2 T fresh ginger, minced

2 T Celtic salt

1 T garlic, minced

1 T plum vinegar

1 T sesame oil

1 t raw apple cider vinegar

½ t chili powder

Combine sauce in a large mixing bowl and add vegetables. Massage the sauce into the vegetables for 2–3 minutes. Place on a dehydrator tray with a Teflex sheet and dehydrate for 1–2 hours at 145°F. Serve warm. Serves 4–6.

# STRING BEAN DAHL

1 C purple string beans
1 C coconut pulp
¼ C coconut water
1 tomato
2 T olive oil
2 t Celtic salt
1 t cumin
¼ t turmeric
⅛ t cayenne
⅛ t coriander
⅛ t mustard seeds

In the blender, combine two string beans with the remaining ingredients until smooth. Add additional water as needed for consistency. Cut remaining string beans in 2" pieces. In a mixing bowl, combine sauce and beans and mix well. Serve with *Chapati*.

# STUFFED TOMATOES

### TOMATOES:

8 tomatoes

Cut in half. Remove the innards.

### STUFFING:

1½ C sunflower seeds, soaked
½ C sun-dried tomatoes, soaked
1½ T white miso
2 T lemon juice
2 T Celtic salt
2 T fresh basil, minced
¼ t hing
1½ t black pepper

Process all ingredients for stuffing in a food processor with the "S" blade. Stuff tomato halves and dehydrate at 145°F for 1 hour. Garnish with fresh parsley.

# Stuffed Vegetables

Red peppers, tomatoes, and/or
zucchinis

Scoop out veggies.

## Stuffing:

2 T olive oil
1½ T pine nuts, unsoaked
¼ C soaked walnuts, crumbled
1 T raisins or currants, soaked
1 t cinnamon
½ t allspice
Celtic salt & pepper to taste
Small bunch parsley, finely chopped

Food-process the ingredients with
the "S" blade to desired mealy
consistency. Stuff veggies with stuffing. Add a dollop of seed cheeze.
Garnish with parsley.

# Sun Burgers

1 C walnuts, soaked

1 C almonds, soaked

1 C pine nuts, unsoaked

½ C olive oil

½ C water

  2 celery stalks, finely chopped

2 T thyme, chopped

3 T sage, chopped

2 T marjoram, chopped

1 t fresh ginger, chopped

1 t cayenne

2 t Celtic salt

Homogenize nuts or blend with olive oil and water until very smooth. Sir in celery, chopped herbs, and remaining ingredients. Cover a counter top with plastic wrap and place dough on it. Cover the dough with another layer of plastic wrap, and with a rolling pin, roll the dough to ½" thickness. With a circular cookie cutter (or lid from a large jar), cut out "burgers" from the dough and place on dehydrator sheets. Dehydrate at 145°F for 1–2 hours. Serve with *Alive Mustard, Living Catsup,* or *Sweet and Hot Barbeque Sauce.*

# Sun Raw Samosas

———————————— 🍎 ————————————

2 C red cabbage or cauliflower

1½ C water

3 T curry

2 T cayenne

1½ C pine nuts, unsoaked

¾ C olive oil

2 cloves garlic, minced

2 T ginger, minced

1 T lemon juice

3 T Celtic salt

3 T curry

1½ C fresh peas

1½ C sweet potatoes, chopped

½ C golden flax seeds, ground

In a blender, process cabbage, water, curry, and cayenne until smooth. Place in a food processor with the "S" blade and blend 2 T Celtic salt, pine nuts, olive oil, garlic, ginger, and lemon juice until smooth. Transfer to a mixing bowl and add fresh peas, sweet potatoes, and remaining Celtic salt and mix well. Place a heaping tablespoon of mixture into hands and form into a ball. Roll in ground flax and place on a dehydrator tray with a Teflex sheet. Form in a triangle and dehydrate at 145°F for 2–3 hours. Remove Teflex sheets and continue dehydrating for 2 hours at 115°F. Serve warm with *Mysore Mint Chutney* (Phase II only).

# TEMPURA VEGETABLES

4 C broccoli tops
1 C cauliflower
½ C pistachios, unsoaked
1 C pine nuts, unsoaked
½ C lemon juice
3 t Celtic salt
½ C olive oil
1 t Chinese 5-spice
1 C water

In high-powered food processor combine pistachios, pine nuts, salt, lemon, 5-spice, and olive oil. Pour water in slowly as mixture blends until a smooth consistency is achieved. Place vegetables in large mixing bowl. Pour sauce onto broccoli and cauliflower and stir thoroughly to ensure that vegetables are well-coated. Spoon vegetables onto Teflex sheets on dehydrator trays and dehydrate for 2 hours at 145°F. Serve warm.

# THAI PATTIES

2 C almonds, soaked
½ C sunflower seeds, soaked
2 carrots
1 zucchini
½ C dulse
½ C parsley
1 T cumin
1 T turmeric
1 t Celtic salt

Process almonds, sunflower seeds, carrots, and zucchini through a Champion Juicer with the solid plate; combine remaining ingredients and mix well. Form into 1½" x ¼" patties and place on a dehydrator tray and dehydrate at 145° for 2–3 hours or until desired moisture is obtained.

# Thai Tempura Vegetables

4 C broccoli tops
1 C cauliflower
½ C pistachios, unsoaked
1 C pine nuts, unsoaked
½ C lemon juice
3 t Celtic salt
½ C olive oil
1 t coriander
2 t cumin
1 cayenne pepper
1 C water

In high-powered food processor combine pistachios, pine nuts, salt, lemon, spices, and olive oil. Pour water in slowly as mixture blends until a smooth consistency is achieved. Place vegetables in large mixing bowl. Pour sauce onto broccoli and cauliflower and stir thoroughly to ensure that vegetables are well-coated. Spoon vegetables onto Teflex sheets on dehydrator trays and dehydrate for 2 hours at 145°F. Serve warm.

# Vegetable Fu Young

### Vegetables:

1 C carrots, shredded
1 C celery, finely chopped
1 C red bell pepper, finely
　　chopped
½ C parsley, finely chopped
¼ C green onions, finely chopped
　　(optional)
½ T fresh ginger, cut into rounds
½ t cayenne

Process all ingredients in a food processor with the "S" blade for 20 seconds.

### Pine Nut Cream:

1 C pine nuts, unsoaked

¾ C almonds, soaked

2 T water

1 T garlic, minced

1 T fresh ginger, finely chopped

1 T flax oil

2 t lemon juice

1 t Celtic salt

Process all ingredients in a food processor with the "S" blade until smooth.

---

1 C Asian bean sprouts, finely chopped

Mix well by hand *Pine Nut Cream,* vegetables, and Asian bean sprouts. Form into nine patties. Dehydrate at 145°F for 2–3 hours and then 115°F for 2–3 hours.

# Vegetable Medley

### Vegetables:

5 stalks of asparagus, cut into 1" pieces

2 tomatoes, diced

1 red bell pepper, cut into fine slivers

⅓ C broccoli, finely chopped

⅓ C fresh basil, finely chopped

⅓ C fresh parsley, finely chopped

⅓ C fresh fennel, finely chopped

Combine in a mixing bowl.

### SAUCE:

1 tomato

¼ C olive oil

¼ C water

2 T lemon juice

2 t fresh ginger, minced

2 t fresh ground black pepper

1 t Celtic salt

1 t oregano

¼ t hing

Blend until smooth; adjust seasoning to your taste. Pour sauce over the vegetables and mix well. Place *Vegetable Medley* in a casserole dish and dehydrate at 145°F for 1–2 hours. Serve over zucchini pasta or as is.

# VEGETABLE TEMPURA

### VEGETABLES:

1 C broccoli florets

1 C zucchini, sliced in ¼" rounds

½ C carrots, sliced in rounds

1 T lemon juice

1 T olive oil

1 T Celtic salt

Combine ingredients in a mixing bowl and marinate for 1 hour.

### PASTE:

½ C golden flax seeds, ground

2 T ginger juice

2 T orange juice (substitute water for Phase I)

2 T water

1 t Celtic salt

½ t fresh ground black pepper

Hand-mix ingredients in a small bowl until they resemble a thin pasty consistency. Toss the paste with the marinated vegetables, making sure it is evenly distributed. Spread on a dehydrator tray and dehydrate at 145°F for 2–3 hours. Serve warm. Serves 2–4.

# ZUCCHINI RATATOUILLE

6 C zucchini, cut into rounds
½ C olive oil
2 T raw apple cider vinegar
1½ C sun-dried tomatoes
1½ C sun-dried tomato soak water
2 T fresh basil, minced
1 T fresh thyme, minced
1 T fresh rosemary, minced
3 t Celtic salt
   Dash of fresh ground pepper

Cut zucchini into rounds using a knife or a mandoline. Toss zucchini in a mixing bowl with olive oil, salt, and a dash of black pepper. Place zucchini on Teflex dehydrator sheets and dehydrate for 1 hour at 145°F. Process the remaining ingredients in a blender until smooth. Toss zucchini with sauce before serving.

# Pâtés and
# Seasoned Nuts

## A NOTE ON MAKING PÂTÉS THAT FIT YOUR BUDGET

Many of the pâté recipes featured are made with pine nuts and macadamia nuts, which are quite expensive. To make these pâtés more affordable, substitute almonds.

# ALMOND PÂTÉ

2 C almonds, soaked
3 carrots
⅓ C celery, finely chopped
¼ C basil, minced
2 T fresh chives, finely chopped (optional)
1½ T ginger, minced
1 t Celtic salt

Process almonds and carrots through a Champion Juicer with the solid plate; combine remaining ingredients and mix well. Serves 4–6.

# ALMOND BROCCOLI PÂTÉ

2 C almonds, soaked
1 C broccoli stalks, finely chopped
1 T red miso
1 t Celtic salt
2 T lemon juice
2 T olive oil
1 T Italian seasoning

Process almonds through a Champion Juicer with the solid plate; combine remaining ingredients and mix well. Serves 4–6.

# ALMOND CARROT PÂTÉ

2 C almonds, soaked
2 C carrots
2 T fresh cilantro, finely chopped
2 T fresh parsley, finely chopped
1 T olive oil
1 T fresh chives, finely chopped
    (optional)
1 t cayenne
1 t Celtic salt

Process almonds and carrots through a Champion Juicer with the solid plate; combine remaining ingredients and mix well. Serves 4–6.

# BLACK OLIVE PÂTÉ

2 C pine nuts, soaked
¾ C black olives
¾ C water
1 avocado
1 C fresh parsley, finely chopped
1 C tomatoes, diced

Process nuts, olives, avocado, and water in a blender until creamy; combine mixture with parsley and tomatoes and mix well.

# Carrot Dill Pâté

3 C macadamia nuts, soaked

4 carrots

5 T fresh dill, finely minced

1 cucumber, finely diced

1 T lemon juice

1 T paprika

1 t Celtic salt

Process macadamia nuts and carrots through a Champion Juicer with the solid plate; combine remaining ingredients and mix well.

# Curried Almonds

4 C almonds, soaked

1 T curry spice

½ C water

2 t Celtic salt

1 t cayenne pepper

Combine all ingredients in a medium-size mixing bowl. Stir well and then place onto dehydrator trays. Dehydrate at 115°F overnight.

# Curried Pâté

1 C almonds, soaked
¾ C carrot pulp
⅓ C fresh chives, minced
    (optional)
½ C zucchini
½ C celery
1 t ginger, minced
3 t turmeric
Dash of cayenne

Process almonds through a Champion Juicer with the solid plate; add remaining ingredients and mix well.

# Curry Dill Pâté

2 C pecans, soaked
2 C cauliflower florets,
    homogenized
1 T curry
1 T dill weed
1 T flax seed oil
1 T lemon juice
1 t Celtic salt

Process almonds and cauliflower through a Champion Juicer with the solid plate; combine remaining ingredients and mix well. Serves 4–6.

# Dulse Sunflower Seeds

3 C sunflower seeds, soaked
1 C dulse flakes
1 T Celtic salt or more to taste

Drain soaked seeds and combine dulse and salt. Dehydrate at 145°F for 2 hours and then 115°F for 8 hours.

# Ginger Almonds

4 C almonds, soaked
3 T ground ginger
2½ T curry powder
1 T Celtic salt
½ t cayenne

Combine all ingredients in a bowl and mix well. Dehydrate at 145°F for 2 hours and then 115°F for 8 hours.

# Hazelnut Pâté

2 C hazelnuts, soaked
1 C parsley, finely chopped
  4 stalks celery, finely chopped
2 T olive oil
2 T lemon juice
  2 t Celtic salt
    Dash of cayenne
    Dash of nutmeg

Process hazelnuts in a food processor with the "S" blade until chunky; transfer to a mixing bowl. Combine with the remaining ingredients and mix well. Serve with crackers or on a bed of lettuce. Serves 4–6.

# Hummus

2 C almonds, soaked
1 C sesame seeds, unsoaked
5 T lemon juice
  1 clove garlic (optional
    or substitute ½ t hing)
1 C water
2 T olive oil
1 T cumin
1½ t Celtic salt
  1 t fresh ground black pepper

In a food processor with the "S" blade, process the almonds until finely chopped. Slowly add ½ C water and mix for 2–3 minutes until creamy. In a blender grind sesame seed dry to powder and then mix with ½ C water and remaining ingredients until the mixture is smooth. (Add more water if necessary.) Add creamed almond mixture and process for 1–2 minutes until the mixture is blended. Sprinkle some fresh finely chopped parsley on top and serve.

# Hummus #2

1 C almonds, soaked
1 C macadamia nuts, unsoaked
1 C white sesame seeds, soaked
5 T lemon juice
   1 clove garlic (optional
   or hing)
1 C water
2 T olive oil
1 T cumin
1½ t Celtic salt
   1 t fresh ground black pepper

In a food processor with the "S" blade, process the almonds and macadamias until finely chopped. Slowly add ½ C water and mix for 2–3 minutes until creamy.

In a blender, mix sesame seeds, ½ C water, and remaining ingredients until the mixture is smooth (add more water if necessary). Add creamed almond mixture and process for 1–2 minutes until blended. Sprinkle some fresh finely chopped parsley on top and serve.

# Imposter "Caramel Corn"

2 C slivered almonds
½ C pumpkin seeds, soaked
½ C raisin soak water (not raisins)
   1 T Celtic salt

Spread a mixture of slivered almonds and pumpkin seeds on Teflex sheets. Mix raisin soak water and salt. Pour over nuts and seeds. Dehydrate at 145°F for 2 hours and then 115°F for 8 hours until completely dry and crispy.

# Intense Italian Pâté

1 C hazelnuts, soaked

½ C sun-dried tomatoes, soaked

⅓ C sun-dried tomato soak water

1 C red bell pepper

2 T olive oil

2 T lemon juice

2 T fresh parsley, finely chopped

½ t Celtic salt

Process all ingredients in a food processor with the "S" blade, add sun-dried tomato soak water for consistency, and mix well. Serves 2–4.

# Mexicali Medley

2 C almonds, soaked

2 C pumpkin seeds, soaked

1 C pine nuts

1 C macadamia nuts

½ C lime juice

1 T Celtic salt

1 T chili spice

2 t cayenne pepper

1 t cumin

Combine all ingredients in a medium-size mixing bowl. Stir well and then place onto Teflex sheets on dehydrator trays. Dehydrate at 145°F for 2 hours and then 115°F for 8 hours.

# Pâté Primavera

1 C pine nuts, unsoaked
1 C walnuts, soaked
½ C olive oil
¼ C lemon juice
¾ C water
1 t peppercorns
½ t fresh rosemary, finely
    chopped

1 C tomatoes, finely chopped
½ C fresh parsley, finely chopped
½ C fresh basil, finely chopped
¼ C fresh oregano, finely
    chopped

Process pine nuts, walnuts, olive oil, lemon juice, water, peppercorns, and rosemary in a food processor with the "S" blade until creamy. Stir in remaining ingredients and mix well.

# Pumpkin Seed Harvest

4 C pumpkin seeds, soaked
2 C white sesame seeds, soaked
⅓ C water
2 t turmeric powder
1½ t Celtic salt

Combine all ingredients in a medium-size mixing bowl. Stir well and then place onto Teflex sheets on dehydrator trays. Dehydrate at 145°F for 2 hours and then 115°F for 8 hours.

# PUMPKIN SEED PÂTÉ

2 C pumpkin seeds, soaked
½ C sun-dried tomatoes, soaked
2 T olive oil
1 T fresh parsley, finely minced
1 T lemon juice
1 t fresh oregano, finely minced
1 t fresh thyme, finely minced
1 t Celtic salt

Homogenize pumpkin seeds and sun-dried tomatoes in a food processor. Add fresh herbs and pâté along with other ingredients. Mix well and serve. It will last for a few days in the refrigerator.

# RED MOUNTAIN TRAIL MIX

2½ C almonds, soaked
2 C pumpkin seeds, soaked
1 C walnuts, soaked
1 C apples, cored
½ C goji berries
1 T Tree of Life Mesquite Meal
2 t cinnamon
½ t allspice
1 t Celtic salt

Place almonds, pumpkin seeds, and walnuts in a food processor and pulse for 45 seconds. Add remaining ingredients and pulse for 15 seconds more. Place mixture onto Teflex sheets on dehydrator trays and dehydrate at 145°F for 2 hours and then 115°F for 8 hours.

# RED TANG PÂTÉ

1 C sunflower seeds, soaked
¾ C red cabbage, finely chopped
⅓ C olive oil
½ C celery, finely chopped
½ C fresh parsley, finely chopped
½ C lemon juice
½ C water
¼ C raw red miso
2 t Celtic salt

Process all ingredients in a food processor with the "S" blade until creamy.

# SAVE THE TUNA SALAD PÂTÉ

1 C almonds, soaked
1 C sunflower seeds, soaked
⅓ C celery, finely chopped
⅓ C pickles, finely chopped (see "Fermented Foods")
2 T lemon juice
1½ T fresh dill, minced
1 T fresh oregano, minced
1 t fresh ground black pepper
1 t sage
1 t kelp granules
½ t Celtic salt

*Optional:*
⅓ C red onions, finely chopped

Process almonds and sunflower seeds through a Champion Juicer with the solid plate; combine the remaining ingredients and mix well. Serve in a nori roll or stuff in a tomato.

# SUNNY BASIL PÂTÉ

1½ C sunflower seeds, soaked
1 C sun-dried tomatoes, soaked
3 stalks of celery
2 carrots
½ C fresh basil, chopped
2 t dried basil
¼ t hing
Celtic salt to taste
Fresh ground black pepper to taste

Process all ingredients in a food processor with the "S" blade until smooth and creamy; add a little water for consistency. Serves 4–6.

# TASTES LIKE REFRIED BEANS PÂTÉ

2 C sunflower seeds, soaked
1 C sun-dried tomatoes, soaked
2 T or to taste Mexican seasoning
1 T red raw miso
1 t cayenne
1 t Celtic salt

Process all ingredients in a food processor with the "S" blade until smooth and creamy; add a little water for consistency. Serves 4–6.

# Taste of India Pâté

I C almonds, soaked

I C sunflower seeds, soaked

½ C fresh parsley, finely chopped

2 stalks of celery, finely chopped

I red bell pepper, finely chopped

2 T lemon juice

I t cumin

I t curry

2 t Celtic salt

*Optional:*

I clove of garlic, minced

Process almonds and sunflower seeds through a Champion Juicer with the solid plate or a food processor with the "S" blade; combine remaining ingredients and mix well. Serves 4–6.

# Thai Seasoned Almonds

3 C almonds, soaked

1–2 T sesame oil

2½ t cumin

1½ t cayenne

1½ t chili powder

I t Celtic salt

Process almonds in a food processor with the "S" blade until they are chunky; in a large mixing bowl, stir the remaining ingredients together and mix well. Place on a dehydrator tray and dehydrate at 145°F for 2 hours and then 115°F for 8 hours.

# Tomato Spice Pâté

2 C sunflower seeds, soaked
½ C sun-dried tomatoes, soaked
1 T fresh ginger, minced
2 t hing
2 t Celtic salt
1 habanero pepper

Process all ingredients in a blender including soak water until smooth and creamy.

# Turmeric Trail Mix

1 C almonds, soaked
1 C sunflower seeds, soaked
1 C pumpkin seeds, soaked
1 T turmeric
1 T curry
1 t Celtic salt

Mix well and dehydrate at 145°F for 2 hours and then 115°F for 8 hours.

# VERY VIVID PÂTÉ

1½ C macadamia nuts, soaked
4 C spinach leaves
¾ C water
¼ C lemon juice
2 T hing
1 T Celtic salt
1 t spirulina powder
1 t cayenne

Process all ingredients in a blender (include only 1½ C spinach) until creamy. Finely chop the remaining spinach into small strips and stir into mixture.

# WALNUT PÂTÉ

2 C walnuts, soaked
1 C leeks, finely chopped
2 T olive oil
1 T Italian seasoning
1 t Celtic salt

Process all ingredients in a food processor with the "S" blade until smooth and creamy; add a little water for consistency.

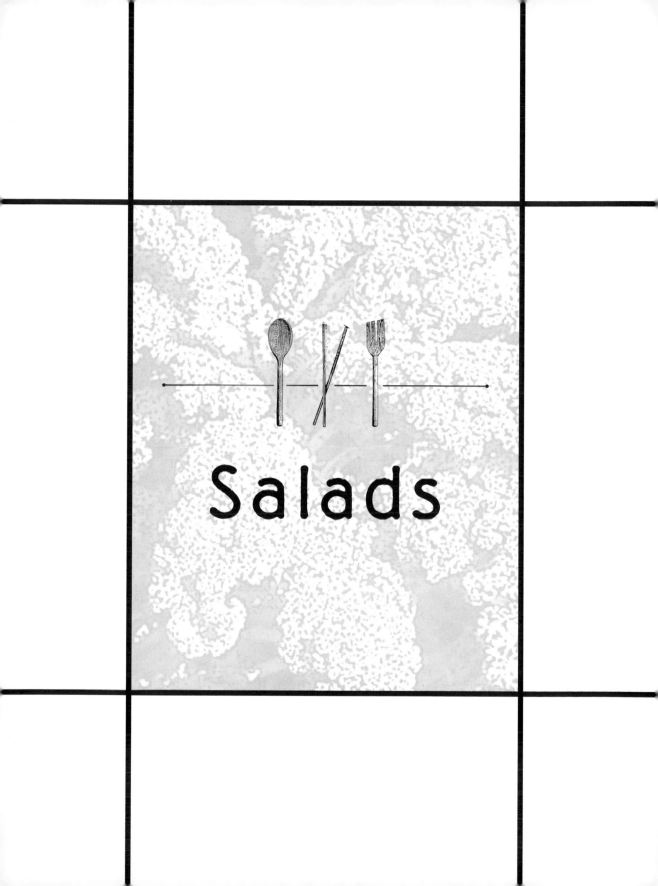

# Salads

## FLOWERS FOR SALADS

Fresh organic flowers are a
wonderful addition to any salad.

Chamomile

Fuchsia

Geranium

Marigolds

Nasturtium

Pansy

Rose Petals

Rosehips

Squash Blooms

Strawberry Leaves

Violet

## GREENS FOR SALADS

Fresh organic greens by themselves
make delicious salads with your
favorite dressing or added to your
favorite salad.

Arugula

Buckwheat Lettuce

Sunflower Greens

Beet Tops

Celery Tops

Butter Lettuce

Dandelion Greens

Sorrel

Purslane

Mint

Mixed Baby Greens

Watercress

Parsley

Cabbage

Chard

Romaine

Lambs Quarter

Kale Leaves

Collard Leaves

# Arugula Cumin Salad

2 C baby arugula
1 C baby spinach
½ C tomato, diced
2 T fresh chives, minced
   (optional)
2 T lemon juice
2 T sunflower oil
1 t cumin
1 t Celtic salt

Combine all ingredients in a large mixing bowl and mix well.

# Arugula Spinach Salad

3 C baby spinach
2 C baby arugula
1½ C avocado, diced
½ C cherry tomatoes, halved
¼ C red onion, thinly sliced
   (optional)
2 T lime juice
½ T fresh jalapeño, seeded and
   minced
1½ t Celtic salt

Combine all ingredients in a mixing bowl and mix well.

## Avocado Salad with Rosemary

2 C avocado, diced
1 C tomatoes, seeded and diced
1 C clover sprouts
1 T rosemary
1½ T lemon juice
1½ T garlic, minced
1 t Celtic salt

Combine all ingredients in a mixing bowl, leaving a slightly chunky consistency.

## Avocado Tomato Salad

1 avocado, mashed
1 tomato, finely diced
½ C dulse, rinsed and chopped

Combine all ingredients in a bowl and mix well. Serve on a bed of lettuce or favorite sprouts. Also, you can roll it up in a nori sheet.

# AVOCADO KALE SALAD

1 bunch dinosaur kale (also
    known as lacinado kale)
1 large tomato
1 avocado
1 stalk celery
¼ C olives
2 T olive oil
2 t lemon juice
1 t salt

*Variations:*
    10 olives any variety
½ C dulse
1 C shredded veggies
½ C pine nuts

Remove main part of kale stem and finely chop leaves into bowl. Add salt and massage well until kale wilts. Add lemon and massage again. Add tomato, olives. Blend avocado, olive oil, and celery to cream and pour over salad. Mix well to completely coat the kale leaves. The order in which you add the ingredients is crucial; if you add the oil too early, the kale will not wilt as well.

Kale is one of the most nutrient-dense items you can buy in your whole-foods store. However, for most people it is too fibrous. At the Tree of Life Café our kale salad appeals to everyone and is a big favorite.

# Bell Pepper Medley

1 C purple bell pepper, julienne
1 C red bell pepper, julienne
1 C yellow bell pepper, julienne
3 T olive oil
2½ T lemon juice
2 T fresh dill, minced
1 T fresh oregano, minced
½ T garlic, minced
1 t Celtic salt
½ t fresh ground black pepper

In a mixing bowl, combine all ingredients and mix well. Marinate in a dehydrator at 145° for 1 hour before serving.

# Cabbage Hemp Salad

2 C red and green cabbage, shredded
3 T fresh cilantro, finely chopped
2 T hemp nuts
2 T hemp oil
2 T olive oil
2 T lemon juice
1 t ginger juice
1 t Celtic salt

Combine cabbage and salt in a mixing bowl and massage the salt into the cabbage. Let sit for 10 minutes. Add remaining ingredients and mix well.

# CARROT DULSE SALAD

2 C carrot, shredded
1 C dulse, chopped and rinsed
½ C snow peas, small julienne
¼ C black sesame seeds
3 T orange juice
2 T green onions, finely chopped
1 T garlic, minced
1 T Celtic salt

Combine all ingredients in a large mixing bowl and mix well. Let marinate for 1 hour before serving. Serves 2–4.

# CAESAR SALAD

3 avocados
⅓ C lemon juice
1 T black pepper
1 T salt
1 t cayenne
3 T olive oil
¼ C water
2 heads romaine lettuce

Blend all ingredients, except lettuce, together in high-power blender. Pour over chopped lettuce and serve immediately.

# Composed Salad

2 handfuls of your favorite
　　sprouts (sunflower is a good
　　choice)
3 large handfuls of fresh baby
　　spinach
2 avocados, cubed
　　Juice of one lemon
　　Pinch of Celtic salt
　　Freshly ground pepper to taste
4 T hemp nuts

Place greens in bowl. Drizzle olive oil and lemon on top. Sprinkle in pepper and salt. Add avocados and sprinkle in hemp nuts. Mix gently with hands. Add tomatoes if you like. Serves 2.

# Cous Cous

1 head of cauliflower
½ C lemon juice
½ C olive oil (optional)
　　Pepper to taste
　　Celtic salt to taste
1 bunch cilantro, finely
　　chopped
1 bunch mint, finely chopped
1 bunch parsley, finely
　　chopped
1 pint cherry tomatoes, seeded
　　and quartered
⅓ C black Moroccan olives,
　　seeded and chopped

Cut cauliflower and place in food processor with "S" blade attachment and blend until a cous cous-like texture is achieved. Place in bowl and add lemon juice, olive oil, salt, and pepper. Mix in herbs, tomatoes, and olives. Stir well and serve chilled. This dish is great served with flax crackers and *Hummus*.

# CRESCENT CUCUMBER SALAD

3 cucumbers, cut into thin
　　rounds
½ C fresh parsley, finely chopped
3 T olive oil
2 T lemon juice
1 t cinnamon
1 t cumin
1 t salt

Toss cucumbers in a mixing bowl with salt and let set for 15 minutes. Drain excess water; add remaining ingredients and mix well. Serves 2–4.

# CUCUMBER AVOCADO SALAD

2 C cucumber, seeded and
　　chopped
1 C avocado, diced
1 C cherry tomatoes
3 T fresh basil, finely chopped
2 T flax oil
1½ T lime juice
1 t Celtic salt

In a mixing bowl, combine all ingredients and mix well. Serves 2–4.

# Cucumber Mint Salad

### Cucumbers:

3 C cucumbers, thinly sliced
2 T lime juice
1½ T fresh mint, minced
1 T fresh ginger, minced
1½ t Celtic salt

Marinate cucumbers in ingredients for 1 hour.

### Spicy Thai Citrus Dressing:

½ C orange juice
½ C lime juice
¼ C raisins
3 T flax oil
1 t Celtic salt
¼ t pepper
1 T jalapeño, finely chopped
1 t garlic

Process all ingredients in a blender and combine with cucumbers and mix well.

# Cucumber Salad

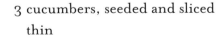

3 cucumbers, seeded and sliced thin
2 T fresh basil, minced
2 T fresh chives, minced (optional)
2 T sunflower oil
½ t Celtic salt

After slicing the cucumbers, massage with salt and allow to "release water" in a strainer for 1 hour. Combine all ingredients in a mixing bowl and serve.

# DANDELION SALAD

1 C dandelion greens, finely
   chopped
1 C romaine lettuce
½ C parsley
½ C pine nuts, unsoaked

Combine all ingredients in a large mixing bowl. Your liver will thank you for this detoxifying salad. Dandelion greens are a little bitter, so we recommend serving this salad with the *Miso Orange Dressing* (Phase II only). The orange helps lighten the taste of the dandelion.

# DANDELION CREAM SALAD

20 dandelion leaves, finely
   chopped (main stem
   removed)
½ C macadamia nuts
¼ C diced red bell pepper
¼ C coconut water
3 T lemon juice
1 t Celtic salt

Massage chopped dandelion leaves well with salt to break down the fiber. Let sit for at least 5 minutes. Blend macadamia nuts with coconut water and lemon to cream. Mix well to coat dandelion with cream and add red bell pepper.

Dandelion is a super-nutritious leafy green, high in minerals and a great liver cleanser. However, it can be a little bitter for most people. This salad is a wonderful way to get the great nutrition of dandelion with a reduction of the bitterness.

# Fiesta Sprout Salad

3 C alfalfa/clover sprouts
1 C tomatoes, diced
½ C olives, pitted and diced
1 large avocado
2 T lemon juice
1½ T fresh oregano, minced

Combine all ingredients in a mixing bowl and mix well. Water may be released from the sprouts, so the salad may need to be strained before serving. Serves 4.

# Fresh Pea Salad

¾ C fresh peas
½ C carrots, diced
¼ C red bell peppers, diced
¼ C fresh cilantro, finely chopped
2½ T lemon juice
2 T flax oil
½ t Celtic salt

Combine all ingredients in a mixing bowl and mix well. Serves 3–4.

# Hemp Kale Salad

1 bunch dinosaur kale (also
　　known as lacinado kale)
1 large tomato, diced
¼ C hemp nuts
3 T olive oil*
2 t lemon juice
1 t Celtic salt

Remove main part of kale stem and
finely chop leaves into bowl. Add
salt and massage well until kale wilts.
Add lemon and massage again. Add
tomato and hemp nuts and mix well.
Finally pour over oil. The order
in which you add the ingredients is
crucial. If you add the oil too early,
the kale will not wilt as well.

   * If you enjoy a rich salad, hemp seed
     oil can be substituted for the olive
     oil; however, beware that hemp oil is
     very strong.

# Israeli Salad

4 radishes, diced
4 tomatoes, diced
3 cucumbers, peeled and cubed
1 C parsley, finely chopped
1 C olive oil
½ C lemon juice
4 T leek, finely chopped
　　(optional)
1 t Celtic salt

Combine all ingredients in a large
mixing bowl and let set for 1 hour
before serving.

# Jicama Picnic Salad

## Salad:

2 C jicama, diced

3 stalks of celery, finely chopped

2 red bell peppers, finely chopped

1 leek, finely chopped (optional)

½ C fresh cilantro, finely chopped

3 T dill

Combine in a mixing bowl.

## Dressing:

½ C raw tahini

2 T lemon juice

1 T white raw miso (substitute with Celtic salt for Phase I)

½ t cumin

⅛ t chili powder

Water for consistency

In a blender, process all ingredients until smooth and creamy. Pour over salad and mix well.

# MARINATED BROCCOLI

4 C broccoli, only florets
(no stems)
⅓ C fresh oregano, minced,
or 2 T dried oregano
⅓ C fresh basil, minced,
or 2 T dried basil
½ C olive oil
¼ C lemon juice

*Optional:*
1 clove garlic, minced

*Variation:*
Substitute fresh lemon grass for the oregano, and lime juice for the lemon juice for a Thai Style Marinated Broccoli.

Combine all ingredients in a large mixing bowl and mix well. Let them marinate overnight in the refrigerator. Warm in a dehydrator before serving for 1 hour at 145°F.

Add ¼ C red bell pepper and serve.

# MARINATED ZUCCHINI

4–5 medium zucchini, peeled
and diced
4 stalks celery, finely sliced
1 leek, finely sliced

MARINADE:
½ C olive oil
½ C lemon juice
1 T thyme
1 T herbs de Provence

Peel the zucchini in order to create as much porous surface area as possible. Marinate the diced zucchini, celery, and leek in the sauce for several hours.

# Mediterranean Sea Vegetable Salad

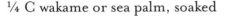

¼ C wakame or sea palm, soaked
¼ C dulse, soaked
½ C sun-dried black olives,
    pitted and chopped
2 T olive oil
2 T lemon juice
6 radishes, finely chopped
2 stalks of celery, finely
    chopped
2 scallions, finely chopped
    (optional)
1 tomato, finely chopped
Dash of cayenne
Sprinkle of sesame seeds

Combine all ingredients in a mixing bowl. Serve on crackers or cucumber rounds.

# Moroccan Olive Salad

1 C fresh peas
½ C carrots, diced
½ C sun-dried black olives, pitted
    and chopped
3 T orange juice
2 T fresh chives, finely chopped
    (optional)

Combine all ingredients in a mixing bowl and mix well.

# Napa Slaw

1 head Napa cabbage, shredded
½ C fresh cilantro, finely chopped
3 T sesame seeds
3 T flax oil
2½ T lime juice
1 T ginger, minced
½ t Celtic salt
¼–½ t cayenne

Toss all ingredients in a large mixing bowl and serve.

# Popeye Salad

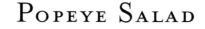

SALAD:
3 C spinach, finely chopped
2 C buckwheat green sprouts, sunflower green sprouts, and mung sprouts
1 red bell pepper, finely chopped

DRESSING:
½ C raw tahini
¼ C lemon juice
¼ C fresh parsley, finely chopped
1 t cayenne
1 t cumin

Process all ingredients in a blender until smooth. Toss salad and mix well. Serves 2.

*Optional:*
½ C orange slices, cut into bite-size pieces.

# RAINBOW SALAD

*Red* ~

    I tomato, diced

*Orange* ~

    I large carrot, cut in rounds
    (to be more exotic, orange
    bell pepper)

*Yellow* ~

    I yellow bell pepper, diced (or
    yellow tomato)

*Green* ~

    6 large kale leaves, finely
    chopped, *and* I avocado,
    diced

*Blue* ~

    blue pansy flowers or other
    blue edible flower

*Purple* ~

    I purple beet, shredded
    and/or I cup dulse, soaked

*White* ~

    I C jicama, diced

Toss all ingredients with *Creamy Miso Dressing* (Phase II only) or *Flax Oil and Ginger Dressing*. Garnish with sesame seeds. Celebrate the Divine within creation as you consume all the color vibrations of the rainbow. Share the experience with a friend, as this salad is a meal for two.

# ROSEMARY BROCCOLI

3 C broccoli, chopped in florets
½ C fresh olives, pitted and diced
2 cloves garlic, minced
3 T olive oil
2½ T lemon juice
2 T fresh rosemary, minced
1½ T Italian seasoning
1 t Celtic salt
Fresh ground black pepper
to taste

Combine all ingredients in a mixing bowl and massage the broccoli. Place in a dehydrator at 145° for ½–1 hour to speed up the marinating process. Serve warm.

# SEA PALM SIMPLICITY SALAD

2 C sea palm, soaked
½ C sesame seeds, soaked
¼ C sesame oil
¼ C lime juice
Pinch of cayenne to taste

If you love sea palm, this is a delicious way to enjoy it.

# Sea Vegetable Salad

1 C dulse, soaked, rinsed and
   chopped
1 C kelp, soaked, rinsed and
   chopped
3 T flax oil
1 T lemon juice
1 t ginger juice

Combine all ingredients in a mixing bowl and mix well. Serves 1–2.

# Sesame Coconut Salad

2 C coconut pulp, julienne
1½ T fresh chives, minced
   (optional)
1½ T sesame seeds
1 T fresh lemon grass, minced
1 T sesame oil
½ t Celtic salt
   Dash of cayenne

Combine all ingredients in a mixing bowl and mix well. Dehydrate for ½–1 hour at 145° to warm. Serves 2–4.

# Sesame Butternut Coleslaw

1 head cabbage, finely chopped
1 C butternut squash, grated
1 C sesame seeds, soaked
½ C parsley
2 C water
1 t cayenne
1 t lemon juice
2 t Celtic salt

Mix by hand the cabbage and squash. In a high-power blender, mix remaining ingredients until smooth and creamy. Stir in with veggies, chill, and serve.

# Sesame Coleslaw

3 C cabbage, shredded
1 C red bell peppers, diced
½ C sesame oil
½ C lime juice
½ C cilantro, minced
½ C white sesame seeds
½ C black sesame seeds
3 T Celtic salt
1 t fresh ginger juice

In large mixing bowl, combine cabbage, oil, salt, cilantro, ginger, peppers, and lime. Mix well and toss with sesame seeds.

# SPICY SPIRULINA CABBAGE

4–5 heads of cabbage
1 bunch dandelion greens
1 C lemon juice
½ C flax or olive oil
1 T spirulina
1 t cayenne pepper
2 t Celtic salt

Chiffonade cabbage and dandelion. Mix lemon juice, spirulina, cayenne, salt, and oil together and pour onto cabbage and dandelion. Massage liquid into greens and allow them to marinate for 2 hours prior to serving.

# SPINACH MASALA SALAD

4 C baby spinach
½ C red bell pepper, finely diced
3 T sunflower oil
1½ T fresh lemon grass, diced
1½ T lemon juice
1 T garam masala
½ T garlic, minced
1 t Celtic salt

Combine spinach and red bell peppers in a mixing bowl. Blend remaining ingredients and toss with spinach. Serves 2–4.

# Spinach Sprout Salad

2 C spinach
2 C sprouts of choice
¼ C olives, pitted
1 medium avocado
1 stalk celery
2 T olive oil
1 T lemon juice
1 t Celtic salt

Massage spinach with Celtic salt until moist. Blend the avocado, celery, lemon juice, and olive oil until creamy. Pour over salad and mix in pitted olives.

# Spontaneous Salad

1 head romaine lettuce
1½ C sun-dried tomatoes
1 C olives, pitted
½ C hemp nuts
½ C almonds, soaked

Chop lettuce, sun-dried tomato, and olives. Mix in other ingredients and serve with olive oil, salt, and lemon.

# STAR ANISE CITRUS SALAD

6 cucumbers
1 C fresh grapefruit juice
⅓ C olive oil
1 T fresh star anise, ground
½ T freshly ground pepper
Celtic salt to taste
⅓ C pistachios

Cut cucumber lengthwise and scoop out seeds. Using a food processor, grate the cucumber into matchstick-size pieces. Whisk together by hand the fruit juice, olive oil, and spices. Pour over cucumbers and mix in nuts by hand. Serve immediately.

# TABOULI #1

4 C parsley, finely chopped
2 C tomatoes, finely diced and
    seeded
1½ large broccoli stems
4 medium lemons
½ C olive oil
2 cucumbers, finely chopped
    and seeded
2 t dried mint
1 t oregano
1½ t Celtic salt
1 t fresh ground black pepper

Chop the broccoli stems into very small pieces using a food processor with the "S" blade. Place in a large bowl and add cucumbers and parsley on top. In a blender, process lemon juice, olive oil, mint, salt, and pepper until smooth. Pour half the dressing over the broccoli mixture and cucumbers, mix, and let marinate for ½ hour. Add the remaining dressing and toss the salad before serving.

# TABOULI #2

4 C parsley, finely chopped
¼ C quinoa, sprouted
4 medium lemons
½ C olive oil
2 cucumbers, finely chopped
2 tomatoes, finely diced
2 t dried mint
1½ t Celtic salt
1 t fresh ground black pepper

Drain quinoa, and with your hands squeeze as much of the moisture out as possible. Put quinoa in a large bowl and place the cucumbers and parsley on top. In a blender, process lemon juice, olive oil, mint, salt, and pepper until smooth. Pour half the dressing over the quinoa and cucumbers and let marinate for ½ hour. Add the remaining dressing and toss the salad before serving.

# TABOULI #3

2 C cucumbers, chopped
1 C tomato, seeded and diced
1 C parsley, finely chopped
2½ T olive oil
2 T lemon juice
1 T fresh oregano, minced
1 T garlic, minced
1 t Celtic salt
½ t cayenne
¼ t fresh ground black pepper

Combine all ingredients in a large mixing bowl and mix well.

# THAI CUCUMBER SALAD

3 cucumbers, thinly sliced
½ C leeks, finely chopped
    (optional)
½ C sesame oil
2 T lime juice
2 T fresh basil, finely chopped
½ T fresh ginger, minced
1 t Celtic salt

In a strainer, allow cucumbers and salt to sit for 1 hour while water drains. Combine all ingredients in a mixing bowl and mix well. Serves 2–4.

# THAI HEMP SLAW

1½ C green cabbage, shredded
1½ C red cabbage, shredded
3 T sesame seeds, unsoaked
3 T fresh cilantro, finely chopped
2 T lime juice
2 T hemp nuts
1½ T hemp oil
1 T fresh ginger, minced
1 T sesame oil
1 t Celtic salt

Combine all ingredients in a mixing bowl and mix well. Serves 1–2.

# The Essence of Spinach Salad

4 C spinach

1 medium avocado, diced

½ C pine nuts, unsoaked

¼ C sun-dried tomato, soaked, finely chopped

¼ C black olives, pitted

2 T olive oil

2 t lemon juice

½ t Celtic salt

Massage spinach with sea salt until moist. Add other ingredients, mix well, and serve.

# Under the Sea Salad

1 C kombu, soaked, rinsed, and cut into small strips

2 C dulse, soaked, rinsed, and cut into small pieces

¼ C sesame seeds

2½ T lime juice

2 T flax oil

2 T fresh chives, minced (optional)

1½ T fresh ginger, minced

1 T garlic, minced

1 T sesame oil

½ t cayenne (optional)

Combine all ingredients in a mixing bowl and mix well.

# Zen Cabbage Salad

2 C green cabbage
¼ C sesame seeds
2 T sesame oil
1 t lemon juice
1 t Celtic salt

Combine cabbage and salt in a mixing bowl. Massage the salt into the cabbage. Let sit for 10 minutes. Add remaining ingredients and mix well.

# Salad
# Dressings

## Avocado Dill Dressing

1 avocado
½ C–1 C water for desired
    consistency
2 T olive oil
2–3 T fresh dill
1–2 T lemon juice
½ t Celtic salt
    Dash of cayenne

*Optional:*
    2 T fresh chives, minced

In a blender, process all ingredients
until smooth and creamy.
Makes 1½ cups.

## Avocado Spinach Dressing

1 large avocado
2 C spinach, finely chopped
½ apple
1 t cayenne
1 t Celtic salt
    Water for consistency

In a blender, process all ingredients
until smooth and creamy.
Makes 2 cups.

# Basic Italian Dressing

2 stalks celery, chopped
1 clove garlic
½ C olive oil
2 T lemon juice
½ T Italian seasoning
½ t Celtic salt

In a blender, process all ingredients until smooth and creamy.
Makes 1 cup.

*Optional:*
⅛–¼ t cayenne

# Blood Orange Vinaigrette

1 blood orange, peeled and
chopped
3 T olive oil
1 T ginger, minced
1 t garlic, minced
1 t Serrano chile, minced
½ t raw apple cider vinegar

In a blender, process all ingredients until smooth and creamy.
Makes ¾ cup.

# Caesar Dressing

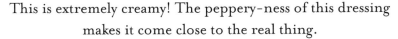

This is extremely creamy! The peppery-ness of this dressing
makes it come close to the real thing.

3 avocados

⅓ C lemon juice

1 T black pepper

1 T salt

1 t cayenne

3 T olive oil

¼ C water

Blend all ingredients together in
high-power blender. Makes 2 cups.

# Coconut Curry Dressing

2 C coconut water

1 C coconut pulp

½ avocado

1 T lemon juice

1 T curry

1 t cumin

1 t coriander

1 t Celtic salt

In a blender, process all ingredients
until smooth and creamy.
Makes 2½ cups.

# CREAMY MISO DRESSING

¼ C flax oil
¼ C lemon juice
2 T water
1 T raw chickpea miso
½ t Celtic salt

In a blender, process all ingredients until smooth and creamy.
Makes ½ cup.

# CREAMY CUKE DRESSING

1 large cucumber
⅓ C flax oil
1 T raw tahini
2 t dill
½ T Celtic salt

In a blender, process all ingredients until smooth and creamy. Makes 1 cup.

# CREAMY DILL DRESSING

½ C olive oil
½ C pine nuts, unsoaked
1 bunch of fresh dill
3 T lemon juice
Freshly ground black pepper
Celtic salt

Blend and enjoy.

# CREAMY TOMATO DRESSING

3 tomatoes
2 T flax oil
½ t Celtic salt
¼ C basil
2 T fresh thyme

In a blender, process all ingredients until smooth and creamy.
Makes 2 cups.

# CREAMY ZUCCHINI VINAIGRETTE

2 C zucchini, chopped
1 T raw apple cider vinegar
1 T olive oil
1 T Italian seasoning
1 t Celtic salt

In a blender, process all ingredients until smooth and creamy. Makes 2 cups.

# CUCUMBER DILL DRESSING

3 cucumbers
3 stalks of celery
½ C olive oil
1 t Celtic salt

In a blender, process all ingredients until smooth and creamy.

*Optional:*

1 clove of garlic

. . . . . . . . . . . . . . . . . . . . . . . . . . .

*Add:*

1 C fresh dill

Pulse a couple of times with the blender. The dill should be chopped but not blended.
Makes 2 cups.

# CURRIED CARROT DRESSING

6 carrots, chopped
2 T sesame oil
1 T ginger juice
1½ t curry
¼ t nutmeg

In a blender, process all ingredients until smooth and creamy.
Makes 2 cups.

# FLAX OIL GINGER DRESSING

1 lemon, peeled
½ C flax oil
1 T ginger juice
1 t Celtic salt

In a blender, process all ingredients until smooth and creamy.
Makes ¾ cup.

# HEMP SEED DRESSING

1 tomato
1 small carrot
½ bell pepper
⅛ C hemp oil
½ T lemon juice
½ t Celtic sea salt

In a blender, process all ingredients until smooth and creamy.
Makes 1½ cups.

*Note:*
Hemp oil is very strong in flavor.

# Italian Dressing

1 large tomato
1 clove garlic
¼ C water
¼ C olive oil
2 T lemon juice
1 t fresh basil
½ t fresh oregano
½ t Celtic salt

In a blender, process all ingredients until smooth and creamy.
Makes 1 cup.

# Lemon Dill Dressing

½ C flax oil
½ C lemon juice
1 T raw tahini
2 t dill
½ t Celtic salt

In a blender, process all ingredients until smooth and creamy.
Makes 1 cup.

# MISO HERB DRESSING

1 C red bell pepper, chopped
½ C olive oil
¼ C water
2 T fresh basil
2 T dark barley raw miso
2 T lemon juice
1 T fresh ginger, minced
1 t fresh thyme

In a blender, process all ingredients until smooth and creamy.

Makes 1 cup.

# MISO ORANGE DRESSING

½ C orange juice, fresh squeezed
½ C olive oil or flax oil
⅛ C lemon juice
2 T chickpea miso

Blend all ingredients. Recommended for the *Dandelion Salad.*

Makes 1½ cups.

# Mock Blue Cheeze Dressing

1 C sesame seeds, soaked and
    homogenized
½ C water
½ C parsley
¼ C olive oil
⅓ C lemon juice
1 T dill
1 T oregano
1 T basil
1½ t Celtic salt

Blend sesame seeds, water, lemon
juice, and salt. Chop and stir in
herbs. Chill and serve.
    Makes 3 cups.

# Moroccan Carrot Dressing

2 C carrots, chopped
2 tomatoes
⅓ C flax oil
1 orange
1 t Celtic salt
1 t allspice
1 t cumin
1 t black pepper or cayenne

In a blender, process all ingredients
until smooth and creamy.
    Makes 2 cups.

# ORANGE DRESSING

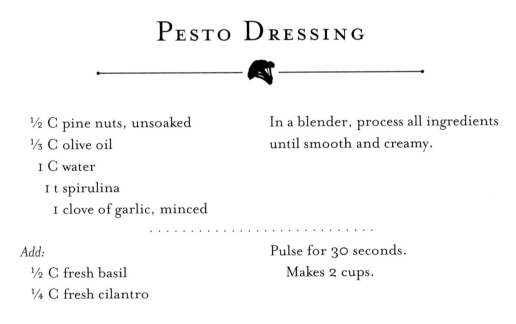

1½ C orange juice
½ C sesame oil
1 t cumin
½ t Celtic salt
Dash cayenne

In a blender, process all ingredients until smooth and creamy.

*Add:*
1 C fresh cilantro

Pulse a couple of times with the blender. The cilantro should be finely chopped but not blended. Makes 2 cups.

# PESTO DRESSING

½ C pine nuts, unsoaked
⅓ C olive oil
1 C water
1 t spirulina
1 clove of garlic, minced

In a blender, process all ingredients until smooth and creamy.

*Add:*
½ C fresh basil
¼ C fresh cilantro

Pulse for 30 seconds. Makes 2 cups.

# RED PEPPER CURRY DRESSING

1 C red bell pepper, chopped
¼ C olive oil
2 T lemon juice
1 T curry powder
½ t Celtic salt

In a blender, process all ingredients until smooth and creamy.
Makes 1¼ cups.

# SPANISH SALSA DRESSING

3 tomatoes
½ C pumpkin seeds or sunflower seeds, soaked
½ C lemon juice
½ C fresh cilantro, finely chopped
¼ C olive oil
1 clove garlic
¼ t cayenne or to taste

In a blender, process all ingredients until smooth and creamy.
Makes 2 cups.

# TAHINI LEMON DRESSING

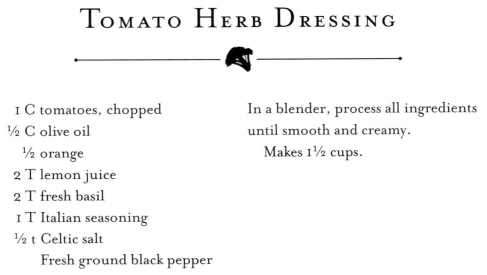

½ C water

2 T raw tahini

1 T lemon juice

1 t Celtic salt

*Optional:*

    1 t garlic, minced

    1 t fresh dill, finely chopped

    1 t fresh chives, finely chopped

In a blender, process all ingredients until smooth and creamy.

Makes ¾ cup.

# TOMATO HERB DRESSING

1 C tomatoes, chopped

½ C olive oil

½ orange

2 T lemon juice

2 T fresh basil

1 T Italian seasoning

½ t Celtic salt

    Fresh ground black pepper

      to taste

In a blender, process all ingredients until smooth and creamy.

Makes 1½ cups.

# Zucchini Herb Dressing

1 C zucchini, chopped
3 T lemon juice
2 T olive oil
1 T fresh basil, finely chopped
1 T fresh chives, finely chopped
½ T fresh thyme, finely chopped
1 t Celtic salt
Dash of cayenne

In a blender, process all ingredients until smooth and creamy.

Makes 1½ cups.

# Zucchini Vinaigrette

2 zucchini
4 stalks of celery
½ C olive oil
½ C water
3 T raw apple cider vinegar
1 T fresh thyme, minced
1 T fresh marjoram, minced
1 t Celtic salt

In a blender, process all ingredients until smooth and creamy.

Makes 2½ cups.

# Chutneys, Salsa,
# Sauces, and
# Spreads

# ALIVE MUSTARD

2 C yellow mustard seeds, soaked
    6–8 hours
1 C raw apple cider vinegar
1 C water
  1 t Celtic salt

In a blender, process all ingredients until smooth and creamy.

# APPLE CHUTNEY

2 apples
1 C cilantro
  1 clove garlic, minced
1 T raw apple cider vinegar
1 T sunflower oil
½ t Celtic salt
    Dash of cayenne
    Dash of cinnamon

Process all ingredients in a food processor with the "S" blade until chunky.

# APPLE PECAN COCONUT CHUTNEY

4 apples, chopped

3 stalks of celery

1 medium radish

Pulp of 3 coconuts,
approximately 3 cups

1 C cilantro

1 C pecans, soaked

1 T fresh ginger juice

2 t garam masala

1 t cardamom

½ t leek

1½ t curry

1 t Celtic salt

½ t fresh ground black pepper

2 cloves of garlic

Process all ingredients in a food processor with the "S" blade until chunky.

# BASIL PESTO

1½ C pine nuts, unsoaked

½ C fresh basil, de-stemmed

¼ C olive oil

3 T lemon juice

1 clove garlic or 1 t hing

2 t Celtic salt

In food processor, combine olive oil and pine nuts by pulsing until nuts are semi-crushed. Add lemon juice, salt, and basil and continue to pulse for an additional 40 seconds. For a creamier consistency, add ½ cup water and 1 additional tablespoon of olive oil.

# Black Olive Salsa

3 tomatoes, chopped

1 cucumber, chopped

1 C Moroccan olives, pitted and
chopped

½ C fresh fennel, chopped

½ C fresh cilantro, chopped

2 t cayenne

2 t cumin

1 t lime juice

1½ t Celtic salt

Stir all ingredients together by hand. Chill and serve.

# Cilantro Pesto

2 C fresh cilantro

1 C fresh basil

1 C walnuts, soaked

¾ C olive oil

2 T lemon juice

2 T fresh sage

1 clove garlic or 1 t hing

2 t Celtic salt

½ t cayenne

Process all ingredients in a food processor with the "S" blade until smooth and creamy.

# COCONUT CHUTNEY

1 apple
1 tomato
1 orange
2 T raisins, soaked
½ C coconut pulp, diced
2 T lemon juice
1 T basil
1 T cilantro
1 t Celtic salt

Blend all ingredients until slightly chunky.

# CREAMY DIJON MUSTARD

¾ C sunflower seeds, soaked
½ C macadamia nuts, unsoaked
¾ C water
1½ T apple cider vinegar
1 t paprika
1 t mustard powder
1½ t Celtic salt

Blend all in a high-power blender, chill, and serve.

# Lemon Tahini Sauce

2 C white sesame seeds, soaked
1 C water
½ C lemon juice
1½ t Celtic salt

*Optional:*
    1 t garlic, minced

In a blender, process all ingredients until smooth and creamy.
Makes 2 cups.

# Living Catsup

1 C sun-dried tomatoes, soaked
1 C tomatoes, diced
1 C water (save soak water from tomatoes)
2 T raw apple cider vinegar
½ t Celtic salt

In a blender, process all ingredients until smooth.

# GROOVY GUACAMOLE

2 ripe avocados
1 tomato, diced
Juice of 1–2 lemons (to taste)
¼ C fresh cilantro, finely chopped
1 clove garlic, minced
1 t cumin
½ t cayenne (or mince in some
fresh, hot chiles!)
½ t Celtic salt
Fresh ground black pepper
to taste

Mash and mix all ingredients with a fork, serve, and stand back! Guacamole is always a big hit—and quick and easy to prepare! You can serve this as a salad or chunky dip, or you can mash it smooth, add water, and use as a salad dressing. Serves 2–4 people.

# GUACAMOLE!

2 ripe avocados
1 tomato, diced
¼ C fresh cilantro, finely
chopped
2 T lemon juice
½ t cumin
½ t hing
½ t Celtic salt

Blend all ingredients, except tomatoes, which should be mixed in by hand.

# MARINARA SAUCE

2 tomatoes

12 sun-dried tomatoes

1 plum (optional;
    Phase II only)

10 strawberries (optional)

¼ C raisins (Phase II only)

½ t jalapeño

½ t Celtic salt

Blend until smooth and serve over *Garden Neatballs* or enjoy with any Italian recipe.

# MEXICALI CRANBERRY SAUCE

2 C fresh cranberries

¾ C raisins, soaked

½ C water

1 C fresh cilantro, de-stemmed
    and minced

2 T lemon juice

2 T sun-dried tomatoes, soaked
    and minced

1½ T Celtic salt

1 T jalapeño, minced

1 t chia seed

1 t chipotle, ground*

Combine cranberries, raisins, jalapeños, chipotle, chia seed, water, salt, and lemon in high-power blender and liquefy. Transfer to bowl and stir in cilantro and tomatoes. Chill for 1 hour prior to serving.

* Not a raw food

# MEXICAN TOMATO SALSA

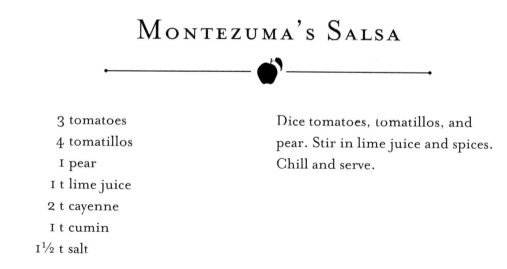

6 tomatoes, diced
½ turnip, finely chopped
1 C cilantro, finely chopped
⅓ C parsley, finely chopped
⅓ C lemon juice
1 t Celtic salt
1 t Mexican spice
½ t cracked red pepper

Combine all ingredients in a large mixing bowl and mix well.

# MONTEZUMA'S SALSA

3 tomatoes
4 tomatillos
1 pear
1 t lime juice
2 t cayenne
1 t cumin
1½ t salt

Dice tomatoes, tomatillos, and pear. Stir in lime juice and spices. Chill and serve.

# Mysore Mint Chutney

½ C raisins, soaked

½ C water

1 apple

2 T fresh mint, minced

1 t fresh ginger, minced

3 black peppercorns

1 t garam masala

½ t cardamom

Process all ingredients in a blender until smooth. Serve with *Sun Raw Samosas.*

# Olive Dip

2 large avocados

2 T lemon juice

1 C Italian black olives, finely chopped

½ C tomatoes, finely chopped

¼ C red bell pepper, finely chopped

¼ C celery, finely chopped

2 T fresh parsley, finely chopped

Mash avocados with lemon juice. Process all ingredients in a blender until chunky.

*Optional:*
Add ¾ C of *Coconut Dream Cream* (Phase I.5).

# PISTACHIO MISO DIPPING SAUCE

1 C pistachio nuts
¼ C olive oil
¼ C water
3 T miso (light or dark)
1½ t Celtic salt

Blend all of the above in a high-power blender and serve with *Nori Rolls*, veggies, or as a salad dressing.

# PLUM CHUTNEY

2 C plums, seeded and diced
¼ C fresh cilantro, minced
2½ T fresh chives, minced
2 T lemon juice
½ t cardamom
½ t cinnamon
¼–½ t cayenne

Combine all ingredients in a mixing bowl and refrigerate for 1 hour before serving. Serves 4.

# SALSA FRESCA

2 C tomatoes, seeded and diced
⅓ C fresh cilantro, finely chopped
1½ T apple cider vinegar
1½ T garlic, minced
1 T lemon juice
1 t Celtic salt

Toss all ingredients in a large mixing bowl and serve.

# SALSA PICANTE

1 C carrot juice
⅓ C sun-dried tomatoes, soaked
2 T flax oil
2 T lemon juice
1½ T chili powder
1 t Celtic salt
½–1 t cayenne
½ t fresh ground black pepper
1 C red bell peppers, diced
1 C cherry tomatoes, quartered
⅓ C fresh cilantro, chopped

In a blender, process carrot juice, sun-dried tomatoes, flax oil, lemon juice, chili powder, salt, cayenne, and black pepper until smooth and creamy. Toss red bell peppers, tomatoes, and cilantro; mix well and serve with *Sun-Dried Tomato Flax Crackers*. Serves 4–6.

# SOUR CREAM

1 C macadamia nuts
½ C sunflower seeds
1 T lemon juice
1 t Celtic salt

Blend in a high-speed blender until smooth.

# SOUR CREAM SAUCE

2 C almonds, soaked
2 T lemon juice
  1 clove garlic, minced
  1 t Celtic salt
  1 t cumin
  1 t fresh ground black pepper
1–3 C water (amount varies with thickness desired—less for thick "sour cream," more for salad dressing)

In a blender, process all ingredients until smooth. Serve chilled or at room temperature.

Wonderful with *Mexican Burritos,* as a topping for *Zucchini Pancakes,* or used as a salad dressing.

*Variation:*
Stir in finely chopped chives.

# SPINACH DIP

2 C spinach
½ C coconut pulp
½ C pine nuts, unsoaked
1 avocado
¼ C lemon juice
¼ C lime juice
⅛ t hing
1 t Celtic salt
¼ t cayenne

In a blender, process all ingredients until smooth and creamy. Add more liquid for dip consistency. Serves 4–6.

# SPINACH BASIL DIP

2 C baby spinach, finely chopped
3 T fresh basil, finely chopped
⅓ C macadamia nuts, soaked
¼ C pine nuts, unsoaked
2 T olive oil
1 T lemon juice
½ t Celtic salt

*Optional:*
½ T fresh lemon grass, minced

Combine spinach and basil in a mixing bowl and set aside. Process remaining ingredients in a food processor with the "S" blade until smooth and toss "cream" with shredded spinach and basil. Serves 4.

# SQUASHO-NACHO CHEEZE

⅔ C butternut squash
2 C fresh cilantro
2 T lemon juice
2 T olive oil
2 t Celtic salt
¼ t fresh ground black pepper
2 red bell peppers, finely
   chopped
2 C golden flax seeds, ground

In your blender, combine everything except the ground flax and minced pepper. Slowly add flax to the mixture as it blends. Spread the combination onto smooth dehydrator sheets all the way to the sides. Sprinkle minced red pepper evenly on top. You can use jalapeño if you like it hot! Dehydrate at 145°F for 2–3 hours. With a knife, cut into fun shapes, and using a spatula, place the shapes on top of stuffed peppers or inside burritos.

# SUN-DRIED TOMATO TAPENADE

1½ C sun-dried tomatoes, soaked
  1 C red bell peppers, chopped
  3 T fresh basil, chopped
  2 T olive oil
1½ T lemon juice
  1 T fresh oregano, chopped
  ½ T fresh sage, chopped
  ½ T fresh thyme, chopped
  ½ t Celtic salt

Process all ingredients in a food processor with the "S" blade until smooth and creamy.
   Serve with crackers.

# Sweet Abundance Stuffing

2 C almonds, soaked
2 C walnuts, soaked
1 C apples, sliced into small,
    thin strips
½ C raisins, soaked
½ C olive oil
2 T fresh sage, minced
1 T fresh thyme, minced
1 T fresh marjoram, minced
1 T fresh oregano, minced
1 T dried poultry seasoning
2 t cayenne pepper
2 t cracked black peppercorns
2 T Celtic salt

In food processor, chop walnuts and almonds until a semi-fine texture has been reached; this is achieved by pulsing the machine's "S" blade for about 1 minute. Next, add apples and 2 T of the soaked raisins. Pulse for another 30 seconds, and then transfer mixture to mixing bowl. Mix in all remaining ingredients by hand and stir well. Form mixture into small loaves (with height no more than 1", length about 5", width about 3") on Teflex sheets on dehydrator trays. Dehydrate for 2 hours at 145°F, then flip loaves over, and removing Teflex, dehydrate at 115°F for 2 hours. Stuffing should be soft and warm when served. Great for holiday parties.

# Sweet & Hot BBQ Sauce

½ C raisins, soaked
1 C soaked sun-dried tomatoes
1 bunch of dill
1 t–1 T apple cider vinegar
Serrano or jalapeño pepper
to taste
Celtic salt to taste

Blend all ingredients in food processor. You may need to add a bit of water or olive oil to thin out.

# Tomato Pizza Sauce

4 large tomatoes, squeeze out
liquid if you prefer a thick
sauce
1½ C sun-dried tomatoes, soaked
½ C olive oil
1 T Italian seasoning
1 T basil
¾ t oregano
1 t Celtic salt
½ t fresh ground black pepper
½ t cayenne

Process all ingredients in a blender until smooth.

*Optional:*
1–3 sweet red or yellow peppers

# TOMATO SALSA #1

4 ripe tomatoes, diced
½ C cilantro, finely chopped
1 t cayenne
1 t hing
2 T lemon juice
Celtic salt to taste

Mix and serve.

*Optional:*
1 clove garlic, minced

# TOMATO SALSA #2

4 tomatoes, seeded and diced
½ C fresh cilantro, finely chopped
1 clove garlic, minced
2 T fresh chives, finely chopped
2 T lemon juice
1 T raw apple cider vinegar
1 t cayenne

Combine all ingredients in a mixing bowl and serve. Serves 2–4.

# TOMATILLO AVOCADO SALSA

2 avocados, diced
2 C tomatillos, chopped
2 T fresh basil, minced
2 T lime juice
1½ T fresh ginger, minced
1 T garlic, minced
½ t Celtic salt

Pulse-chop in a food processor with the "S" blade the tomatillos, lime juice, ginger, garlic, and salt. Pour into a mixing bowl; add the avocado and fresh basil and stir. Chill 1 hour before serving to thicken. Serves 2–4.

# TOMATILLO SAUCE

2 C tomatillos, chopped
½ C fresh cilantro, chopped
2 T lemon juice
2 T raisins, soaked
1 T olive oil
1 T fresh jalapeño, seeded
    and chopped
1 T garlic, minced
1 t Celtic salt

Process all ingredients in a food processor with the "S" blade until slightly chunky. Serve as a salsa with burritos. Serves 4.

# ULTIMATE ITALIAN RED SAUCE

2 C sun-dried tomatoes, soaked
  1 tomato
1 C sun-dried tomato soak water
2 T olive oil
2 T lemon juice
2 T fresh parsley, finely chopped
2 T fresh basil, finely chopped
1 T oregano
  1 t Celtic salt
  1 t thyme
¼ t marjoram
¼ t rosemary
¼ t sage

In a blender, process tomato, sun-dried tomatoes, and remaining ingredients until smooth. Add more sun-dried tomato soak water for a thinner consistency. A thicker sauce is used for a lasagna, whereas a thinner sauce could be used for zucchini pasta.

# WASABI SAUCE

  1 T horseradish or wasabi powder
½ C cucumber juice
  1 T Celtic salt

Mix together in a bowl until creamy and serve.

# Yellow Bell Pepper Curry Sauce

2 C yellow bell pepper, chopped
2 T olive oil
2 T raisins, soaked
1½ T lemon juice
1 T ginger juice
1 T curry
2 t cumin
1 t Celtic salt

Process all ingredients in a blender until smooth and creamy.

# Zesty Catsup

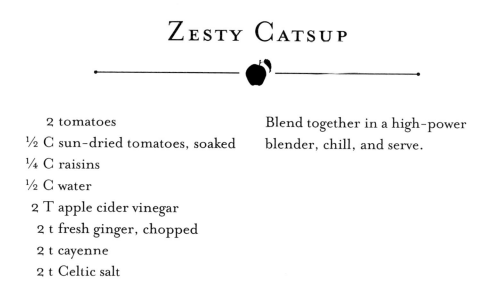

2 tomatoes
½ C sun-dried tomatoes, soaked
¼ C raisins
½ C water
2 T apple cider vinegar
2 t fresh ginger, chopped
2 t cayenne
2 t Celtic salt

Blend together in a high-power blender, chill, and serve.

# Soups

## HOW TO MAKE WARM SOUP:

When you want winter comfort food, you can have warm soup (even in live-food cuisine). To achieve this, warm the water used in the recipe to a temperature just under boiling.

# CARROT SOUP WITH ARUGULA SALSA

### SOUP BASE:

4 C carrot juice

1 T ginger juice

### ARUGULA SALSA:

3 C arugula, finely chopped

1 C broccoli, finely chopped

1 C cauliflower, finely chopped

½ C carrots, diced

¼ C olive oil

4 T lemon juice

¼ t fresh ground black pepper

Pinch of cayenne

Celtic salt to taste

Place one-third of salsa in a blender and process until smooth; pour into soup base and mix well. Combine all ingredients in a large mixing bowl and mix well. Garnish with arugula.

# CHINESE CREAM OF CUCUMBER SOUP

4 C cucumber, peeled with
   zebra stripes
2 C coconut water
2 C coconut pulp
½ C olive oil
½ C orange juice
2½ T Celtic salt
  1 t star anise
  1 t fennel seed
  5 drops liquid stevia

Combine all ingredients in blender on high until smooth.

# COCONUT CELERY SOUP

**PART 1:**

Pulp of 2 coconuts
4 C coconut water
  3 stalks of celery
  1 zucchini, remove dark
    green skin
½ t cinnamon

In a blender, process all ingredients until smooth.

**PART 2:**

2 zucchini, remove dark skin

Peel zucchini and discard the dark green skin. Continue to peel the zucchini thinly. Add the thin slices to Part 1 and serve.

# Cream of Carrot Soup

3 carrots, chopped

2 stalks of celery

2 C almonds, soaked

2–3 cloves of garlic

2 C water

1½ C orange juice

1 t nutmeg

In a blender, process all ingredients until smooth and creamy.

# Cream of Tomato Soup

1 tomato

½ C macadamia nuts, soaked

½ C sun-dried tomatoes

1½ C sun-dried tomato soak water

½ t Celtic salt

½ t basil

In a blender, mix all ingredients and serve.

# Curried Carrot Avocado Soup

3 C carrots, chopped
2 C water
  2 avocados
  1 clove of garlic
3 t ginger juice
1 t lemon juice
1 t curry powder
½ t cumin
½ t Celtic salt
¼ t cayenne
¼ t fresh ground black pepper

In a blender, process all ingredients until smooth and creamy.

# Fennel Soup

  2 C fennel bulb, chopped
  1 C tomato
1½ T lemon juice
  ½ T garlic, minced
  ½ t oregano
  ½ t sage
  ½ t Celtic salt
  ½ C avocado, diced
  ½ C cucumber, diced
  ⅓ C red bell pepper, diced

In a blender, process fennel, tomato, lemon juice, garlic, oregano, sage, and Celtic salt until smooth and liquefied. Strain the mixture and stir in avocado, cucumber, and red bell peppers. Garnish with fresh herbs. Serves 2–3.

# Fruity Cream of Tomato Soup

2 tomatoes

2 tomatillos

¼ lime

10 strawberries, chopped

10 raspberries, chopped

¼ C leeks, chopped

Pulp from 1 young coconut

¼ C raisins (Phase II only)

1¼ C macadamia nuts, unsoaked

1½ t Celtic salt

2 t jalapeño, chopped (optional)

¼ C cilantro, chopped

Blend tomatoes, tomatillos, lime, coconut pulp, and macadamia nuts in a high-power blender until smooth. Stir in raisins, strawberries, raspberries, leeks, and jalapeño. Add salt and cilantro to taste.

# Gazpacho Soup

3 C heirloom or black plum
    tomatoes, chopped
1 C sun-dried tomatoes
1 C zucchini, chopped fine
1 C celery, chopped
2 t cayenne pepper
1½ t black pepper
½ t white pepper
1 t hing
2 T chives, fresh
2 T salt
⅓ C lime

Combine celery, sun-dried tomatoes, and tomato soak water in blender until creamy. Add lime, salt, and spices, mixing for additional 30 seconds. Next, add chopped tomatoes and chives and mix for 20 seconds. Soup should be slightly chunky. Serve immediately.

# Ginger Jai Bisque

1 C pumpkin, seeded
1 C coconut water or purified
    water
1½ C pine nuts, unsoaked
1 T leeks, minced
2 t fresh ginger, minced
1½ t Celtic salt
1½ t cumin
1½ t cayenne pepper
1 t fenugreek seeds, ground

Blend all ingredients together in high-power blender for 1 minute or until creamy.

# Green Campfire Stew

2 C avocado

2 C water

1 C fresh cilantro, de-stemmed
    and minced

1 C celery

½ C kale, de-stemmed

½ C lemon or lime juice

2 T Celtic salt

1 t cayenne pepper

1 hot pepper, seeded

Combine all ingredients in blender and mix until thoroughly creamy. Serve immediately.

# Miso Noodle Soup

2½ C water

1½ C coconut pulp

1½ t dark barley miso

1½ t Celtic salt

½ t ginger, minced

Place coconut pulp on cutting board. Using cleaver or long chef's knife, cut into thin noodle-like strips, at least 1½" long. In blender, combine miso, ginger, water, and salt until smooth. Pour into serving bowl and stir in coconut noodles.

*Optional:*
Use warm, not boiling, water during the winter for a very satisfying experience.

# PINE NUT CREAM OF TOMATO SOUP

4 tomatoes
3 stalks of celery
1 C water
¾ C pine nuts, unsoaked
2 T lemon juice
1 t basil
1 t oregano
2 t Celtic salt
¼ t fresh ground black pepper
¼ t cinnamon

In a blender, process all ingredients until smooth and creamy.

# THICK AND CHUNKY TOMATO SOUP

4 tomatoes
2 avocados
2 stalks celery
½ head cauliflower
2 zucchini
½ C olive oil
1 T basil
1 T oregano
½ T rosemary
1½ t Celtic salt

Chop and marinate the cauliflower, zucchini, and celery in olive oil and rosemary, and then dehydrate for 2–3 hours (until soft). Puree the tomato and avocado, and stir in softened veggies and herbs. Salt to taste and garnish with basil.

# SIMPLE CREAMY TOMATO SOUP

4 C vine-ripened tomatoes
   Freshly ground pepper
   Celtic salt
1 C pine nuts
  1 big bunch of dill, chopped

Blend tomatoes, salt, and pepper. Add pine nuts and dill. Pulse. Serve with a smile.

# SQUASH BISQUE

1 C butternut squash, peeled
   and chunked
1 red bell pepper, seeded
   and chopped
2 stalks of celery
1 tomato
2 T parsley, minced
2 T cilantro, minced
1 T olive oil
2 C water
1 t Celtic salt
1 t fresh ground black pepper
   Dash of cayenne

Combine all ingredients, except parsley and cilantro, in your blender until smooth and creamy. Add parsley and cilantro and serve in a hollowed butternut squash.

# ZEN GAZPACHO

5 C vine-ripened tomatoes
¼ cup olive oil
1 jalapeño, seeded and diced,
  or to taste
  Dash of cumin
  White pepper to taste
  Celtic salt to taste
2 avocados, cubed
3 cucumbers, seeded and
  cubed
  Bunch of cilantro, chopped
  Handful of mint, chopped
3 T fresh lime juice

Blend tomatoes, olive oil, jalapeño, and spices. Mix in avocados, cucumbers, mint, and cilantro. Chill. Add lime juice before serving.

# Crackers, Chips, and Jerkys

# ALMOND SEED CRACKERS

6 C flax seeds, soaked
4 C almonds, soaked
4 C carrot pulp
2 C parsley, finely chopped
1 C sesame seeds, soaked
1 C pumpkin seeds, soaked
  6 stalks of celery, finely
    chopped
6 T lemon juice
3 T Celtic salt
3 T powdered kelp

Process almonds and carrots through a Champion Juicer with the solid plate; combine all ingredients in a large mixing bowl and mix well. Spread the dough on a dehydrator tray with a Teflex sheet approximately ¼" thick; score crackers with a spatula. Dehydrate at 145°F for 2–3 hours, then turn over, remove Teflex, and continue dehydrating for 6–8 hours at 115°F or until desired moisture is obtained. Store in glass jars. Makes 9 trays of 14"× 14".

# BASIC CRACKERS

2½ C water
1½ C flax, powdered
  1 C almonds, soaked

¼ C olive oil
2 T salt
1 T cumin

Combine almonds, water, olive oil, salt, and cumin in high-power blender. Mix thoroughly and transfer to bowl. Stir in flax meal slowly. Scoop about 1 cup of mixture onto Teflex on each of 3 to 4 dehydrator trays and spread out to all corners evenly. Score cracker mixture using a spatula. Dehydrate at 145°F for 2–3 hours, then turn over, remove Teflex, and continue dehydrating for 6–8 hours at 115°F or until desired moisture is obtained. Store in the refrigerator and consume within two weeks.

# Basic Veggie Chips

4 C radish, butternut squash, or yam sliced into thin "chips"
¾ C olive oil
2 T salt
1 t cayenne pepper

Begin by slicing root vegetable of choice with a mandoline or food processor. Place chips into shallow casserole dish. In bowl, combine remaining ingredients and mix well before pouring over chips. Massage chips to ensure that each one is covered with sauce/marinade. Place chips onto mesh dehydrator trays and dehydrate for 2 hours at 145°F and then 115°F for 2 more hours or until crispy. Store in refrigerator for up to one month.

# Basic Veggie Jerky

### Vegetables:

2 red bell peppers

2 eggplants

1 medium butternut squash

5 zucchini

### Marinade:

½ C olive oil

¼ C lemon juice

1 T Celtic salt

Blend marinade in high-power blender or by hand until ingredients are thoroughly mixed. Peel and slice vegetables into ½"-thick strips. Place into shallow, rectangular dish (a casserole dish works well) and cover with marinade. Massage liquid into veggies, ensuring that both sides of each vegetable are covered with liquid. Store in the refrigerator for 24 hours to allow time for the flavor to soak in. Next, place vegetables on Teflex sheets in the dehydrator. Dehydrate at 145°F for 2–3 hours and then 115°F for 10 hours. Stores well in sealed jars in the refrigerator for up to 3 weeks.

# "Cheeze" -n- "Crackers"

15 nori sheets
  1 recipe of *Pâté Primavera* or any
    basic pâté (choice may
    depend on Phase)

Topping Suggestions:
black and white sesame seeds
soaked pumpkin seeds
sun-dried tomatoes
dried herbs
olives

Place nori sheets onto dehydrator trays. Spread thin layer of pâté onto nori, no more than ⅛" thick. Sprinkle on toppings as colorful garnishes. Dehydrate for 2–3 hours at 145°F and then 5–6 hours at 115°F.

This recipe yields nori crackers that taste essentially like cheeze and crackers. They are great as travel snacks, as substantive, lively hors d'oeuvres, and in children's school lunches. Also great when paired with other dips, spreads, and pâtés. Enjoy!

# CONFETTI CRACKERS

2½ C water
2 C flax, powdered
1 C almonds, soaked
¼ C white sesame seeds
¼ C black sesame seeds
¼ C olive oil
2 T salt

Combine almonds, water, olive oil, and salt in high-power blender. Mix thoroughly and transfer to bowl. Stir in flax meal slowly. Scoop about 1 cup of mixture onto Teflex on each of 3 to 4 dehydrator trays and spread out to all corners evenly. Score cracker mixture using a spatula. Sprinkle sesame seeds on crackers as a fun decoration. Dehydrate at 145°F for 2–3 hours, then turn over, remove Teflex, and continue dehydrating for 6–8 hours at 115°F or until desired moisture is obtained. Store in the refrigerator and consume within two weeks.

# GREEN WONDER WAFERS

1 C almonds, soaked
½–¾ C coconut water
¼ C spirulina, blue-green algae, or favorite green powder
3 T olive oil
1 t Celtic salt

Process almonds through a Champion Juicer with the solid plate; combine remaining ingredients and mix well. Spread on a dehydrator tray with a Teflex sheet about ¼" thick and dehydrate at 145°F for 1–2 hours or until desired consistency is obtained.

# ITALIAN CRACKERS

2½ C water

1½ C flax, powdered

½ C almonds, soaked

¼ C olive oil

3 T Italian seasoning

2 T Celtic salt

1 T fresh basil, minced

Combine almonds, water, olive oil, salt, Italian seasoning, and basil in high-power blender. Mix thoroughly and transfer to bowl. Stir in flax meal slowly. Scoop about 1 cup of mixture onto Teflex on each of 3 to 4 dehydrator trays and spread out to all corners evenly. Score cracker mixture using a spatula. Dehydrate at 145°F for 2–3 hours, then turn over, remove Teflex, and continue dehydrating for 6–8 hours at 115°F or until desired moisture is obtained. Store in the refrigerator and consume within two weeks.

# ITALIAN SUN-DRIED TOMATO FLAX CRACKERS

4 C flax seeds, soaked

2 C sun-dried tomatoes, soaked and blended

2 T Italian seasoning

1 T olive oil

1 t Celtic salt

1 t cayenne

Combine all ingredients in a large mixing bowl and mix well. Spread mixture approximately ¼" thick on dehydrator trays with a Teflex sheet. Keeping hands wet will help in the spreading of the flax seeds. Dehydrate at 145°F for 2–3 hours, then turn over, remove Teflex, and continue dehydrating for 6–8 hours at 115°F, or until desired moisture is obtained. Store in glass jars.

# KALE CURRY CRACKERS

2 C golden flax seeds, ground
1 C almonds, soaked
1 C kale, homogenized
1 T curry
1 t cumin
1 t Celtic salt

Process almonds and kale through a Champion Juicer with the solid plate; combine remaining ingredients and mix well. Spread mixture approximately ¼" thick on dehydrator trays with a Teflex sheet. Keeping hands wet will help in the spreading of the flax seeds. Dehydrate at 145°F for 2–3 hours, then turn over, remove Teflex, and continue dehydrating for 6–8 hours at 115°F, or until desired moisture is obtained. Store in glass jars.

# SAVORY CRACKERS

6 C flax seeds, soaked

6 C pecans, soaked

6 zucchini

2 T Celtic salt

2 T dried Italian seasoning

Process pecans and zucchini through a Champion Juicer with the solid plate; combine remaining ingredients and mix well. Spread mixture approximately ¼" thick on dehydrator trays with a Teflex sheet. Keeping hands wet will help in the spreading of the flax seeds. Dehydrate at 145°F for 2–3 hours, then turn over, remove Teflex, and continue dehydrating for 6–8 hours at 115°F, or until desired moisture is obtained. Store in glass jars.

# Spicy Southwestern Jerky

### Vegetables:

4 red bell peppers

2 eggplants

1 medium butternut squash

10 zucchini

### Marinade:

½ C olive oil

¼ C lemon juice

1 T Celtic salt

1½ T chili spice powder

1 t cayenne pepper

1 t paprika

Blend marinade in high-power blender until ingredients are thoroughly mixed. Peel and slice vegetables into ½"-thick strips. Massage liquid into veggies, ensuring that both sides of each vegetable are covered with liquid. Place into shallow, rectangular dish (a casserole dish works well) and cover with marinade. Store in the refrigerator for 24 hours to allow time for the flavor to soak in. Dehydrate at 145°F for 2–3 hours and then 115°F for 10 hours.

# Sun-Dried Tomato Flax Crackers

6 C flax seeds, soaked

2 C sun-dried tomatoes, soaked

1 C celery juice

1 C fresh parsley, minced

3 T Celtic salt

1 T Italian seasoning

3 cloves garlic, minced

Process sun-dried tomatoes in a blender, adding soak water until the mixture is a thick liquid. In a large bowl, combine flax seeds, sun-dried tomatoes, and remaining ingredients. Spread mixture as thin as possible, approximately ¼" thick, on dehydrator trays with a Teflex sheet. Keeping hands wet will help in the spreading of the flax seeds. Dehydrate at 145°F for 2–3 hours, then turn over, remove Teflex, and continue dehydrating for 6–8 hours at 115°F, or until desired moisture is obtained.

# Sweet and Sour Jerky

### Vegetables:

2 red bell peppers

2 large sweet potatoes, sliced thin into "chips" with a mandoline

1 medium butternut squash

5 zucchini

### Marinade:

½ C olive oil

½ C lemon juice

½ C raisins, soaked

½ C water

2 T fresh ginger, minced

1½ T Celtic salt

1 T red pepper flakes

Blend marinade in high-power blender until ingredients are thoroughly mixed. Peel and slice vegetables into ½"-thick strips. Massage liquid into veggies, ensuring that both sides of each vegetable are covered. Place into shallow, rectangular dish (a casserole dish works well) and cover with marinade. Store in the refrigerator for 24 hours to allow time for the flavor to soak in. Dehydrate for up to 20 hours at 100°F.

# TASTE OF INDIA FLAX CRACKERS

4 C flax seeds, soaked

3 C almonds, soaked

4 stalks of celery, finely chopped

1½ C parsley, finely chopped

½ C olive oil

4 C carrot pulp

4 T lemon juice

3 T Celtic salt

1 T curry

2 t cumin

2 t ginger

1 t coriander

2–4 cloves of garlic

Process almonds and carrots through a Champion Juicer with the solid plate; combine all ingredients in a large mixing bowl and mix well. Spread mixture approximately ¼" thick on a dehydrator tray with a Teflex sheet; score crackers with a spatula. Dehydrate at 145°F for 2–3 hours, then turn over, remove Teflex, and continue dehydrating for 6–8 hours at 115°F, or until desired moisture is obtained.

# TOASTIES

1 C sesame seeds, soaked
½ C grapefruit juice
2 T caraway seeds
2 T poppy seeds
1½ C golden flax seeds, ground

In a blender, process sesame seeds with grapefruit juice until smooth. Add poppy seeds and caraway seeds and process for 2–3 minutes more. Place in a medium-size bowl and mix in flax until a dough consistency is obtained. Shape dough into a loaf, slice into bread slices approximately ¼" thick, and place on a dehydrator sheet. Dehydrate at 145°F for 2–3 hours and then 115°F for 1–2 hours, or until desired moisture is obtained.

# TOMATO BASIL FLAX CRACKERS

2 C flax seeds, soaked
2 medium tomatoes
¼ C basil, chopped
1 T Celtic salt
½ T black pepper, ground

Blend all ingredients in food processor. Spread evenly on Teflex sheets. Be sure that they aren't too thick or too thin. Dehydrate at 145°F for 2–3 hours, then turn over, remove Teflex, and continue dehydrating for 6–8 hours at 115°F, or until desired moisture is obtained.

# Tomato Spice Crackers

2 C sun-dried tomatoes, soaked
1½ C flax, powdered
1 C almonds, soaked
¼ C olive oil
2 T Celtic salt
1 T cumin
1 t cayenne pepper

Combine almonds, tomato soak water, olive oil, salt, cayenne, and cumin in high-power blender. Mix thoroughly and transfer to bowl. Cut tomatoes into dime-size pieces and stir into mixture. Next, stir in flax meal slowly. Scoop about 1 cup of mixture onto Teflex on each of 3 to 4 dehydrator trays and spread out to all corners evenly. Score cracker mixture using a spatula. Dehydrate at 145°F for 2–3 hours, then turn over, remove Teflex, and continue dehydrating for 6–8 hours at 115°F, or until desired moisture is obtained. Store in the refrigerator and consume within two weeks.

# Bread

# APPLE CINNAMON BREAD

2 C golden flax seeds, ground
1 C almonds, soaked
½ C raisins, soaked
1 C apple, blended
1 apple, grated
2 t cinnamon
½ Celtic salt
½ vanilla bean

Grind flax seeds in a coffee grinder or a blender (do not grind the flax seeds until they are superfine; the thicker the mixture, the better the bread). Process almonds in a food processor with the "S" blade until meal-like. Process raisins, apple, and vanilla bean in a blender until smooth; add some of the raisin soak water to blend. Combine all the ingredients in a mixing bowl; add cinnamon, salt, and mix well. Form into two loaves approximately 4"× 8"× 1" and slice into ¼" pieces. Dehydrate at 145°F for 2–3 hours and then 115°F for 2 hours, or until desired moisture is obtained.

# APRICOT BREAD

———————— 🍎 ————————

2 C golden flax seeds, ground
1 C almonds, soaked
½ C dried apricots, soaked
1 T orange zest
1½ t cinnamon
1 t Celtic salt
½ vanilla bean

Grind flax seeds in a coffee grinder or a blender (do not grind the flax seeds until they are superfine; the thicker the mixture, the better the bread). Process almonds in a food processor with the "S" blade until meal-like. Process apricots and vanilla bean in a blender until smooth; add some of the almond soak water to blend. Combine all the ingredients in a mixing bowl; add orange zest, cinnamon, salt, and mix well. Form into two loaves approximately 4" x 8" x 1" and slice into ¼" pieces. Dehydrate at 145°F for 2–3 hours and then 115°F for 2 hours, or until desired moisture is obtained.

# BUTTERNUT CHALLAH

1 C butternut squash

½ C almond flour*

½ C Brazil nuts

¾ C ground flax seeds

1 T Tree of Life mesquite
pod meal

1 T cinnamon

1 t Celtic sea salt

3 grains buckwheat, soaked**

\* To make almond flour, blend 2½ C soaked almonds with 2 cups of water in a blender. Strain the mixture through a fine-mesh straining bag. Use the liquid as almond mylk. Dehydrate the almond pulp on a Teflex sheet at 145° for 2–3 hours, or until dry.

\*\* For a bread to be considered a traditional Challah it must contain a grain. We have added three grains of buckwheat to meet the criteria.

Process almond flour, Brazil nuts, and squash individually with the "S" blade of a food processor. Hand-mix processed ingredients with spices and salt until thoroughly mixed. Add ground flax seed and mix well by hand until mixture is sticky. Form into two loaves and dehydrate at 145°F for 2–3 hours and then 115°F for 2 hours, or until desired moisture is obtained. Or separate dough into three equally sized balls. Roll into three strands, pinching them together at the top to hold. Braid the three strands until the end and then stick the ends under the bread and pinch together. Place on a dehydrator sheet and dehydrate for 2–3 hours at 145° until the bread is a little crusty on the outside.

# CAROB HAZELNUT BISCOTTI

3 cups hazelnut flour*

1½–2 C nut mylk or water

½ C raisins, soaked

3 T golden flax seed, powdered

⅓ C raw carob powder

2 t cinnamon

1 t Celtic salt

---

* To make hazelnut flour, blend 2½ C soaked hazelnuts with 2 cups of water in a blender. Strain the mixture through a fine mesh bag. Use the liquid for nut mylk. Dehydrate the hazelnut pulp on a Teflex sheet at 145°F for 2–3 hours, or until dry.

Combine hazelnut flour, ground flax seeds, cinnamon, and salt in a large mixing bowl. Add 1 C liquid and remaining ingredients and hand-mix before adding additional liquid. The liquid amount will vary depending on the dryness of the nut pulp. The flax can take a little time to fully absorb the liquid. The mixture is ready when it all holds together easily in one ball without crumbling. Form mixture on a dehydrator tray with a Teflex sheet or parchment paper into a loaf approximately 4" × 10" × 1". Dehydrate at 145°F for half an hour in the form of a loaf before cutting into slices about ½" thick. Lay slices flat on dehydrator sheet with mesh screen only and dehydrate at 145°F for 2–3 hours and then 115°F for 2 hours, or until desired moisture is obtained.

*Notes:*

This is very crisp and crunchy biscotti, which goes well with a glass of the mylk created with the nut pulp used in this recipe.

# CARROT BREAD

———————— 🍎 ————————

3 C carrot pulp
½–1 C raisins, soaked and pureed
1 vanilla bean
1 t spice of your choice: nutmeg,
    pumpkin pie spice, or
    cinnamon
Pinch of Celtic salt
¼ C golden flax seeds, ground

In a mixing bowl, mix all ingredients by hand until they form a dough-like consistency. If the mixture is too sticky, add more flax. If it is too dry, add a bit of water or coconut water. Form into a small loaf. Using a serrated knife, slice into toast-size pieces. Place on dehydrator trays and dehydrate at 145°F for 2–3 hours and then 115°F for 2 hours, or until desired moisture is obtained. The slices should still be a bit soft and bread-like when removed. Store in refrigerator. These are delicious topped with a coconut icing.

# Carrot Dill Bread

2 C golden flax seeds, ground
1 C almonds, soaked
1½ C carrot, finely grated
1 C apple, grated
1 T dill
1 T Celtic salt

Grind flax seeds in a coffee grinder or a blender (do not grind the flax seeds until they are superfine; the thicker the mixture, the better the bread). Process almonds in a food processor with the "S" blade until meal-like. Process carrot and apple in a blender until smooth; add some of the almond soak water to blend. Combine all the ingredients in a mixing bowl; add dill, salt, and mix well. Form into two loaves approximately 4" × 8" × 1" and slice into ¼" pieces. Dehydrate at 145°F for 2–3 hours and then 115°F for 2 hours, or until desired moisture is obtained.

# Carrot Nut Bread

2 C golden flax seeds, ground
1 C almonds, soaked
1½ C carrot, finely shredded
½ C raisins, soaked
1 t cinnamon
¼ t cardamom
¼ t nutmeg
1 t Celtic salt

Grind flax seeds in a coffee grinder or a blender (do not grind the flax seeds until they are superfine; the thicker the mixture, the better the bread). Process almonds in a food processor with the "S" blade until meal-like. Process raisins and carrot in a blender until smooth; add some of the raisin soak water to blend. Combine all the ingredients in a mixing bowl; add spices, salt, and mix well. Form into two loaves approximately 4" × 8" × 1" and slice into ¼" pieces. Dehydrate at 145°F for 2–3 hours and then 115°F for 2 hours, or until desired moisture is obtained.

# Chapati

1 C buckwheat, sprouted and
   dehydrated
2 C sesame seeds
⅔ C golden flax seeds
¼ C lemon juice
1 C carrot-celery juice
1 T cumin
2 t hing
2 t Celtic salt

Process the buckwheat, flax, and sesame in a blender until flour consistency. In a large mixing bowl, combine the flour with the cumin, hing, and Celtic salt. Slowly add the lemon juice and carrot-celery juice, adding only enough to create coherent but pliant dough. Place a large ball of dough on a Teflex sheet, lay another Teflex sheet on top of the dough, and use a rolling pin to create a ¼"-thick circle. Remove the top sheet. Use a cookie cutter or wide-mouthed jar lid to create circular pieces of dough and dehydrate on a mesh sheet for 1–2 hours at 145°F. Chapati should still be pliant, not crunchy or doughy. Serve with Indian curry dishes.

# CRANBERRY BREAD

2 C golden flax seeds, ground
1 C almonds, soaked
¾ C fresh cranberries
¼ C grapefruit juice
1 T orange zest
1½ t cinnamon
1 t Celtic salt
½ vanilla bean

Grind flax seeds in a coffee grinder or a blender (do not grind the flax seeds until they are superfine; the thicker the mixture, the better the bread). Process almonds in a food processor with the "S" blade until meal-like. Process cranberries, juice, orange zest, and vanilla bean in a blender until smooth; add some of the almond soak water to blend. Combine all the ingredients in a mixing bowl; add cinnamon, salt, and mix well. Form into two loaves approximately 4" × 8" × 1" and slice into ¼" pieces. Dehydrate at 145°F for 2–3 hours and then 115°F for 2 hours, or until desired moisture is obtained.

# CRANBERRY CAROB CHALLAH

1½ C butternut squash, peeled, seeded, chopped, and firmly packed

½ C raisins, soaked

1 C fresh cranberries

3 t cinnamon

1 t allspice

½ t nutmeg

¼ t cloves

1 t vanilla, optional

2 C almonds, soaked

2 t raw carob powder

1¾ C buckwheat, soaked, sprouted, dehydrated, and ground into flour

½ C golden flax seeds, ground

1½ t Celtic salt

¼ C additional buckwheat flour, for rolling and shaping

*Optional:*

1 C almonds, ground

1–2 T raw carob powder

Process butternut squash in a food processor with the "S" blade until finely ground. Add raisins and cranberries and process until well mixed. Add cinnamon, allspice, cloves, nutmeg, vanilla, and almonds and process until smooth. Add the carob to synergistically transform the spices (the carob mellows them). Process again until mixed well. Combine in a large mixing bowl and slowly add the ground buckwheat flour into the mixture, turning the bowl to aid the process until all the flour is incorporated in the dough. Add ground flax seeds and salt and mix until the dough comes together and begins to hold a ball shape. Turn dough onto a surface lightly dusted with buckwheat flour. Knead the dough until it has a bread-like consistency. Form dough into desired shape: round for desserts and biscotti or braided for challah. The dough can be rolled in ground almonds and raw carob powder for a different flavor. Place on a dehydrator tray and dehydrate at 145°F for 2–3 hours.

# Foccacia

2 C golden flax seeds, ground
1 C almonds, soaked
1 C apple, grated
  1 large tomato
2 T olive oil
2 T fresh basil, finely chopped
1 T Celtic salt

Grind flax seeds in a coffee grinder or a blender (do not grind the flax seeds until they are superfine; the thicker the mixture, the better the bread). Process almonds in a food processor with the "S" blade until meal-like. Process apple, tomato, and olive oil in a blender until smooth; add some of the almond soak water to blend. Combine all the ingredients in a mixing bowl; add basil, salt, and mix well. Form into two loaves approximately 4"× 8"× 1" and slice into ¼" pieces. Dehydrate at 145°F for 2–3 hours and then 115°F for 2 hours, or until desired moisture is obtained.

# Herb Seed Bread

1¼ C golden flax seeds, ground
1 C pecans, soaked
1 C apple, grated
½ C coconut water
1 T poppy seeds
1 T thyme
2 t rosemary
2 t sage
1 t Celtic salt

Grind flax seeds in a coffee grinder or a blender (do not grind the flax seeds until they are superfine; the thicker the mixture, the better the bread). Process pecans in a food processor with the "S" blade until meal-like. Combine all the ingredients in a mixing bowl; add remaining ingredients and mix well. Form into two loaves approximately 4" × 8" × 1" and slice into ¼" pieces. Dehydrate at 145°F for 2–3 hours and then 115°F for 2 hours, or until desired moisture is obtained.

# INDIAN FLAT BREAD

1 cauliflower

1 carrot

2 C golden flax seeds

1 C sunflower seeds, soaked

1½ C water

2 t turmeric

1 t cinnamon

1 t Celtic salt

Process cauliflower and carrot through a Champion Juicer with the solid plate; combine with remaining ingredients and mix well. Spread mixture onto dehydrator sheet with either a Teflex sheet or parchment paper. Spread thinly to cover, but leave no spots uncovered or they will tear later. Dehydrate at 145°F for 1 hour. Flip over onto mesh sheet and dehydrate the other side for approximately 2 more hours.

# INDIAN FLAT BREAD #2

2 C carrot pulp

1 C flax seeds, ground

1 C coconut pulp

1½ C water

½ C sunflower seeds, soaked

1 T curry

1 t Celtic salt

*Optional:*
Add sesame seeds.

Process all ingredients in a blender until smooth. Spread dough approximately ¼" thick on a dehydrator tray with a Teflex sheet. Dehydrate at 145°F for 1–2 hours, turn the dough over and remove Teflex sheet, and continue dehydrating at 115°F for 2–4 hours, or until desired moisture is obtained.

# ITALIAN BREAD

2 C golden flax seeds, ground
1 C pecans, soaked
1 C apple, grated
½ C coconut water
1 T Italian seasoning
1 t Celtic salt

Grind flax seeds in a coffee grinder or a blender (do not grind the flax seeds until they are superfine; the thicker the mixture, the better the bread). Process pecans and apple in a food processor with the "S" blade until meal-like. Combine in a mixing bowl; add remaining ingredients and mix well. Form into two loaves approximately 4" × 8" × 1" and slice into ¼" pieces. Dehydrate at 145°F for 2–3 hours and then 115°F for 2 hours, or until desired moisture is obtained.

# PUMPKIN BREAD

2 C golden flax seeds, ground
1 C pecans, soaked
1 C fresh pumpkin
1 C apple, grated
½ C coconut water
1 T orange zest
2 t cinnamon
1 t Celtic salt

Grind flax seeds in a coffee grinder or a blender (do not grind the flax seeds until they are superfine; the thicker the mixture, the better the bread). Process pecans in a food processor with the "S" blade until meal-like. Process pumpkin in a blender with coconut water until smooth. Combine in a mixing bowl; add remaining ingredients and mix well. Form into two loaves approximately 4" × 8" × 1" and slice into ¼" pieces. Dehydrate at 145°F for 2–3 hours and then 115°F for 2 hours, or until desired moisture is obtained.

# Pumpkin Seed Bread

2 C golden flax seeds, ground
1½ C pumpkin seeds, soaked
¼ C grapefruit juice
1 t cinnamon
1 t ginger juice
½ t allspice

Process all ingredients except flax seeds in a food processor with the "S" blade. Place dough into a large mixing bowl and knead the ground flax seeds into the dough. Form into two loaves and slice into ¼" pieces. Dehydrate at 145°F for 2–3 hours and then 115°F for 2 hours, or until desired moisture is obtained.

# Sun-Dried Tomato Bread

2 C golden flax seeds, ground
1 C pecans, soaked
1 C apple, grated
½ C coconut water
½ C sun-dried tomato, soaked
1 T basil
1 T oregano
1 T Celtic salt

Grind flax seeds in a coffee grinder or a blender (do not grind the flax seeds until they are superfine; the thicker the mixture, the better the bread). Process pecans in a food processor with the "S" blade until meal-like. Process sun-dried tomatoes in a blender with soak water until smooth. Combine all the ingredients in a mixing bowl; add remaining ingredients and mix well. Form into two loaves approximately 4"× 8"× 1" and slice into ¼" pieces. Dehydrate at 145°F for 2–3 hours and then 115°F for 2 hours, or until desired moisture is obtained.

# SACRED CHALLAH

2 C almond flour *

1½ C coconut water, or raisin
    soak water

¾ C golden flax seeds, ground

½ C raisins, soaked

2 t cinnamon

1½ t Celtic salt

1 t nutmeg or pumpkin spice

3 grains buckwheat, soaked **

½ C flax seeds, ground for cutting
    board

*Optional:*

1 apple, shredded

½ C almonds or pecans, soaked
    and finely chopped, to add
    texture and crunch

⅓ C Turkish apricots, soaked and
    chopped or

⅓ C raisins, soaked

  * To make almond flour, blend 2½ C
    soaked almonds with 2 cups of water
    in a blender. Strain the mixture
    through a fine mesh bag. Use the
    liquid as almond mylk. Dehydrate
    the almond pulp on a Teflex sheet at
    90° for 8–10 hours, or until
    completely dry.

** For a bread to be considered a tradi-
    tional Challah it must contain a
    grain. We have added three grains of
    buckwheat to meet the criteria.

Process raisins and apricots in a food processor with the "S" blade; transfer to a large mixing bowl and mix in cinnamon, salt, and nutmeg. Slowly add the flax meal, almond flour, buckwheat grains, and water. Add additional flax meal if consistency is not doughy. Form into two loaves and dehydrate at 145°F for 2–3 hours and then 115°F for 2 hours, or until desired moisture is obtained. Or separate dough into three equally sized balls. Roll into three strands and pinch them together at the top to hold. Braid the three strands until the end and then stick the ends under the bread and pinch together. Place on a dehydrator sheet and dehydrate for 2-3 hours at 145° until the bread is a little crusty on the outside.

*Optional:*
Glaze the outside of the bread with a few drops of olive oil before dehydrating. Or when bread is done, use a coconut cream icing.

# SWEET SACRED CHALLAH

———————— 🍎 ————————

2 C golden flax seeds, ground
¾ C pecans, soaked
½ C sesame seeds, soaked
½ C figs, soaked
1 t Celtic salt
½ t allspice
½ t cinnamon
½ t cardamom
½ t nutmeg
3 grains buckwheat, soaked*

\* For a bread to be considered a traditional Challah it must contain a grain. We have added 3 grains of buckwheat to meet the criteria.

Grind flax seeds in a coffee grinder or a blender (do not grind the flax seeds until they are superfine; the thicker the mixture, the better the bread). Process pecans in a food processor with the "S" blade until meal-like. Process figs in a blender with soak water until smooth. Combine all the ingredients in a mixing bowl; add remaining ingredients and mix well. Form into two loaves and dehydrate at 145°F for 2–3 hours and then 115°F for 2 hours, or until desired moisture is obtained. Or separate dough into three equally sized balls. Roll into three strands and pinch them together at the top to hold. Braid the three strands until the end and then stick the ends under the bread and pinch together. Place on a dehydrator sheet and dehydrate for 2–3 hours at 145°F until the bread is a little crusty on the outside.

*Optional:*
Using a pastry brush, brush the outside of the bread with olive oil or coconut oil.

# TORTILLAS

1 C golden flax seeds, soaked
½ ripe avocado
Celtic salt to taste
Water for consistency

*Variations:*
Add different spices and vegetable pulp for a completely different taste.

Blend ingredients in Vita-Mix or blender, adding water to create a smooth batter. Spread ½ C batter evenly on Teflex sheets—to a thickness of about ¼" and 6" in diameter. The thinner your batter, the less time it will take to dehydrate. Dehydrate at 95° for 2–3 hours, flip the tortillas over and remove the Teflex sheet, and continue dehydrating 2–3 hours more until the tortillas are soft and flexible. Remove the tortillas from the dehydrator before they are crisp. Makes ten 6" tortillas.

Tired of salads? How about a burrito! If you are looking for a crowd-pleasing meal, this is the one! For best results, dehydrate *Tortillas* the night before you plan to use them—fill with salads, *Guacamole!, Salsa Fresca,* and *Sour Cream.* See *Mexican Burritos.*

# Zucchini Bread

2 C pecans, soaked
½ C raisins, soaked
1 C zucchini
1¼ C golden flax seeds, ground
2 t cinnamon
1 t Celtic salt
½ vanilla bean

Process raisins, zucchini, and vanilla bean in a blender until smooth; add some of the raisin soak water to blend. Process pecans in a food processor with the "S" blade until meal-like. Grind flax seeds in a coffee grinder or a blender. Combine all the ingredients in a mixing bowl; add cinnamon and salt and mix well. Form into two loaves and slice into ¼" pieces. Dehydrate at 145°F for 2–3 hours and then 115°F for 2 hours, or until desired moisture is obtained.

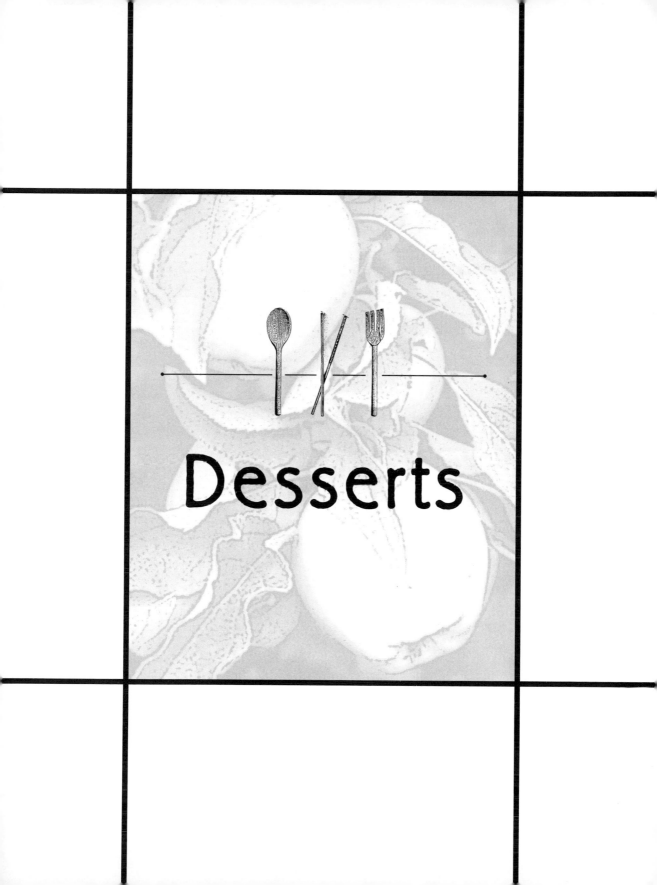

# Desserts

# Apple Spice Bars

2 C apples, finely chopped
3 C coconut pulp, blended
¼ C raw tahini
2 T almond butter
2 t cinnamon
1 t allspice
1 t nutmeg

Combine all ingredients in a mixing bowl and mix well. Form into bars and roll in finely chopped pecans or pine nuts. Refrigerate until cold and serve.

# "Baked" Apples

6 apples
2 C raisins
1 T cinnamon
2 t ground cloves
2 C water

Cut apples in half and hollow out seeds. Dehydrate at 145°F for 2 hours. In blender, mix all remaining ingredients and soak dried apples in mixture for ½ hour. Place apples back in the dehydrator after soaking and spoon the raisin mixture into the hollowed-out halves. Dehydrate an additional 4 hours and serve warm.

# Blueberry Cream Pie

CRUST:

2 C pecans, soaked
½ C raisins, soaked
1 T cinnamon

Process all ingredients in a food processor with the "S" blade until they form a ball. Form crust in a 9" glass pie pan and dehydrate for 1–2 hours at 145°F.

FILLING:

2 C blueberries
1½ C coconut pulp
2 T coconut butter
½ t cinnamon

Process all ingredients in a blender until smooth. Pour filling into pie pan and chill for one hour before serving. Garnish with blueberries and cinnamon. Serves 6–8.

# Bliss Balls

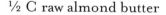

½ C raw almond butter
½ C raw tahini
¼ C pine nuts or hemp seeds, unsoaked
¼ C raw carob powder
1 t vanilla extract or 1 soaked vanilla bean
½ t cinnamon
½ t nutmeg
¼ t fresh ground ginger

Combine all ingredients in a large mixing bowl. Form into balls and roll in carob powder or hemp seeds.

# CAROB CREAM ÉCLAIRS

### ÉCLAIR SHELLS:

1¾ C butternut squash

Pulp of 4 coconuts

1 avocado

1½ t cinnamon

1 t Celtic salt

1 t nutmeg

2½ C golden flax seeds, ground

Process all ingredients, except flax, in a food processor with the "S" blade until smooth. Place in a large bowl and mix in ground flax seeds. Roll into small balls and flatten into small round patties 3" in diameter and ¼" thick. Place on a dehydrator sheet with a Teflex sheet and dehydrate at 145°F for 1–2 hours, or until desired moisture is obtained.

### COCONUT CREAM FILLING:

2 C coconut pulp

½ C coconut butter

½–¾ C coconut water

¼ C raw carob powder

1 vanilla bean

1 t cinnamon

½ t allspice

Blend all ingredients in a blender until thick and smooth. Adjust consistency with coconut water. Refrigerate for 2 hours. Fold éclair shells in half and fill with 1 T of coconut cream filling.

# CAROB CRÈME PIE

### CRUST:

2 C pecans, soaked
½ C raisins, soaked

Process pecans and raisins in a food processor with the "S" blade until the ingredients form a ball. Press mixture into a 9" glass pie plate and place in a dehydrator for 1 hour at 145°F.

### FILLING:

3 C coconut pulp
½ C coconut water
6 T raw carob powder
2 T coconut butter
¼ t Celtic salt

Process all ingredients in a blender until smooth. Pour into pie plate and chill before serving.

# CAROB COOKIES

1 C almonds, soaked
1 C coconut pulp, blended
1 C apple, grated
2 T golden flax seeds, ground
1½ T raw carob powder
1 t cinnamon
¼ t Celtic salt
½ vanilla bean

Process almonds in a Champion Juicer with the solid plate; combine remaining ingredients in a mixing bowl. Form dough into 1" cookies and place on a dehydrator tray. Dehydrate at 145° for 2–3 hours or until desired moisture is obtained. The cookies should still be moist.

# CAROB FUDGE

1 C raw carob powder
½ C almonds, chopped and
   soaked
½ C coconut oil
½ t vanilla
   2 dried apricots, soaked

Blend in food processor with "S" blade. Spread batter ½" thick in 4" × 7" glass pan. Refrigerate until coconut butter sets the batter into a fudge-like consistency. Cut into 20 squares.

# CAROB MINT FLAT BARS

1 C almonds, soaked
1 C raw carob powder
½ C pine nuts
½ C coconut water
¼ C chia seeds
1 T vanilla
   4 drops mint essential oil

*Optional:*
   1 t fresh ginger, grated

Process almonds and pine nuts in a food processor with the "S" blade, then add remaining ingredients and mix well. Spread thin on a dehydrator tray with a Teflex sheet and score the mixture into bars. Dehydrate for 2–3 hours at 145°F and then 115°F for 3–4 hours.

# CARROT CAKE

Take a 6" cheezecake pan
(collapsible) and line it with plastic
wrap; set aside.

### FIRST LAYER:

3 C walnuts, soaked
1 C raisins, soaked
1 vanilla bean
1 t cardamom or garam masala
1 t Tree of Life mesquite
    pod meal
Pinch of salt
Coconut water, if needed

Blend ingredients, making sure that
the consistency is like thick oatmeal,
not as thick as dough. It should not
stick to a spoon if turned upside
down. Press half of this mixture into
the bottom of the cheezecake pan.

### MIDDLE LAYERS:

3 C carrot pulp
2 C diced apple

Press the carrot pulp in firmly as the
next layer. Next, the diced apples.
Then the rest of the nut mixture. It
should fill the entire pan. Press
everything down firmly.

### BOTTOM LAYER (OPTIONAL):

Any pie crust recipe

You may then add the last layer,
which is actually the bottom of the
cake. Press firmly in. This layer is
not necessary.

Fold remaining plastic wrap over the cake and chill overnight or for at least 4 hours. Place plate on top, flip, and release cake, which should stand nicely on its own. Frost with your favorite coconut icing and garnish.

# Carrot Pudding

1 C carrot pulp
1 C coconut pulp
1 vanilla bean
1 t spice of choice: cardamom, cinnamon, anise, nutmeg, or pumpkin pie spice

Blend until creamy and chill.

# Carrot Truffles

2 C carrot pulp
1 C carob
½ C raisins, soaked
1 t pumpkin pie spice or Tree of Life mesquite pod meal

Combine ingredients. Roll into balls and chill. Or, you can dehydrate them. You may wish to add a dollop of your favorite coconut icing.

# CHAI SPICE WAFERS

2 C almond pulp (the leftovers
from almond mylk)
1 C hulled sesame seeds, soaked
1½ C coconut water
1 vanilla bean, soaked
overnight
1 T chai spice (see Resources
Directory)

Process all ingredients in a blender
until smooth. Spread the mixture
about ⅛" thick on a dehydrator tray
with a Teflex sheet. Dehydrate at
145°F for 2–3 hours and then
115°F for 2–3 hours, or until
desired moisture is obtained. They
should be crispy.

# CHERRY TRUFFLES

4 C coconut pulp
4 C almonds, soaked
7 Bing cherries, pitted
½ t cinnamon
½ vanilla bean, soaked

2 C Bing cherries, pitted

Process coconut pulp, 7 cherries,
almonds, cinnamon, and vanilla
bean in a food processor with the
"S" blade until mixture is smooth
and forms a large ball. Form into
round balls approximately 1½" in
diameter and place a cherry in the
center of each truffle. Place on a
dehydrator tray and dehydrate at
105° for 30 minutes. Makes
approximately 20–30 truffles.

# "CHOCOLATE PEANUT BUTTER" PIE

### CRUST:

2 C pecans, soaked

½ C raisins, soaked

2 T Tree of Life mesquite pod meal

2 T raw carob powder

2 t cinnamon

1 t nutmeg

Process all ingredients in a food processor with the "S" blade until a dough-like consistency is obtained. Press into a 9" glass pie pan and refrigerate for 1 hour.

### FILLING, LAYER 1: SWEET "PEANUT" BUTTER

1 C raw almond butter

⅓ C water

½ C raisins, soaked

2 t Celtic salt

Process all ingredients in a blender including the soak water until creamy. Spread mixture into pie pan.

### FILLING, LAYER 2: CHOCOLATESQUE SAUCE

1 C raw carob powder

4 black olives

1 C water

½ C olive oil

½ C raisins, soaked

1 T Tree of Life mesquite pod meal

1 t spirulina

½ t Celtic salt

Process all ingredients in a blender including the soak water until creamy. Pour sauce over peanut butter. Retain ½ cup.

### FILLING, LAYER 3: COCONUT CREAM

2 C coconut pulp
1 C coconut water
¼ C raisins, soaked
1 T Tree of Life mesquite
  pod meal
1 t Celtic salt

Process all ingredients in a blender including the soak water until creamy. Pour 2 C of coconut cream over the *Chocolatesque Sauce*.

Pour ½ C *Chocolatesque Sauce* into the center of the pie in a circular shape. Using a chopstick, slowly swirl the sauce into a spiral shape. Dust with carob powder and refrigerate for 1 hour before serving.

# CINNAMON RAISIN BISCOTTI

3 C almond flour*
½ C raisins, soaked
1–1½ C almond mylk, coconut
  water, or water
3 T golden flax seeds, ground
2 t cinnamon
1 t Celtic salt

* To make almond flour, blend 2½ C soaked almonds with 2 cups of water in a blender. Strain the mixture through a fine-mesh straining bag. Use the liquid for almond mylk. Dehydrate the almond pulp on a Teflex sheet at 145° for 2–3 hours, or until dry.

Combine almond flour, ground flax seeds, cinnamon, and salt in a large mixing bowl. Add 1 C liquid and remaining ingredients and hand-mix before adding additional liquid. The liquid amount will vary depending on the dryness of the nut pulp. The flax can take a little time to fully absorb the liquid. The mixture is ready when it all will hold together easily in one ball without crumbling. Form mixture on a dehydrator tray with a Teflex sheet or parchment paper into a loaf approximately 4" × 10" × 1". Dehydrate at 145° for ½ hour in the form of a loaf before cutting into slices about ½" thick. Lay slices flat on dehydrator sheet with mesh screen only and dehydrate at 145°F for 2–3 hours and then 115°F for 2 hours, or until desired moisture is obtained.

*Notes:*
This is a very crisp and crunchy biscotti that goes well with a glass of the mylk created for the nut pulp used in this recipe.

# CINNAMON ROLLS

## DOUGH:

½ C almond flour

1 C powdered flax seeds

1 C fresh young coconut pulp

1 fresh vanilla pod, soaked 8 hours

1 C fresh young coconut water

Blend ingredients in food processor with the "S" blade, adding coconut water until achieving the consistency of dough. Sprinkle an additional ½ cup powdered flax seeds on a cutting board. Press dough out by hand into a square.

FILLING:

2 C coconut pulp or *Coconut Dream Cream*

1 T cinnamon

1 t nutmeg or 3 drops nutmeg oil

\* To make almond flour, blend 2½ C soaked almonds with 2 cups of water in a blender. Strain the mixture through a fine-mesh straining bag. Use the liquid for almond mylk. Dehydrate the almond pulp on a Teflex sheet at 145° for 2–3 hours, or until dry.

Blend ingredients in food processor with the "S" blade, or for extra creaminess blend in a high-power blender. Spread the cream completely over the dough. If you are on Phase II, you may wish to sprinkle finely chopped strawberries or goji berries on top of the cream layer. Roll dough and cut into 1" pieces. Dehydrate at 110° for 5 hours. Comfort food is here!

# Coconut Apple Pie

1 C almonds

3 T raisins

1 C apple, shredded

1 C coconut pulp

¼ C coconut water

2 T coconut butter

1 T Tree of Life mesquite pod meal

1 t Celtic salt

Homogenize almonds and raisins and press into pie plate. Shred apple and sprinkle over almond crust. Blend coconut pulp, coconut water, coconut butter, mesquite, and salt and pour over shredded apple. Chill for 1 hour and serve.

# COCONUT CREAM PIE

CRUST:

1 C almonds, soaked

2 T raisins, soaked (Phase II only)

1 T Tree of Life mesquite pod meal

½ T Celtic salt

Homogenize ingredients in a food processor or high-power juicer to make crust. Press crust firmly into pie plate.

FILLING:

2 C coconut pulp

4 T coconut water

1 T coconut butter

Blend in a high-power blender coconut pulp, butter, and water, adding coconut water until achieving desired consistency. Pour the cream into the crust. Chill for 1 hour and serve with fresh berries.

# Heavenly Dream Cake

### Coconut Cream Filling:

2 C coconut pulp
1½ C coconut water
1 C macadamia nuts, unsoaked
¾ vanilla bean
1 t Celtic sea salt
2 T Tree of Life mesquite
    pod meal
½ C raisins, soaked
⅛ C raisin soak water
½ t allspice
1 t cinnamon
½ t stevia

Put all above ingredients in a food processor with "S" blade and blend well.

### Granola Cream:

1 C almonds, soaked
½ C sunflower seeds, soaked
½ T Tree of Life mesquite
    pod meal
½ T cinnamon
1 C coconut pulp
1 t Celtic sea salt
¼ vanilla bean

Put almonds in a food processor with "S" blade and process until small almond chunks are formed. Put in bowl and add whole sunflower seeds. Blend remaining ingredients and mix with almond/sunflower mixture. Combine coconut cream with granola cream and mix well.

## CAROB CAKE LAYERS:

2 C macadamia nuts, unsoaked

1 C almonds, soaked

1½ C coconut butter

½ C pine nuts

2 C coconut pulp

½ vanilla bean

Put above ingredients in a food processor with "S" blade and blend well. Add the following ingredients and blend again:

2 C raw carob powder

2 T Tree of Life mesquite
   pod meal

1 C fresh raspberries

½ t cinnamon

½ t Celtic salt

Spread a portion of the carob mixture onto a Teflex sheet on a dehydrator tray. Spread the mixture to 9" diameter and approximately ¾" thick.

Place a 9" springform pan over the mixture and press down. Scrape away excess mixture around the outer edges of the pan. Lift off springform pan. You will have a perfect circular carob cake layer. Repeat for an additional two trays.

Dehydrate for 2 hours at 145°F and then 115°F for 10 hours. Flip layers at 5 hours. When complete let cool. Refrigerate for a few hours; do not stack cake layers.

## LAYERING:

Put one carob cake layer on plate. Spread a ½" layer of coconut cream filling on top. Place second cake layer on top of coconut filling. Spread coconut filling over cake and repeat for third layer of carob cake. Spread filling around edges of cake. Refrigerate for at least 2 hours.

Makes one 9" layer cake.

# KEY LIME PIE

CRUST:

2 C pecans, soaked
½ t nutmeg
¼ t fresh ground black pepper
¼ t Celtic salt

Process all ingredients in a food processor with the "S" blade until the mixture becomes sticky and forms a ball. Press into pie plate and chill while making the filling.

FILLING:

½ avocado
½ C coconut water
Pulp of 1 coconut
4 T lemon juice
4 T lime juice
½–1 vanilla bean
½ t Celtic salt
¼ t stevia
1 t psyllium

In a blender, process all ingredients except psyllium until smooth and creamy. Add psyllium and mix well. Pour filling into crust and chill.

# PISTACHIO PLEASURE

2 C coconut pulp
1½ C coconut water
1 small avocado
½ C raw pistachios, unsoaked
½ C raisins, soaked
½ vanilla bean
1 t Celtic salt

Process all ingredients in a blender until smooth and creamy. For a mousse-like texture, refrigerate for at least 1 hour before serving.

# PUMPKIN PIE

### FILLING:

1 medium pumpkin, peeled (try the Japanese squash variety)

1½ C pine nuts

¾ C coconut water or water

1 T coconut butter

3 t cinnamon

1 t nutmeg

2 T pumpkin pie spice

4 dried apricots, soaked

Blend pumpkin in a food processor with the "S" blade until relatively smooth. Place in a glass bowl with coconut water or water. Place bowl in dehydrator for 5 hours at 140°. Make sure that the water does not dry up. The pumpkin should always be covered by water. (The water stops the food temperature from increasing to the point of enzyme destruction.) Remove from dehydrator, and blend in a high-power blender. (Only a high-power blender will make it very creamy.) Blend in remaining ingredients.

### CRUST:

2 C flax, powdered

½ C hemp seeds

½ C *Almond Mylk*

2 T coconut butter, melted

1 t Celtic salt

Mix by hand flax, hemp seed, salt, and coconut butter until you achieve the consistency of coarse corn meal. Add *Almond Mylk* or coconut water and mix. Press into glass 10" pie plate.

Pour filling into crust and serve warm or chilled.

# STRAWBERRY DREAM PIE

## CAROB CRUST:

1½ C almonds
1 C raw carob powder
3 T coconut butter
1 t Celtic sea salt
Coconut water to bind

In a food processor combine ingredients, adding coconut water until the mixture starts to form a ball. Press crust into pie plate, all the way to the top edge.

## FILLING:

2 pints strawberries
6–8 young coconuts, pulp
3 T coconut butter
1 vanilla bean
Pinch of Celtic salt
½ C coconut water

Place ingredients in a food processor and blend, adding coconut water until reaching a very smooth and creamy consistency. Pour into pie crust and chill overnight. Garnish with fresh lavender or other seasonal flowers and strawberry slices.

# TAHINI TRUFFLES

1 C raw tahini
½ C raw carob powder
Stevia to taste for sweetness

Form into balls and chill until served.

# Jams, "Sweet" Sauces, and "Sweet" Spreads

# Basic Nut Spread

1 C nut of choice, soaked
¾ C coconut water, or water
    for Phase I
2 vanilla beans

In a blender, process all ingredients until smooth and creamy.

*Variations:*
If you prefer chunky spread, reserve a portion of nuts. Process them with the "S" blade until chunky and add to the mixture. This spread can be easily transformed into a glaze, an icing, or even porridge by playing with variations of nuts, consistency, and spices. Hazelnuts with orange zest, pecans with pumpkin pie spices, or walnuts with cinnamon are some of the possible combinations.

# Butternut Marmalade

1 C butternut squash
2 C coconut water
¼ C orange zest

In a blender, mix all ingredients until smooth and creamy.

# CAROB GRAPEFRUIT SYRUP

2 grapefruits, peeled
3 apples, diced
2 stalks celery, diced
3 C coconut pulp
½ C coconut water
1 t raw carob powder

In a blender, process all ingredients until smooth. Serve with *Zucchini Pancakes.*

# "CHOCOLATE" SAUCE

½ C raw carob powder
½ C raisins, soaked
⅓ C olive oil
4 black olives
2 T aloe vera gel
1 t mesquite
1 t spirulina
½ t Celtic salt

In a blender, process all the ingredients until smooth.

# Coconut Butter Icing

Pulp of three young coconuts
1 vanilla bean
3 T coconut butter

Blend well in high-power blender until creamy. Chill until ready to use.

*Variations:*
For a sweeter frosting add raisin water or coconut water.
   Play with spices, mesquite powder, or rose or lavender essence.

# Coconut Cream Cheeze

3 C coconut pulp, or 1 C
   macadamia nuts, unsoaked
3 T lemon juice
½ t olive oil

In a blender, mix all ingredients until smooth and creamy.

# Coconut Cream Icing

3 C coconut pulp
¼ C flax oil
   1 t Celtic salt

In a blender, process all the ingredients until smooth and creamy. Store in the refrigerator; keeps for 4 days.

# Coconut Dream Cream

1 C macadamia nuts, unsoaked
2 C coconut pulp
1½ C coconut water
¼ vanilla bean
¼ t Celtic salt
1 T mesquite (Phase I.5) or
  1 t green stevia powder
  (Phase I)

Process all ingredients in a blender until smooth and creamy, adding more coconut water for consistency. Serving suggestion: Pour over sliced strawberries.

# Coconut Orange Sauce

3 C coconut pulp
2 carrots
1 orange
1½ C coconut water
1 T orange zest
½ t Celtic salt
½ t ginger
½ vanilla bean

Process all ingredients in a blender until smooth and creamy. Add more or less coconut pulp for thicker or thinner sauce.

# CRANBERRY SWEETHEART JAM

1 C fresh cranberries, dehydrated
2 C coconut pulp, or 2 C
    macadamia nuts, unsoaked
¼ C coconut water
2 fresh vanilla beans

Dehydrate cranberries at 115° for 2 hours until they are like puffs of air. In a blender, mix half the cranberries with the remaining ingredients. Transfer to a mixing bowl. Crumble the remaining cranberries by hand and sprinkle over jam. Stir and serve.

# I CAN'T BELIEVE IT'S NOT BUTTER!

½ C coconut butter
    Pulp of 4 coconuts
1½ lemons, peeled
½ C flax oil
1 t Celtic salt

Process all ingredients in a blender until thick and smooth.

# La Crème de la Crème

2 C coconut pulp, or 1 C
    macadamia nuts, unsoaked
2 C coconut water
2 fresh vanilla beans
½ t Celtic salt

In a blender, mix all ingredients
until smooth and creamy.

# Lemon Drop Cream

1 recipe of *La Crème de la Crème*
1 t lemon zest

In a blender, mix all ingredients
until smooth and creamy.

# Orange Dream Cream

1 recipe of *La Crème de la Crème*
¼ C carrots, butternut squash,
    or acorn squash
1 T orange zest

In a blender, mix all ingredients
until smooth and creamy.

# Pecan Nut Sauce

2 C pecans, soaked
1 C coconut water
½ C water
¼ t cinnamon
1 vanilla bean

Process all ingredients in a blender until smooth and thick.

# Rich Nut Frosting

Pulp of three young coconuts
1 C Brazil or macadamia nuts, unsoaked
3 T coconut butter
1 vanilla bean
Coconut water

Blend in high-power blender, adding coconut water for consistency. This is very rich, and makes an amazing cake frosting or filling.

# Simplicity Sauce

2 C nut or seed of choice, soaked
1 C coconut water

Process all ingredients in a blender until smooth and creamy.

# STRAWBERRY SAUCE

1 pint strawberries
Pulp of one young coconut
¼ C macadamia or Brazil nuts,
   unsoaked
1 vanilla bean

Blend.

# SWEET SIAM SAUCE

1 C coconut water
¾ C pecans, soaked
¼ C flax oil
¼ C raisins, soaked
1 T coconut butter
2 t lime leaf, minced
2 t Celtic salt

Process all ingredients in a blender
until smooth. Serves 2–4.

# Porridge
# and Breakfast
# Dishes

# Apple Cinnamon Porridge

3 C almonds, soaked
1 apple
1 T cinnamon
1 t Celtic salt

Process all ingredients in a blender until smooth and creamy. This porridge is great on a cold morning. It also goes well with some ginger added.

# Apple Spice Porridge

2½ C coconut water
2 C almonds, soaked
1 C coconut pulp
1 C apple, chopped
2 T raw carob powder
1 T cinnamon
1 t nutmeg

Process all ingredients in a blender until smooth and creamy. Serve with plum sauce. Serves 4–6.

# AUTUMN MORNING PORRIDGE

2 C butternut squash, peeled and
   cubed

1 C walnuts, soaked

1 C coconut water

2 vanilla beans

2 t cinnamon

2 t orange zest

Process all ingredients in a blender
until smooth and creamy.

# BUCKWHEATIES

2 C buckwheat groats, sprouted

Drain and rinse several times, place
on dehydrator tray with a Teflex
sheet, and dehydrate at 105° for
3–6 hours. Be sure to rinse the
buckwheat several times, otherwise it
very easily ferments.

# BUTTERY BUTTERNUT PORRIDGE

2 C butternut squash, peeled and
    chunked
Pulp of 3 coconuts, or 1 C
    macadamia nuts, unsoaked
¾ C coconut water, or water
    2 vanilla beans

Process all ingredients in a blender
until smooth and creamy.

# CINNAMON "TOASTED" PECAN

# BUCKWHEATIES

2 C *Buckwheaties*

CINNAMON TOASTED PECANS:
2 C pecans, soaked
1 T lemon juice
1 T cinnamon

Process pecans and lemon juice in a
food processor with the "S" blade
until chunky; toss pecans in cinnamon. Mix in *Buckwheaties* now or
wait until after nuts are dehydrated.
Place mixture (with or without
*Buckwheaties*) on a dehydrator tray
and dehydrate at 105° for 2–3
hours. If you haven't already, mix in
*Buckwheaties*. Serve with nut mylk.

# COCO MAC PORRIDGE

Pulp of 4 young coconuts
½ C macadamia nuts, unsoaked
½ vanilla bean
½ t Trec of Life mesquite
pod meal
Pinch of salt
Coconut water, if needed
(water for Phase I)

Blend and serve.

*Phase II variations:*
Add carob, pears, or other sweet fruit.

*Phase I variations:*
Add cardamom or strawberries, even pumpkin pie spice for a different flavor.

# CRANBERRY HAZELNUT PORRIDGE

2 C fresh cranberries
2 C coconut pulp
1 C hazelnuts, soaked
¾ C coconut water
1 vanilla beans

In a blender, process 1½ C coconut pulp with the coconut water and vanilla bean until smooth and creamy. Process hazelnuts, cranberries, and remaining coconut pulp in a food processor with the "S" blade until chunky. Combine in a mixing bowl and mix well.

# CREAMY COCONUT CUSTARD

Pulp of 4 coconuts
½–¾ C coconut water
I vanilla bean
¼ t cinnamon

Process all ingredients in a blender until smooth and creamy. Add more coconut water if needed. To be used as a thin custard with *Buckwheaties* or your favorite porridge.

# FIVE-LAYER BREAKFAST QUICHE

Prepare each portion of the quiche separately and layer just prior to serving.

### LAYER 1: PECAN CRUST

2 C pecans, soaked
¼ C grapefruit juice
½ t marjoram
¼ t sage
¼ t thyme

Process all ingredients in a food processor with the "S" blade until smooth. Press into 9-inch pie plate to form crust. Dehydrate at 145°F degrees for ¼ hour for a firmer crust.

## Layer 2: Sesame Seed Cream

1½ C sesame seeds, soaked
½ C grapefruit juice or lemon
1 clove garlic
1 T sesame oil
½ t Celtic salt

1 T parsley, finely chopped

Process all ingredients but parsley in a blender until smooth and creamy. Add parsley and mix well.

## Layer 3: Thinly Sliced Tomatoes

2 tomatoes, sliced

## Layer 4: Squash Scramble

½ small butternut squash
½ medium-size cauliflower
1 T olive oil
1 clove garlic
½ t Celtic salt
¼ t nutmeg
Pinch of fresh ground black pepper

Process all ingredients in a food processor with the "S" blade until mixture resembles a scrambled texture.

## Layer 5: Savory Pecan Topping

1 C pecans, soaked
2 T lemon juice
1 T olive oil
1 t Celtic salt
1 t cumin
¼ t fresh ground black pepper
¼ t hing
¼ t marjoram
¼ t oregano
¼ t sage
¼ t turmeric

Process all ingredients in a food processor with the "S" blade until crumbly. Spread on dehydrator tray with a Teflex sheet and dehydrate for 1 hour at 105°F.

Layer quiche in pie plate as numbered or any which way you please! Dehydrate completed pie for ¼ hour at 145°F for warm quiche—also wonderful served cold!

# Granola

1 C almonds, soaked
1 C coconut pulp
1 T Tree of Life mesquite
   pod meal
1 T pumpkin pie spice
1 t Celtic salt

Process ingredients until chunky and dehydrate for 3 hours at 145°F and then 2–3 hours at 115°F. Serve with fresh nut/seed mylk.

# Granola Bars

1 recipe *Granola*
¾ C freshly ground flax meal
¼ C coconut water, purified
   water, or fresh juice
¾ C coconut, pulp finely chopped
   and dehydrated (optional)

Place fully dehydrated granola in medium mixing bowl. Stir in flax meal and mix well. Finally, stir in liquid and mix thoroughly. Using a tablespoon to help with measuring, scoop a heaping portion (about 2 tablespoons) of mixture into your hands and form into a 5"-long, 1"-high bar. Place onto mesh dehydrator tray and top with coconut flakes if desired. Dehydrate for 2 hours at 145°F and then 115°F for 4–5 hours or until dry. Stores well in refrigerator for up to 2 weeks.

# KASHI

2 C buckwheat, sprouted
2 T coconut butter
 1 t Celtic salt

Soak and sprout the buckwheat groats for about two days until they have long "tails." Drain soak water. Place in glass dish and cover completely with water. Place bowl in dehydrator for 5 hours at 140°F. Remove from dehydrator and drain any water. Stir coconut butter and salt into the buckwheat. Enjoy as a breakfast cereal or add it to soups. Kashi may even be blended into a creamy porridge.

# Nutty Granola

2 C almonds, soaked
1 C raw pumpkin seeds, soaked
1 C sunflower seeds, soaked
  2 apples, shredded
1 T cinnamon
  1 t Celtic salt

Process almonds in a food processor with the "S" blade until chunky; pour into a mixing bowl. Process pumpkin seeds and sunflower seeds in a food processor until chunky and combine with almonds. Chop apples into large pieces and process in a food processor until shredded. Add cinnamon and salt and mix well. Spread mixture on a dehydrator tray with a Teflex sheet and dehydrate at 145°F for 3 hours and then 10 hours at 115°F, or until desired moisture is obtained. Be sure to dehydrate until all the water is removed from the granola. Store in glass jar. Granola will last 1–3 months, so make lots! Serve with *Almond Mylk.*

# Peace and Love Porridge

1 C almonds, soaked
    Pulp of 3 coconuts
1 C coconut water
¼ C cranberries, fresh or
    self-dehydrated
  1 vanilla bean
  1 t Celtic salt

In a blender, process ¾ C almonds, pulp of three coconuts, coconut water, and ⅛ C cranberries until smooth and creamy. Process remaining almonds and cranberries in a food processor with the "S" blade until chunky. Combine all in a mixing bowl and stir. Serve garnished with several whole almonds and cranberries.

# Pecan Porridge

2 C pecans, soaked
1 C coconut water or water
½ t Celtic salt
½ t cinnamon
  ½ vanilla bean

Process all ingredients in a blender until smooth and creamy.

# SAVORY SPICY PECAN LOAF

1 C pecans, soaked
2 T lemon juice
2 T water
1 T olive oil
2 t Celtic salt
2 t cumin
¼ t hing
¼ t oregano
¼ t thyme
¼ t turmeric
⅛ t marjoram
⅛ t sage

Process all ingredients in a food processor with the "S" blade until smooth. Form mixture into a loaf and serve. The special blend of spices creates a taste quite reminiscent of sausage.

# SQUASH SCRAMBLE

2 butternut squash, peeled and
  chopped
1 stalk of celery, chopped
¼ C fresh cilantro
2 T lemon juice
2 t Celtic salt
2 t paprika
1 t fresh ground black pepper
1 avocado

Process squash in a food processor with the "S" blade until finely chopped. Add celery, cilantro, lemon juice, and spices until well combined. Finally add the avocado and process until all is combined. Serves 2–4.

# Sweet-n-Spicy "Roasted" Almond Buckwheaties

2 C *Buckwheaties*

ALMONDS:
1 C almonds, soaked
2 T lemon juice
½ t cinnamon
¼ t allspice
¼ t cayenne

Process all ingredients in a food processor with the "S" blade until chunky. Hand mix with *Buckwheaties*. Spread on a dehydrator tray and dehydrate at 105° for 1–2 hours.

Serve with a nut mylk or a creamy desert.

# Tum-Yum Yogurt

2 C coconut water, or water
1 C walnuts, soaked
¼ C fresh lemon juice
1 T fresh ginger juice
2 vanilla beans

Process all ingredients in a blender until smooth and creamy. Serves 2.

# Zucchini Pancakes

6 medium zucchinis, grated

2 avocados

3 stalks of celery

4 prunes

1–1½ C ground golden flax seeds

1 C sunflower seeds, soaked

1 t cinnamon

½ t allspice

1 vanilla bean

1 t Celtic salt

PART 1:

Grate zucchini in a food processor with the grating blade; add salt and set aside for 20 minutes. Process the remaining ingredients (except the ground flax seeds) in a food processor with the "S" blade until smooth.

PART 2:

Squeeze the moisture out of the zucchini with your hands. Place the zucchini in a large bowl and add the remaining ingredients (except the ground flax seeds) and mix well. Slowly add the ground flax seeds to the mixture until it all stays together enough to form a ball. Form the dough into smaller balls and flatten into 3" rounds about ¼" thick. Place on a dehydrator tray and dehydrate at 145°F for 2–3 hours.

# Nut Mylks
# and Kefir

# NUT MYLKS

HOW TO MAKE NUT AND SEED MYLKS

1. Soak nuts or seeds in filtered water for recommended amount of time: See Soaking and Sprouting Chart on pages 157–159.

2. Soak any dried fruit (Phase II only) that you wish to add to your recipe for 4–6 hours.

3. Drain nuts, seeds, and soaked fruit. Combine all ingredients, adding spices. Add water, coconut water, or fruit soak liquid so that your mixture will have enough of a liquid consistency to strain—about 1 cup nuts or seeds to 2 cups liquid.

4. Using a blender or food processor with the "S" blade, process all ingredients until smooth.

5. Strain ingredients through a piece of cheesecloth or nylon stocking. You'll have to squeeze a lot to get all the liquid out. You may want to make a nut mylk bag using a nylon small-holed mesh fabric. Make the bag a 4"× 6" rectangle. The bag is easy to wash by hand or in a washing machine and to reuse.

6. Enjoy your fresh mylk over granola, with dessert, or alone.

7. Dehydrate the "pulp" that is left after straining. Spread pulp on a Teflex sheet. Dehydrate at 110°F for about 8 hours or until totally dry and flaky. Sprinkle the pulp on top of desserts or use as "flour" in bread recipes. No Waste!

# ALMOND CHAI

3 C *Almond Mylk*
3 T raisins, soaked (optional)
2½ T raw carob powder
1½ T ginger juice
1 T cinnamon
1 T nutmeg
½ T cardamom

Process all ingredients in a blender until smooth. Chill for 1–2 hours before serving.

# ALMOND CRÈME

2 C almonds, soaked
1¾ C water
1 T flax oil
1 t vanilla extract or ½ vanilla bean, soaked overnight
1 t Celtic salt

Follow instructions above. It's the best non-dairy creamer. Perfect for tea parties. Save the almond pulp for *Chai Spice Wafers.*

# ALMOND MYLK

1 C almonds, soaked
3 C coconut water

Follow instructions above.

*Variation:*
½ vanilla bean
2 t cinnamon

# ALMOND MYLK #2

1 C almonds, soaked
2 C water
2 C coconut water
½ vanilla bean
¼ t Celtic salt

Follow instructions above.

# ALMOND MESQUITE MYLK

1 C almonds, soaked
3 C coconut water
1 T Tree of Life mesquite
    pod meal
1 t cinnamon

Follow instructions above.

# ALMOND CARDAMOM MYLK

1 C almonds, soaked

2 C water

2 C coconut water

1 t cardamom

Follow instructions above.

# AMBROSIA ELIXIR

½ C macadamia nuts, unsoaked

2½ C coconut water

½ C coconut pulp

¼ vanilla bean

½ t Celtic salt

Follow instructions above.

*Optional:*

½ t Tree of Life mesquite
pod meal

# Black Sesame Seed Mylk

2 C black sesame seeds, soaked

1 C water

1 C coconut water

1 t mesquite

1 t carob

1 t cardamom

1 t Celtic salt

Blend sesame seeds with water using high-speed blender. Strain and blend with other ingredients.

# Calcium Coconut Mylk

2 C coconut water

1 C coconut pulp

¼ C sesame seeds

1 t mesquite

½ t Celtic salt

¼ vanilla bean

Process all ingredients in a blender until smooth and serve immediately.

# Chai Nut Mylk

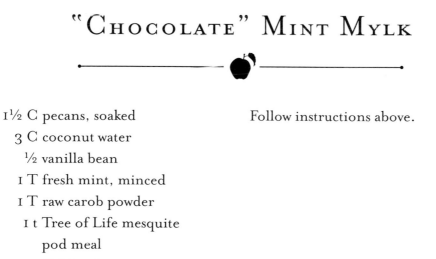

1¼ C almonds or pecans, soaked

2½ C coconut water

¼ C raisins, soaked

1" of vanilla bean

1 T Celtic salt

1 t garam masala

1 t ginger

1 t cinnamon

½ t cardamom

Follow instructions above.

# "Chocolate" Mint Mylk

1½ C pecans, soaked

3 C coconut water

½ vanilla bean

1 T fresh mint, minced

1 T raw carob powder

1 t Tree of Life mesquite
    pod meal

1 t Celtic salt

Follow instructions above.

# Hazelnut Mylk

1 C hazelnuts, soaked

3 C coconut water or water

1 apple

1 t cinnamon

¼ t nutmeg

Dash of Celtic salt

Follow instructions above.

# Lavender Mylk

1 C almonds or pecans, soaked

2½ C coconut water

¼ vanilla bean

1 t lavender flowers

1 t salt

Follow instructions above. It is best to serve this mylk within 4 hours, as the lavender flavor increases in a short amount of time and may over-power other ingredients.

# Macadamia Chai

1 C macadamia nuts, unsoaked
2 C water
1 C coconut water
2 t cinnamon
1 t cardamom
½ t ginger juice
¼ t fresh ground black pepper

Follow instructions above.

# Mesquite Vanilla Almond Mylk

1½ C almonds, soaked
2½ C water
¼ vanilla bean
1 t Tree of Life mesquite
     pod meal
1 t Celtic salt

Follow instructions above.

# Pecan Carob Mylk

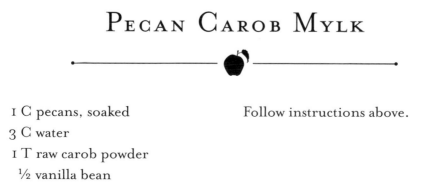

1 C pecans, soaked
3 C water
1 T raw carob powder
½ vanilla bean
¼ t Celtic salt

Follow instructions above.

# Pecan Nut Mylk

1 C pecans, soaked
3 C water or coconut water
2 T Tree of Life mesquite
   pod meal
2 t cinnamon
½ t cardamom
1 vanilla bean

Follow instructions above.

# Strawberry Almond Mylk

1 C almonds, soaked
2 C coconut water
1–2 C strawberries, to taste
1 vanilla bean

Follow instructions above.

# Walnut Mylk

1 C walnuts, soaked
3 C coconut water
1 vanilla bean

Follow instructions above.

# KEFIR

Kefir is a fermented food that adds healthy bowel flora to our intestines, stabilizes digestive function, and has an extensive range of other health benefits. Making kefir requires special "grains" known as "kefir grains" which aid in the fermentation process. High-quality kefir grains are only available through select suppliers (see Resources Directory).

The "kefir grains" are actually a culture of healthy bacteria and yeast, which can live indefinitely. The process of making kefir involves creating an environment with a base such as nut or seed mylk (traditionally raw milk), in which the healthy bacteria and yeast can proliferate. When consumed in the form of a drink, known as "kefir," these healthy bacteria and yeast have tremendous healing power and benefit the body in many ways. The kefir creates a healthy mucous lining in the colon, which acts as a good medium to support the growth of beneficial bowel flora. Kefir helps to prevent parasitic infections and cancer, as well as constipation.

Because of kefir's ability to establish healthy bowel flora, it is beneficial in preventing many gastrointestinal disorders. Some researchers have found that kefir also exudes bacterial inhibitory factors, which prevent the growth of harmful bacteria. In this sense, it actually acts as a natural antibiotic. Some studies show that kefir whey neutralizes most pathogenic bacteria within 24 hours. Various medical reports suggest that kefir has been helpful in the treatment of psoriasis, eczema, allergies, migraines, gout, rheumatic arthritic conditions, candidiasis, and colitis. The World Health Organization has even reported that kefir has been used effectively in the treatment of tuberculosis and typhoid fever. Additional studies suggest that diarrhea caused by *E. coli* bacteria in newborn infants has been successfully controlled with kefir. Other studies show that kefir helps to heal urinary tract infections and even prostate problems. Kefir may also be important in the alleviation of anxiety. Interestingly enough, those put on a kefir diet consistently have less anxiety. This may be because the fermentation process produces high levels of tryptophan, which converts into serotonin in the brain, thus producing a relaxing effect.

The kefir grains produce right-rotating L(+) lactic acid, which is an important constituent of the human body. It is particularly important in the prevention of cancer and has been used experimentally with success in the treatment of cancer. In addition, right-rotating lactic acid may help maintain healthy functioning of the heart. According to some researchers, the cells of the heart muscle obtain their energy primarily from right-rotating lactic acid.

Although many people are concerned about acidity, my experience is that many people are actually too alkaline. Acidity from healthy lactic acid helps bring their pH back to the normal range needed for optimal health. The acidity of kefir is as low as a pH of 3, consisting of .85-1.5% lactic acid. The normal healthy human pH for optimal brain function as discussed earlier is 7.46. Many people I test have a pH of 7.5-7.65, and the kefir helps to bring the pH back into the normal range.

Kefir has many nutritional benefits as well. Kefir is a complete protein and rich in many vitamins. The fermentation process actually increases the amount of vitamins, especially the B vitamins. Kefir is an excellent source of $B_{12}$ and is high in vitamins $B_1$ and $B_6$.

Kefir creates what are known as "ferments," which act as super metabolizers that assist with nutrient assimilation as well as digestion. The traditional term "ferment" refers more specifically to enzymes. Kefir actually creates many enzymes that can be absorbed as healing forces. As discussed earlier, enzymes are the key to building and maintaining good health. These enzymes are actually vortexes of energy that help with many aspects of our metabolism. Since, in my experience, many people become enzyme-deficient as they age, I consider fermented foods, and especially kefir, an essential part of my total health program.

The exact origin of kefir is unknown. Some believe it may have come from Russia, while others suggest Turkey. We can say, however, that kefir originated somewhere in the northern Caucasus Mountains. Legend has it that the prophet Mohammed received kefir grains directly from Allah. According to *The Body Ecology Diet* by Donna Gates, kefir was brought to the United States in 1960 from Russia.

Kefir is traditionally made from raw milk. We do not use any products from cows or goats in Rainbow Green Live-Food Cuisine, but instead have found that any nut or seed mylk such as almond, sesame, and sunflower mylks can be made into kefir. In addition there is some evidence to suggest that kefir made from dairy products may block the absorption of vitamin C. When one is taking high amounts of vitamin C for therapeutic reasons it's probably best to eat less dairy-based kefir. Because kefir bacteria produce an acid condition in the mouth it is good to brush your teeth after drinking kefir.

Kefir provides a sour taste, which is very balancing from both the Chinese and Ayurvedic perspectives. Kefir is also cooling and is good for calming pitta during the summer. As kefir is a fermented food, it is offered as part of the Phase I.5 cuisine. Unlike seed cheeze and rejuvelac, kefir is a controlled fermentation process in which a specific culture is introduced, therefore unfriendly bacteria are not encouraged to grow.

High-quality kefir grains contain:

1. *Streptococcus lactis,* which produces lactic acid, aids digestion, inhibits harmful microorganisms, and produces bacteriolysins.

2. *Lactobacillus plantaturum,* which makes lactic acid, fights against *Listria monocytogenes,* and makes plantaricin that inhibits microorganisms which cause spoilage.

3. *Streptococcus cremoris,* which has similar properties as *S. lactis.*

4. *Lactobacillus casei,* which produces large quantities of L(+) lactic acid; colonizes well in the gastrointestinal tract; creates a favorable medium for other healthy bacteria to grow; inhibits putrefaction; increases immune function; and inhibits pathogenic bacteria and helps protect against bacterial infections.

5. *Streptococcus diacetylactis,* which produces $CO_2$ in the kefir; makes diacetyl, which gives the kefir its characteristic odor; and has general properties similar to *S. lactis.*

6. The yeasts: *Saccharomyces florentinus* and *Leuconostoc cremoris,* which do not cause candida.

We recommend purchasing kefir starter grains from two sources: Dominic Anfiteatro and Lifeway. (Please see Resources Directory.)

There is a variety of kefir recipes in this section. We hope you enjoy these recipes and reap the many wonderful benefits of kefir.

## KEFIR PREPARATION PROCESS

1. First, make any seed or nut mylk with *warm* water. Follow the instructions "How to Make Nut and Seed Mylks" at the beginning of this section. It is best to use plain, unseasoned mylk made with water to begin the kefir process.
2. Follow the instructions provided with the kefir starter grains that you purchase.
3. Kefir may also be made by adding ¼–½ cup of previously made kefir to the seed mylk. Although this is an easy and efficient way to make kefir, it is not recommended for those with candida.

You can experiment by adding any of your favorite spices to the finished kefir, or by adding flavorings such as peppermint and vanilla extracts. You may want to sweeten the kefir with stevia. In order to preserve the integrity of the culture, do not blend for more than 30 seconds.

# CAYENNE ALMOND KEFIR

4 cups almond kefir
Pinch of cayenne

# Cinnamon Almond Kefir

4 C almond kefir
2 T cinnamon

# Mint Sunflower Kefir

4 C sunflower kefir
   Dash of peppermint oil
   or ¼ cup fresh mint leaves

Blend for 30 seconds and serve.

# Vanilla Almond Kefir

4 C almond kefir
1 T vanilla extract

# Vanilla Sunflower Kefir

4 C sunflower kefir
2 T vanilla extract
½ T licorice root powder

# Warming Almond Kefir

4 C almond kefir
I t cinnamon
I t ginger powder

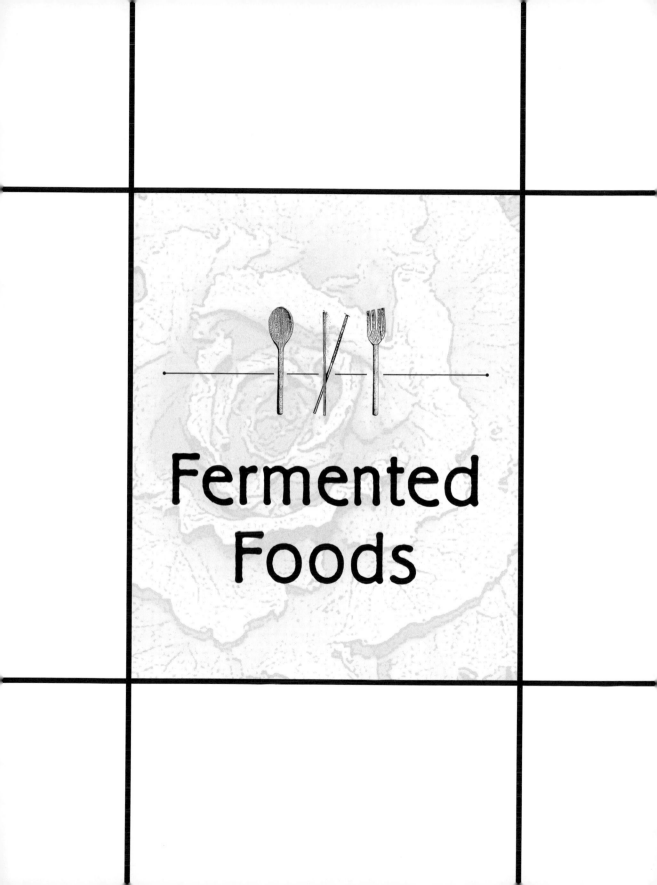

# Fermented Foods

# HOT-N-SPICY KIM CHEE

4 C green cabbage, shredded
(save 3–4 outer leaves)
2 C Napa cabbage, shredded
2 C carrots, grated
1 C daikon radishes, grated

Mix vegetables in large bowl.

4 jalapeño chiles
2 T ginger, grated
1 T miso (any type)

Blend chiles, ginger, and miso with 2 C water and stir into mixed vegetables.

Spoon mixture into crock or gallon glass container. Pound mixture to release juices and remove all air. Top off (to cover cabbage) with a little water if mixture is dry. Cover with outer cabbage leaves to create a tight seal with edge of container. Set a plate on top of cabbage leaves and weigh down with suitable-sized rocks (or other object). Leave Kim Chee in warm (60–70°F) place for 5 days. Do not uncover during this period. After 5 days remove covering, scraping away top layer of vegetables (do not be concerned if you see mold; remove top layer and the rest is good to eat). Kim Chee will become acidic as it ferments, but it takes on a sweeter smell and flavor when it is ready to eat. If you have never tasted Kim Chee, Rejuvenative Foods sells a raw version that you might want to try to help you determine when your own batch is done.

# PICKLED GINGER

One 32-ounce glass container
One fine-mesh bag for straining
  2 C fresh young ginger, thinly
     sliced
  1 C apple cider vinegar
  1 C purified water
  ½ C raisins, soaked
  ½ C beets, shredded
   1 t coriander seeds

Blend raisins and beets with water in a high-power blender and pour through a fine mesh strainer into glass container. Add ginger, coriander, and vinegar. Store in refrigerator for at least 4 days prior to using. Keeps for months when stored at or below 45°F.

Pickled ginger is an essential flavor for creating unique, Japanese-inspired dishes such as seaweed salad and nori rolls. The commercially-available pickled ginger often contains both artificial colors and saccharin, deeming it far from being raw or healthful. Our raw recipe creates sweet, tangy pink ginger that is better than anything else out there!

# Pickled Vegetables

4 carrots, cut into rounds

4 whole dried chiles

2 zucchini, cut into rounds

2 cucumbers, finely chopped

2 red bell peppers, finely
chopped

4 cloves garlic

3 sprigs of fresh oregano

2 T coriander seeds

2 T cumin

2 T fresh ground black pepper

1½ T Celtic salt

Raw apple cider vinegar

Add all dry spices to a gallon jar and place vegetables on top. Fill the jar two-thirds full of raw apple cider vinegar. Fill the last third with water and close the jar; shake well. Keep in the refrigerator, shaking every day for at least 1 week before eating.

# SAUERKRAUT

4 C green cabbage, shredded
2 C Napa cabbage, shredded
2 T ginger, grated
1 T raw white miso
2 t whole caraway seeds

Spoon mixture into crock or gallon glass container. Pound mixture to release juices and remove all air. Top off (to cover cabbage) with a little water if mixture is dry. Cover with outer cabbage leaves to create a tight seal with edge of container. Set a plate on top of cabbage leaves and weigh down with suitable-sized rocks (or other object). Leave Sauerkraut in warm (60–70°F) place for 5 days. Do not uncover during this period. After 5 days remove covering, scraping away top layer of vegetables (do not be concerned if you see mold; remove top layer and the rest is good to eat). Sauerkraut will become acidic as it ferments, but it takes on a sweeter smell and flavor when it is ready to eat. If you have never tasted Sauerkraut, Rejuvenative Foods sells a raw version that you might want to try to help you determine when your own batch is done.

# Mixed Vegetable Sauerkraut

4 C red cabbage, shredded

2 C carrots, grated

2 C beets, grated

¼ C fresh dill weed, finely
chopped

1 T raw red miso

Spoon mixture into crock or gallon glass container. Pound mixture to release juices and remove all air. Top off (to cover cabbage) with a little water if mixture is dry. Cover with outer cabbage leaves to create a tight seal with edge of container. Set a plate on top of cabbage leaves and weigh down with suitable-sized rocks (or other object). Leave Sauerkraut in warm (60–70°F) place for 5 days. Do not uncover during this period. After 5 days remove covering, scraping away top layer of vegetables (do not be concerned if you see mold; remove top layer and the rest is good to eat). Sauerkraut will become acidic as it ferments, but it takes on a sweeter smell and flavor when it is ready to eat. If you have never tasted Sauerkraut, Rejuvenative Foods sells a raw version that you might want to try to help you determine when your own batch is done.

# Essential Oil Delicacies

## HELPFUL HINTS FOR USING ESSENTIAL OILS IN CUISINE

- Essential oils must come from a pure and reliable source, especially if you are using them in food. The company Tree of Life uses is Elizabeth Van Buren. They sell only high-quality, therapeutic oils. (See Resources Directory for ordering information.)
- Essential oils are a wonderful and exotic way to add flavor to food.
- To dispense oil, tap the bottom of the bottle lightly and one drop will come out.
- Caution: some essential oils are very strong, so go one drop at a time! It may overwhelm the recipe.
- Store oil in a cool, dark place. Heat and light destroy the beneficial effects.

# APRICOT DELIGHT

3 dried apricots, soaked
¾ C water
½ C macadamia nuts
1 drop of lemon grass oil

Process macadamia nuts in a food processor with the "S" blade until a fine meal. Add apricots and water and blend until smooth and creamy. Stir in lemon grass oil. *Apricot Delight* can be poured over morning fruit or a dessert.

# BAVARIAN GINGER FUDGE

½ C almond butter

½ C tahini

¼ C carob powder

4 dried apricots, soaked,
or 3 drops stevia

1 t pure vanilla or ½ vanilla
bean, soaked

2 drops ginger oil

1 drop nutmeg oil

Blend soaked apricots and stir in remaining ingredients. Roll into 1" balls. Try rolling balls in extra carob, hemp seed, or chopped nuts.

# COCO ORANGE CRÈME

1 C water or coconut water

1 C tahini or pine nuts, unsoaked

3 T carob powder or more to
taste

3 drops orange oil

Blend all ingredients, except essential oil, in a food processor with the "S" blade. Stir in orange oil by hand.

# CRANBERRY YLANG YLANG CREAM

¾ C fresh cranberries
½ C pine nuts, unsoaked
½ C macadamia nuts, unsoaked
2–3 T coconut water or water
1 drop ylang ylang oil

Process pine nuts and macadamia nuts in a food processor with the "S" blade until powdery. Add cranberries and water until smooth. Stir in ylang ylang oil.

# DESERT SAGE DRESSING

½ C hemp or flax oil
½ C lemon juice
1 T flax seed, ground
1 t Celtic salt
½ t fresh oregano
½ t fresh basil
2 drops sage oil

Whip ingredients in a blender and serve over your favorite salad.

# ESSENTIAL ALMOND MYLK

Any *Almond Mylk* recipe
2 drops of your favorite essential oil

Stir in oil by hand.

# FENNEL DREAM CREAM

1 C water or coconut water
1 C tahini or pine nuts, unsoaked
2 drops fennel oil

Blend all ingredients, except essential oil, in a food processor with the "S" blade. Stir in fennel oil by hand. A delicious licorice taste.

# LEMON POPPY SEED BISCOTTI

2½ C golden flax seeds, finely ground in a coffee grinder or blender
½ C slivered almonds
10 drops lemon essential oil or lemon essence
½ C poppy seeds
¾ C coconut water

*Variation:*
Add ¾ C apricots, blended (Phase II only)

In a large bowl, mix all the ingredients until they are firm but not too dry. Shape into an oval approximately 8" x 6" and 1" thick. Place on a dehydrator tray and dehydrate at 145°F for 1 hour. Remove from dehydrator and turn the dough over, then cut the oval into smaller pieces ¾" thick and separate on the tray. Continue dehydrating for 8–10 hours at 115°F or until desired moisture is obtained.

# LONGEVITY DRESSING

1 C carrot juice
¾ C blend of macadamia nuts and
    pine nuts, unsoaked
½ C water
  1 t lemon zest
  1 t Celtic salt
  3 drops orange oil or dill oil
  1 drop ginger oil

Place all ingredients, except essential oils, in blender and blend until smooth and creamy. Stir in essential oils by hand.

# MAGIC DRAGON FOOTPRINTS

½ C macadamia nuts, unsoaked
½ C walnuts or pine nuts,
    unsoaked
½ C goji berries, soaked
½ C raisin soak water or ¼ C
    raisins, soaked
  2 T flax powder
½ t blue-green algae
  2 drops peppermint oil

Using a food processor with "S" blade, blend ingredients, except essential oil, until creamy. Stir in essential oil by hand. Roll dough into balls. Be creative in making footprints or simply flatten balls. Refrigerate. Kids love following the magic dragon!

# Nut Mylk Extraordinaire

1 serving *Almond Mylk* or *Black Sesame Mylk*

1 drop lavender, orange, nutmeg, lemon, rose, or fennel oil

Stir essential oil into nut mylk by hand. Enjoy!

# Nutmeg Dream Cream

1 C water or coconut water

1 C tahini or pine nuts

2 drops nutmeg oil

Blend all ingredients, except essential oil, in a food processor with the "S" blade. Stir in nutmeg oil by hand.

*Variation:*
For a sweeter taste add 3 drops of lime oil or 3 drops of spearmint oil.

# ORANGE ESSENCE CREAM

1 C apple
¾ C fresh cranberries
½ C pine nuts
½ C macadamia nuts, unsoaked
2–3 T coconut water or water
2 drops orange oil

Blend ingredients in a food processor using the "S" blade. Add essential oil and stir in by hand.

# RASPBERRY LEMON JEWEL BARS

1 C Brazil nuts, unsoaked
1 C raspberries
2 T tahini (may use powdered flax as a substitute)
2 T lemon zest
5 drops mandarin essential oil
1 drop nutmeg essential oil

Blend Brazil nuts with "S" blade of food processor. Stir in remaining ingredients by hand. Serve bars immediately or dehydrate at 130°F for two hours, turning bars over and dehydrating for another two hours at 115°F.

# ROYAL CRANBERRY SPREAD

1 C cranberries, softened *
½ C pine nuts, unsoaked
   1 medium red apple, finely
      diced (omit for a Phase I
      recipe)
½ C goji berries, soaked 1 hour
   1 drop rose or geranium oil

  * To soften cranberries, place them
    in a small glass dish. Put them in the
    dehydrator for 1 hour at 145°F.

In a high-power blender, blend pine nuts. You may also blend goji berries or leave them whole for flecks of color. Mix in by hand apple for chunky texture, or blend with pine nuts for smooth texture. Stir in essential oil by hand. Serve over flax meal or granola. Makes 2 cups.

# WIZARD MINT WHIP

  2 apples
½ C coconut water
¾ C avocado
  1 drop peppermint oil
    (only 1 drop)

Using a food processor with the "S" blade, pulse the apple and avocado. Stir in coconut water and 1 drop of peppermint oil. Chill. Serve this cooling delicacy in the summer.

*Variation:*
¼ C goji berries for sweetness and a splash of color

*Appendix*

# Raising Rainbow Babies

**W**hat a blessing it is to nourish our babies with organic living foods that will strengthen them physically, mentally, emotionally, and spiritually. Not only is it possible; it is optimal. Babies are so full of life force and develop at such a miraculous rate. A well-balanced, 100% raw, organic diet of fruit, vegetables, nuts, and seeds provides them with the uncompromised nourishment that will support them in creating a lifetime of well-being.

Breast milk is the perfect "live-food" nutrition for infants. Whenever possible, breast milk should be the main dietary component for the first year of life or longer. If breast milk is not always available, parents do not have to succumb to the use of infant formula. There is not a single brand that is appropriate nutrition for an infant. They do not contain the GLA and DHA which are so important. Breast milk is perfectly formulated for maximum neurological growth. (For the most comprehensive medical information available on healthy vegan and live-food pregnancy and nursing, please see *Conscious Eating.*)

When it is time to introduce food, even the youngest babies can be nourished with living foods. For most babies, it is appropriate to introduce "solid" live food around six months of age, as they become inquisitive at mealtime, their digestion is stronger, and the swallowing reflex is well developed. The beginning of the teething process is a sign that the baby may be ready for solid food. As progressively more teeth come into place, chunkier textures of solid foods can be introduced, as well as an increased number of different types of food. The appearance of teeth suggests that the enzyme systems have begun to manifest, making it appropriate to introduce certain foods.

A baby is in the kapha phase of life, according to the Ayurvedic dosha system. This means that his system is cold, damp, and mucus-forming and the digestion is fragile. Therefore, baby's diet must be anti-kaphagenic—warming and drying. Particularly in the first two years, a child's food should be warm, approximately 100–105°F, blended, with certain warming spices added. At the beginning of baby's life his digestive fire is just being ignited. If the food is too cold or too concentrated, it can extinguish the digestive fire. The spices we recommend blending into the food in moderation are ginger, cardamom, cilantro, cumin, cinnamon, nutmeg, peppermint, and chamomile. The two best are ginger and cardamom. To warm the temperature of the food, you can place blended food on the stove on low heat, stirring until it is warm to the touch. Food can also be placed in the dehydrator before blending, for two hours at 115°F. This works especially well for more fibrous foods like broccoli. Some foods, like avocados, can be placed in the sun while still in the skin.

We do not recommend feeding baby any soy products. The reasons are fivefold. (1) Soy is kaphagenic—damp and cold. (2) Soy has an excess of copper, manganese, aluminum, and estrogen. (3) Because 70% of soy is genetically modified, it is one of the top ten allergenic foods. (4) Soy is not meant to be used as a regular food, but as a condiment, as it is highly processed and denatured. (5) Soy is high in estrogen and may be hormonally unbalancing for the child.

As parents, we may not have made a complete transition to a live-food diet. We may have "food issues" that make a live-food diet a process. An infant is born free of food issues and programmed food preferences. For an infant who delights in the unimpeded, natural, joyful flow of life, a raw-food diet supports them in sustaining this "unadulterated" experience. In fact, your infant's dietary patterns can even support you in making shifts in your own nutritional choices.

Because infants who are given a live-food diet are getting such a pure nutritional start and they haven't compromised their system with a lifetime of poor nutritional habits, they do not need to adhere to the Phase I Rainbow Green Live-Food Cuisine. Rather, a lenient Phase II diet is appropriate. This section, "Raising Rainbow Babies," is not meant to be a comprehensive guide to nourishing children. Rather, it aims to inspire parents to have the confidence and creativity to raise a rainbow baby with live foods. For comprehensive information on the hows and whens of feeding your infant, we recommend the book *Super Baby Food* by Ruth Yaron (F.J. Roberts Publishing Company). It is a complete vegetarian guide, containing much useful information that is easily adaptable to a live-food diet. Unfortunately, there is no other comprehensive information of which we are aware to support parents in raising babies live from first bite. This is breakthrough information.

Currently, the Tree of Life Foundation is conducting research on the health and growth patterns of young children nourished with live foods. The preliminary research suggests that the general growth patterns of live-food children fall into the average to above-average range.

The following live foods and live-food recipes are some age-appropriate ideas for your rainbow baby that will help him/her to develop good nutritional habits, healthy taste buds, and a strong constitution. The recipes written in *italics* can be found throughout this book. These recipes are offered in the age-appropriate categories so that you and your infant can share a live-food meal together. Enjoy!

## Age-Appropriate Foods Table

| | | | |
|---|---|---|---|
| **Under 6 Months** | fresh young coconut water<br><br>wild-crafted red bananas<br><br>apple, peeled | pear, peeled<br><br>cucumbers, peeled<br><br>ripe avocado | *Almond Mylk*<br>(as breast milk supplement if necessary) |
| **6 Mos & Older** | papaya<br><br>mango | sapote<br><br>winter squash | |
| **7 Mos & Older** | coconut pulp (blended)<br><br>apricots, (fresh or dried that have been soaked and blended) | peaches<br><br>flax seeds, powdered | local bee pollen<br><br>chlorella<br><br>spirulina |
| **8 Mos & Older** | almonds<br>pistachios<br>sesame seeds (tahini)<br>pumpkin seeds<br>sunflower<br>hemp<br>chia | apple, peeled<br>fig, peeled<br>kiwi, peeled<br>plums, peeled<br>grapes, peeled<br>raisins, soaked<br>currants, soaked<br>cherries, pitted<br>olives, pitted | broccoli<br>okra<br><br>raw carob<br>mesquite |
| **9 Mos & Older** | pineapple<br>beets<br>carrots<br>summer squash<br>turnips<br>rutabaga | rhubarb<br>asparagus<br>cauliflower<br>eggplant<br>Brussels sprouts<br>spinach | kale<br>sea vegetables<br>celery<br>buckwheat |

| 10 Mos & Older | sprouts, ground greens, massaged | red pepper macadamia nuts | Brazil nuts |
|---|---|---|---|
| 1 Year & Older | citrus fruits<br>tomatoes<br>strawberries<br>blueberries<br>cranberries<br>goji berries<br>other berries<br><br>pecans<br>walnuts<br>pine nuts | Allium family:<br>garlic, leek,<br>shallots, onions<br>(in strict moderation)<br><br>Potent spices:<br>cayenne, chile<br>peppers, black<br>pepper, hing,<br>wasabi, etc.<br>(in strict moderation) | apple cider vinegar<br>(and other vinegars)<br><br>miso<br><br>fermented foods<br><br>raw honey<br>(not recommended) |

# UNDER 6 MONTHS

Ideally an infant can be exclusively breast-fed until at least four or six months of age (or even longer); however, when this isn't possible, the following live foods are recommended as supplements to breast milk. Consult a live-food-oriented physician before completely weaning an infant less than nine months off of breast milk and solely employing a live-food diet. If your infant can be exclusively breast-fed, you may choose to wait to introduce food until baby is at least six months old.

When feeding an infant, remember to thoroughly mix all "solid" foods with water (in a blender or with a fork) until they are of "liquid" consistency. At this stage, feed baby a mono diet (one type of food per meal). When introducing new foods to your baby, introduce one new food every two to four days. This allows you to reasonably deduce what food may be the cause of an allergic reaction. Allergic reactions (whether age-related or not) often occur in infants. If you notice symptoms such as rashes, unexplained irritability, or circles under the eyes, please consult a holistic physician. It is possible to do allergy testing.

FOODS:

Fresh young coconut water

Wild-crafted red bananas (lower
in sugar than organic farm-
raised)

Ripe avocado

Cucumbers, peeled

Apples, peeled

Pears, peeled

RECIPES:

*Almond Mylk* (as breast milk
supplement if necessary)

## 6 MONTHS AND OLDER

This may be the appropriate time in your infant's life to introduce "solid" food. A mono diet is still best for most meals. In addition to the above list, the following are considered "first foods" that should be completely blended, adding water if necessary, to a liquid consistency.

FOODS:

Papaya

Mango

Sapote

Winter squash

RECIPES:

*Buttery Butternut Porridge*

## 7 MONTHS AND OLDER

At this stage, begin to introduce gentle combinations of blended foods.

FOODS:

coconut pulp (blended thoroughly
with water until creamy)

Apricots, fresh or dried, that have
been soaked and blended

Peaches

Flax, powdered

Local bee pollen

Chlorella

Spirulina

RECIPES:

## GREEN POWER BANANAS

1 wild-crafted red banana
1 t chlorella or spirulina

Mash green powder evenly into banana, adding water until reaching liquid-like consistency.

## BUZZIN' BANANAS

1 wild-crafted red banana
2 t local bee pollen

Soak bee pollen in water and mash until liquefied. Mash evenly into banana, adding water until reaching liquid-like consistency.

## FLAX BANANAS

1 wild-crafted red banana
1 T flax seeds, ground
Pinch of cardamom

Mash powdered flax seeds evenly into banana, adding water until achieving liquid-like consistency.

## OCEAN AVOCADO

½ avocado
½ t kelp powder

Mash kelp powder evenly into avocado, adding water until achieving liquid-like consistency.

## CUKE AVO BLEND

¼ avocado
⅛ cucumber

Blend, adding water until achieving liquid-like consistency.

## FRUITY COCONUT WATER

Water of 1 fresh young coconut
½ C age-appropriate fresh fruit
    or ¼ C dried age-appropriate
    fruit, soaked

Blend ingredients until completely smooth.

## APRICOT FLAX TEETHING BISCUITS

2 C flax seeds, ground
1 C dried apricots, soaked
1 C or more fresh young
    coconut water

Blend all ingredients in food processor, adding coconut water to desired consistency. Place batter in small rounds on Teflex sheet and dehydrate at 145°F for 2 hours. Flip biscuits over and dehydrate at 115°F for 4 hours more or until very hard. As your child gnaws on the biscuit, it will soften enough to be swallowed safely when pieces come off. Of course, never leave baby unattended while eating. Biscuits will store for several weeks so you may wish to increase the recipe if you have a large dehydrator and can make them in bulk.

ADDITIONAL RECIPES:

*La Crème de la Crème*

## 8 MONTHS AND OLDER

As your infant may now have a couple of teeth, allow the consistency of food to become slightly chunkier. Make sure that your child's swallowing reflex is good and that she uses her teeth well before moving to foods with more fiber or which are more complex. Offer small bite-size pieces of soft finger foods. Give baby a little something to sink her teeth into and practice feeding herself. Begin adding mild spices and herbs to some food combinations. For most meals stick with monofoods or simple combinations. Some of the fancier recipes are offered as special treats that can be more frequently incorporated as baby gets older.

FOODS:

Easily digestible nuts: almond, pistachio

Easily digestible seeds: sesame (tahini), pumpkin seed, sunflower, flax, hemp, chia

Nut butter thinned with coconut water (use age-appropriate nuts)

Fig, peeled or blended

Kiwi, peeled

Plums, peeled

Grapes, peeled (Concord are easiest to remove the skins)

Raisins, soaked

Currants, soaked

Cherries, pitted

Olives (pitted and blended or finely chopped. We recommend Kalamata olives from Tree of Life which are cured in Celtic sea salt. See Resources Directory.)

Broccoli, marinated in oil, then blended

Okra

Raw carob powder

Mesquite powder

RECIPES:

### BANANA SUPERFOOD

1 wild-crafted red banana
1 t flax seed, powdered
1 t spirulina or chlorella
1 t bee pollen, soaked and liquefied

Mash all ingredients together until evenly mixed.

## BANANA-N-BUTTER

1 wild-crafted red banana
1 T raw almond butter (may be
    thinned with coconut water)
Pinch of cinnamon

Cut banana in small chunks. Mix by hand the almond butter, coconut water, and cinnamon and smear on top of banana chunks. A fun and messy meal.

## CUKE AVO SALAD

½ avocado, diced
¼ cucumber, diced
2 T flax oil
1 t Celtic sea salt, or to taste

Mix all ingredients and serve as finger food.

## SWEET APRICOT ALMOND COOKIES

2 C almonds, soaked
1 C dried apricots, soaked
1 C coconut pulp
½ C currants, soaked
1 C fresh young coconut water
½ T vanilla extract or 1 vanilla
    bean
1 t almond extract
1 t nutmeg
1 t cinnamon

Blend all ingredients in food processor. Drop batter on Teflex sheet in heaping tablespoons. Slightly flatten cookies with a spoon so they will fit in dehydrator. Dehydrate 2 hours at 145°F. Flip cookies over and continue to dehydrate at 115°F for another 4–6 hours. Cookies will store refrigerated for a week or longer. Makes 45–50 cookies.

### SALAD DRESSINGS
*Avocado Dressing*

*Creamy Cuke Dressing*

## CRACKERS

*Green Wonder Wafers*

## BREAD

*Apple Cinnamon Bread*

*Apricot Bread*

*Carrot Bread*

*Carrot Dill Bread*

*Carrot Nut Bread*

*Cranberry Carob Challah*

*Indian Flat Bread*

*Sacred Challah*

*Tree of Life Challah*

*Tortillas*

## DESSERTS

*Apple Spice Bars* (do not roll in
     pecans or pine nuts; substitute
     chopped almonds)

*"Baked" Apples*

*Carob Cookies*

*Carob Coconut Cream Éclairs*

*Carob Fudge*

*Chai Spice Wafers*

*Cherry Truffles*

*Cinnamon Raisin Biscotti*

*Cinnamon Rolls*

*Coconut Apple Pie*

*Coconut Cream Pie*

*Pistachio Pleasure*

*Tahini Truffles*

## JAMS, "SWEET" SAUCES, AND "SWEET" SPREADS

*Basic Nut (or Seed) Spread*

*"Chocolate" Sauce*

*Coconut Butter Icing*

*Coconut Cream Icing*

*Plum Raisin Syrup*

*Simplicity Sauce*

## PORRIDGE AND BREAKFAST DISHES

*Apple Cinnamon Porridge*

*Apple Spice Porridge*

*Peace and Love Porridge*

*Zucchini Pancakes*

## NUT MYLKS

*Almond Cardamom Mylk*

*Almond Crème*

*Almond Mesquite Mylk*

*Calcium Coconut Mylk*

*Lavender Mylk*

*Mesquite Vanilla Almond Mylk*

*Vanilla Almond Mylk*

## ESSENTIAL OIL DELICACIES

*Wizard Mint Whip*

*Bavarian Ginger Fudge*

# 9 MONTHS AND OLDER

## FOODS:

Pineapple

Beets (blended or finely shredded)

Carrots (blended, as they can be a
   choking hazard)

Summer squash

Turnips

Rutabaga

Rhubarb

Asparagus

Cauliflower

Eggplant (softened by marinating in
   Celtic sea salt and flax oil)

Brussels sprouts

Spinach (blended or softened by
   massaging with Celtic sea salt. Let sit
   for 30 minutes. Add bit of flax oil and
   marinate for 1 hour. Finely chop.)

Kale (prepare as for spinach)

Sea vegetables
   (soaked and finely chopped)

Celery (best juiced or blended)

Buckwheat groats
   (sprouted and blended)

## RECIPES:

### GREEN JUICE

cucumber

celery

kale

Juice all ingredients. Make enough to share. You may be surprised what your infant will drink if he sees you enjoying it first.

*Almond Carrot Pâté* (omit chives)

*Sesame Coconut Salad*

*Avocado Spinach Dressing*

*Squasho-Nacho Cheeze* (blend all
    ingredients)

*Coconut Celery Soup*

*Kale Curry Crackers*

*Bliss Balls* (use hemp seeds rather
    than pine nuts)

*Carrot Pudding*

*Carrot Truffles*

*Buttery Butternut Porridge*

# 10 MONTHS AND OLDER

By now your baby probably has some upper and lower teeth. Introduce chunkier foods and recipes for baby to enjoy.

### FOODS:

Sprouts, ground

Greens, marinated and/or
    massaged with Celtic salt to
    soften, or blended

Brazil nuts, blended (in moderation)

Macadamia nuts, blended
    (in moderation)

Red pepper, blended or finely
    chopped

### RECIPES:

#### SUPER GREEN JUICE

cucumber

celery

kale

spinach

dandelion greens

sprouts

parsley

Juice all ingredients. Make enough to share. You may be surprised what your infant will drink if he sees you enjoying it first.

*Ocean Rolls*

*Thai Patties*

*Save the Tuna Pâté*

*Crescent Cucumber Salad*

*Marinated Broccoli*

*Thai Hemp Slaw*

*Mysore Mint Chutney*

*Plum Chutney* (omit chives)

*Squash Bisque*

*Indian Flat Bread #2*

*Almond Flax Crackers* (powder flax and blend all ingredients)

*Apricot Delight*

# 1 YEAR AND OLDER

Some foods have certain properties that may cause allergies to develop later in life if introduced too early. For this reason, it is recommended that the foods on this list not be introduced until your baby is at least one year old. Some foods are too "strong," such as the Allium family and certain spices, and they should be strictly minimized until your child is old enough to make his or her own responsible food choices. Foods should still be cut into small bite-sized pieces, and greens should be blended or finely chopped and softened by massaging with Celtic sea salt, and then marinated in avocado or oil. Never leave baby unattended while eating.

FOODS:

Citrus fruits

Tomatoes

Strawberries

Blueberries

Cranberries

Goji berries

Other berries

High-fat nuts: pecans, walnuts, pine nuts

Allium family: garlic, leek, shallots, onions (in strict moderation)

Potent spices: cayenne, chile peppers, black pepper, hing, wasabi, etc. (in strict moderation)

Apple cider vinegar (and other vinegars)

Miso

Fermented foods

Raw honey (Not recommended in Rainbow Green Live-Food Cuisine, but if you are using it, wait until baby is at least one year.)

RECIPES:

## MY FIRST BIRTHDAY "CAKE"
### (REALLY, IT'S A PIE)

*Crust:*

2 C almonds, soaked 12 hours

1 C dried apricots, soaked 3
hours

1 C dried shredded coconut,
soaked 3 hours

½ C apricot soak water

½ T vanilla extract or 1 vanilla
bean

1 t almond extract

1 t nutmeg

1 t cinnamon

½ C fresh young coconut water

Blend all ingredients, adding the coconut water slowly to achieve a consistency that can be pressed into a crust. Make the pie in a plastic bowl (rather than glass), about 6" wide and 3" deep. Press the crust into the bowl between ¼" and ½" thick. (Use the leftover crust batter to make dehydrated cookies.) Dehydrate crust at 145°F for 2 hours. Then turn the dehydrator down to 115°F and continue dehydrating for another 4–6 hours. Remove crust from dehydrator and serve warm or refrigerate for at least 1 hour.

*Filling:*

1 wild-crafted red banana,
sliced

½ mango, diced

1 kiwi, diced

10 strawberries, sliced

Fill crust with bite-sized diced fruit in layers. Use banana on bottom layer to keep the crust crustier.

*Coconut Butter Icing:*

3 C coconut pulp
½ C dried apricots, soaked
¼ C flax oil
1 t Celtic salt

Blend all ingredients in a high-power blender. Only these industrial blenders have the capacity to whip the coconut into a creamy consistency. Blend until entirely creamy. Cover top of pie completely with coconut icing.

*Decoration:*

Decorate the top with raspberries
and one beeswax birthday candle.

One of the joys of your baby's first birthday is watching him respond to his birthday cake. Will he delicately pluck off the raspberry garnish one by one or will he lunge for it with both little hands, delighting in the sensation of icing between the fingers? Either way, offering baby his own special age-appropriate birthday treat will ensure that you do not have to be concerned that he will not leave enough intact for others to share. Party-goers will enjoy any one of the pies or cakes that you select from the Desserts section of this book.

## FRUIT LEATHER

Use any fruit.

Blend in food processor, adding water only if necessary. Spread evenly on Teflex sheets. Dehydrate until dry but still tacky.

## STRAWBERRIES WITH ALMOND BUTTER

6 strawberries
2 T almond butter

Simply smear almond butter on the strawberry. This is an easy and delicious snack.

## SALSAMOLE

2 avocados, diced
1 tomato, diced
2 T flax oil
2 T lime juice (or more to taste)
1 t Celtic sea salt (or more
   to taste)

This recipe yields enough for you to share the meal with your baby. Parents may enjoy *Salsamole* with any flavor flax crackers.

## LEMONADE

2 C water
Juice of one lemon
Stevia to taste (about 5 drops)

### ENTREES

Aloo Paleek
Chili
Classic Neatballs
Falafel
Garden Neatballs
Lasagna
Malai Kofta
Mashed Taters

Mediterranean Patties (omit garlic)
Pizza
Popeye's Spinach Pie
Spinach Tostada
Stuffed Tomatoes
Sun Burger
Sun Raw Samosas (omit garlic)
Zucchini Ratatouille

### PÂTÉ

Almond Broccoli Pâté
Black Olive Pâté
Carrot Dill Pâté
Hummus (omit garlic)
Pâté Primavera

Pumpkin Seed Pâté
Red Tang Pâté
Sunny Basil Pâté
Tastes Like Refried Beans Pâté
Very Vivid Pâté

## SALADS

Avocado Salad with Rosemary

Avocado Tomato Salad

Cabbage Hemp Salad

Carrot Dulse Salad

Cous Cous

Cucumber Avocado Salad

Cucumber Mint Salad

Fiesta Sprout Salad

Israeli Salad

Under the Sea Salad (omit chives
and garlic)

Marinated Broccoli

Mediterranean Sea Vegetable Salad

Napa Slaw

Sea Palm Simplicity Salad

Sea Vegetable Salad

Star Anise Citrus Salad

Tabouli

## SALAD DRESSINGS

Creamy Miso Dressing

Creamy Tomato Dressing

Creamy Zucchini Dressing

Miso Orange Dressing

Moroccan Carrot Dressing

Orange Dressing

Pesto Dressing

Spanish Salsa Dressing

Tahini Lemon Dressing

## CHUTNEYS, SALSA, SAUCES, AND SPREADS

Alive Mustard

Apple Chutney

Black Olive Salsa

Cilantro Pesto

Coconut Chutney

Creamy Dijon Mustard

Lemon Tahini Sauce

Living Catsup

Groovy Guacamole

Guacamole!

Marinara Sauce

Mexican Tomato Salsa

Olive Dip

Pistachio Miso Dipping Sauce

Salsa Fresca

Sour Cream

Sour Cream Sauce

Spinach Basil Dip

Spinach Dip

Sun-Dried Tomato Tapenade

Tomato Pizza Sauce

Tomato Salsa #1

Tomatillo Avocado Salsa (omit garlic)

Tomatillo Sauce

Ultimate Italian Red Sauce

Zesty Catsup

## SOUPS

Cream of Broccoli Soup

Cream of Carrot Soup

Cream of Cauliflower Soup

Cream of Tomato Soup

Fruity Cream of Tomato Soup

Mexican Avocado Soup

Miso Soup

Pine Nut Cream of Tomato Soup

Thick and Chunky Tomato Soup

Tomato Soup

Simple Creamy Tomato Soup

Squash Bisque

Zen Gazpacho

## CRACKERS

Taste of India Flax Seed Crackers (powder the flax seeds)

Tomato Basil Flax Crackers (powder the flax seeds and blend all ingredients)

## BREADS

Chapati

Cranberry Bread

Lemon Poppy Seed Biscottis

Focaccia

Herb Seed Bread

Italian Bread

Pumpkin Bread

Pumpkin Seed Bread

Sun-Dried Tomato Bread

Sweet Sacred Challah

Zucchini Bread

## DESSERTS

Blueberry Cream Pie

Bliss Balls

Carob Cream Pie

Carob Mint Flat Bars

Carrot Cake

"Chocolate Peanut Butter" Pie

Key Lime Pie

Strawberry Dream Pie

## JAMS, "SWEET" SAUCES, AND "SWEET" SPREADS

Butternut Marmalade

Carob Grapefruit Syrup

Coconut Cream Cheese

Coconut Dream Cream

Coconut Orange Sauce

I Can't Believe It's Not Butter

Lemon Drop Cream

Orange Dream Cream

Pecan Nut Sauce

Rich Nut Frosting

Strawberry Sauce

Sweet Siam Sauce

## PORRIDGE AND BREAKFAST DISHES

Autumn Morning Porridge

Coco Mac Porridge

Pecan Porridge

Savory Spicy Pecan Loaf

Squash Scramble

Tum-Yum Yogurt

## NUT MYLKS

Almond Chai

Ambrosia Elixir

Chai Nut Mylk

"Chocolate" Mint Mylk

Hazelnut Mylk

Macadamia Chai

Pecan Nut Mylk

Pecan Carob Mylk

Walnut Mylk

## FERMENTED FOODS

Pickled Vegetables

Sauerkraut

Mixed Vegetable Sauerkraut

## ESSENTIAL OIL DELICACIES

Apricot Delight

Coco Orange Crème

Longevity Dressing

Magic Dragon Footprints

*Appendix*

# Traveling in the Raw

*"One of the best ways to get one's culinary needs fulfilled
is to take care of them oneself."*
—*Gabriel Cousens*

Following the Rainbow Green Live-Food Cuisine while traveling, be it a short trip or a long holiday, can be a challenge when you first begin. In this section we give you some basic hints and tips that we have discovered over the years of following a raw-food diet. They make planning your trip simple and the whole experience one of joy.

In Appendix III of this book you will find a section with hints and tips minimizing jet stress, including airplane Yoga. We also recommend that you read the section in *Conscious Eating* on traveling in the raw.

The tips below can be applied when making fast raw food for when you are on the go!

## PLANNING YOUR TRIP

Traveling in the raw, like eating in the raw, is all about good planning—from what to take to where to get your fresh supplies along the way. There are many good resource guides for health food stores, both in print format and on the Internet. In the back of this book you can also find a comprehensive list of resources for stocking up on your bulk items.

Where there are no health food stores along the way, you can usually find supermarkets with a limited organic range such as avocados, organic baby greens, carrots, and sprouts. This can be supplemented with various foods that travel well (as described in this section).

If you would like to eat out at a restaurant, call ahead of time and be specific as to your dietary requirements. If you are specific, you will find that most good restaurants will be happy to cater for your needs. This also applies to eating out at the homes of non-raw friends and relatives. If you are not able to plan ahead, you can request a plain salad and add your own dressing, avocado, and dehydrated seed mix.

## BASIC EQUIPMENT

Your choice of equipment will vary depending on your mode of travel and the space you have available. If you are flying it is not possible to take any form of cutting utensils apart from plastic knives on the plane, but you can take them in your suitcase. Here are some general suggestions:

- Containers that seal well are important. A good-size container will double as your preparation and eating bowl and the lid as your cutting board.
- Plastic cups or glass jars with screw-on lids to mix your green drinks and dressings.
- Utensils—knife, fork, spoon (take plastic when flying).
- Chopsticks.
- Roll-up chopping mat, available from most supermarkets.
- Wellness Portable water filtration system,* which filters out the majority of contaminants, saving you from carrying large amounts of water everywhere you go.

- Tribest Personal Blender,* essential for longer trips for grinding your flax seeds and creating yummy dressings for your salads. An inverter can be bought with this product that allows use in car, boat, RV, and camper.
- High-quality knife with plastic cover.
- Iodine is a useful addition for washing your veggies.
- Travel Yoga Mat.*
- Jet Stress Kit* (see Appendix III).

\* These items are available from the Tree of Life Health Store, www.treeoflife.nu.

## BASIC TRAVEL FOODS

There are some basic foods that should be in everyone's travel pack, because they do not require any major preparation. See the Resources section for companies that sell high-quality food items from sea vegetables to nuts and seeds.

- Nuts and Seeds provide that nutrient density we crave while traveling (take a plastic cup or glass jar for soaking).
    - Almonds
    - Hemp Seeds*
    - Macadamia Nuts
    - Sunflower, Sesame, and Pumpkin Seeds
- Superfoods* are essential on trips where food choice may be limited, providing all your nutrient needs in compact packages.
    - Green Powders—Spirulina, Vitamineral Green, Pure Synergy, and Chlorella
    - Bee Pollen
    - Goji Berries
    - Coconut Oil—for both external and internal use
- Nut Butters* are great for dipping with veggie sticks or mixing into simple salad dressings with water, lemon, and salt.

- Almond
- Sesame Tahini
- Celtic Sea Salt* is the best salt available, providing trace minerals. Added to water, it helps with hydration.
- Olive Oil*—Choose only organic stone-pressed.
- Apple Cider Vinegar (Phase I.5)
- Sea Vegetables
    - Whole Dulse
    - Dulse Flakes
    - Nori Sheets—Great for wrapping up your salads.
- Olives* provide a nutrient-dense food that will satisfy you on the go.
- Miso (Phase I.5)
- Flax Seeds*—Ideally ground fresh, but for short trips of a few days you can take pre-ground flax seeds.
- Vegetables/Fruits that travel well:
    - Cabbage, Carrots, Bell Pepper
    - Avocado, Apples, Grapefruit, Raisins

\* These items are available from the Tree of Life Health Store, www.treeoflife.nu.

## FOODS THAT REQUIRE PRE-PREPARATION

If you have time it is useful to stock up on some dehydrated goodies. Recipes can be found throughout the book.

- Seasoned Nuts
- Trail Mixes
- *Imposter "Caramel Corn"*
- Crackers
- *Green Wonder Wafers*
- *Veggie Chips*

- Jerkys
- Granolas
- Granola Bars
- *Magic Wands*

# "FAST FOOD"

Many of us lead a busy lifestyle that does not allow time for preparing the more elaborate recipes found in this book. Whether traveling cross-country or journeying through your busy day, you can be nourished by Rainbow Green Live-Food Cuisine. There are many recipes in this book that are relatively fast and easy to prepare.

When "on the go," wrapping your favorite raw foods in nori sheets, collard greens, or cabbage leaves makes a great meal and minimizes preparation and clean-up! It allows you to be creative and use whatever you have in the fridge. Try making *Noritos.*

There many salads that can be prepared very quickly yet provide that satisfaction you are looking for. Some of them don't mind marinating, so you can prepare your lunch in the morning. We suggest the following "all you need is a knife" recipes:

- *Arugula Cumin Salad*
- *Arugula Spinach Salad*
- *Avocado Kale Salad*
- *Avocado Tomato Salad*
- *Cabbage Hemp Salad*
- *Zen Cabbage Salad*
- *Carrot Dulse Salad*
- *Composed Salad*
- *Cucumber Avocado Salad*
- *Hemp Kale Salad*
- *Mediterranean Sea Vegetable Salad*
- *Moroccan Olive Salad*

- *Napa Slaw*
- *Rainbow Salad*
- *Sea Palm Simplicity*
- *Spinach Masala Salad*
- *Spinach Sprout Salad*
- *Tabouli #3*
- *Thai Hemp Slaw*
- *The Essence of Spinach*

Fast Food Tip: Make a batch of pâté or a dressing that will last you a few days.

## SUMMARY

With a little planning and use of the guidelines found in this section, you will find that traveling in the raw is actually a great deal of fun and can work for you. Traveling in the raw is simple—no cooking utensils, little clean-up, and you get to feel great because you can stick to a cuisine that works for you and your body without the need to compromise. After a while it will become second nature and give you an amazing sense of empowerment in caring for yourself!

*Appendix*

# PREVENTING
# JET STRESS

Though I don't particularly enjoy flying, I've become what some folks might consider a "frequent flyer" out of necessity of my life work. Part of my lifestyle is presenting and attending health- and spirituality-oriented workshops that happen to be located in faraway places. Because I know that there are health hazards to flying, I have developed an ongoing interest in minimizing the harmful effects of air travel and have created, at the insistence of some of my patients and friends, a jet stress prevention program.

Not everyone agrees on the exact cause for jet stress. Some people say that it is primarily related to the disruption of the circadian biological cycles caused by rapidly traveling through the time zones. The more time zones we travel through at one time, the more our circadian biological rhythms are disrupted. Our daily circadian rhythms include blood pressure, eyesight, mental functioning, energy levels, alertness, sleep/wake cycles, digestion/elimination cycles, temperature cycles, a 24-hour metabolic cycle, sense of time, and acupuncture meridian energy cycles.

Jet stress also affects the ultradian cycles second to second such as heartbeat, pulse, respiration, cell division, and brain waves. Moving through a time zone causes a cellular confusion that manifests various symptoms as the body's homeostasis begins to shift into the new time frame and rhythm. The time it takes to reset all the biological rhythms is considered by some as both the definition of and the main cause for jet stress.

Some of the early symptoms of jet stress that people may experience are fatigue, disorientation, decreased mental and physical ability, mental confusion, poor digestion, constipation, and other forms of bowel and urinary dysfunctions. Other symptoms that may not occur immediately are generalized decreased energy and vital force resulting in decreased sexual interest, decreased work capacity, physical incoordination, insomnia, headache, malaise, lack of clarity in thinking, and loss of appetite. The book *Overcoming Jet Lag* by Dr. Charles Ehret and Lynne Scanlon reports current research suggesting that it may take between two days to two weeks to completely recover from all the symptoms of jet stress. The research reported in *Overcoming Jet Lag* says that traveling north to south does not seem to produce as much jet stress as traveling east to west. This is because one is not crossing any time zones. The research also suggests that traveling east to west results in 30–50% less jet stress symptoms than traveling west to east.

Peter Lindeman, a sophisticated biophysics researcher who developed one of the first experimental anti-jet-stress devices, gives another view. He states that the primary three causes are:

1. Stress derived from movements detected by the inner ear
2. Stress from the human body rapidly cutting through magnetic fields
3. Stress from physical vibrations

Cellular confusion caused by these mechanical micro movements is experienced by the body as a peculiar and unusual stress. In a personal communication Lindeman shared that the cause for this cellular confusion is the eye perceiving that nothing is moving while the inner ear is picking up the micro movement vibrations of the jet. These two opposite messages create what might be called a dysynchronous subliminal stress that throws the cells into shock and confusion. Riding in a jet creates a discrepancy in the body's basic spatial and balancing orientation. Experiencing this nervous system dysynchronicity for an extended time is particularly stressful. While flying the body receives information input that says "stillness is movement." This in itself is stressful. It takes some time after landing to readjust to "stillness is stillness and movement is movement." With a lot of flying, the body loses its trust in the continuity of sensory information and on a subtle level may enter a state of constant stress. Without proper rest between flights, most flight personnel may suffer from this chronic stress.

An additional stress is the rapid crossing of the magnetic lines of the Earth, which Peter Lindeman believes creates a "magnetic burn" on the subtle energy system. It may take several days for the system to rebalance from the "magnetic burn." While flying, we are no longer being harmonized by what has been named the Schumann resonance of 7.83 hertz, an emanation given off by the Earth itself. Stress to the body results from being disconnected from the Earth frequency emanations, which have been biologically programmed in us for millennia. This may also explain why there is more stress flying east to west or west to east rather than north-south. East-west or west-east flights generally cut across the magnetic lines, and north-south flights are usually parallel to them. Just exactly how we are affected is not known, but research has certainly established that body function is definitely affected by these magnetic fields. We simply are not biologically designed to fly in airplanes at high speeds such as the Concorde and therefore need to know how to compensate for this.

The vibration of jet engines sets up a variety of additional stresses on the nervous system. There is the actual physical sensation of being vibrated for the duration of the flight. Every cell is shaken. Often people can feel the buzzing for hours after the flight has landed, until the cells undergo a change back to their normal state. There is also a general background noise of 20–50 decibels that cannot be ignored. In addition, there are non-sound vibrations of the jet engine that are transferred to the passenger seat.

Lindeman theorizes that there are also secondary stresses from crossing time zones and the static-electric fields moving across the fuselage as the plane discharges them through special devices. It is not known exactly what sort of effect this has, but moving fields do affect the body.

There are some additional biological stresses of flying that affect one's health: increased radiation exposure, dehydration, low oxygen content inside the airplane, and lack of physical activity. The higher up in the atmosphere, the more cosmic radiation we receive. In a routine flight from Los Angeles to San Francisco I was able to measure a tenfold increase in radiation with a mini-Geiger counter. It jumped from 12 to 125 radiations per minute when we leveled off at the maximum flight pattern. This correlates with the fact that flying personnel are exposed to higher rates of radiation than those working on the ground. This is a potential problem because as we already know, continual low-level radiation produces free radicals.

Another stress is that the atmosphere of the airplane is dry and lower in oxygen than the atmosphere on the ground. It is equivalent on the average to 8,000 feet altitude. The pilots, thank goodness, get a higher $O_2$ concentration. Although the air has been immeasurably improved since smoking was disallowed on many flights, the air situation is still a potentially unhealthy one. In addition, the air is recirculated, so we are exposed to everyone's viruses and bacteria. This is especially so when combined with lack of exercise to keep the circulation moving. Low oxygenation of the blood coupled with a tendency to get dehydrated leads to sludgy blood and the danger of blood clotting, especially in the legs. Lack of exercise and the shallow breathing due to sitting most of the time slow circulation and further contribute to the lower energy of the system.

The result of all these stress factors is severe cellular stress, confusion, and poor biological functioning. In this multi-faceted stressed-out state, the cells do not function correctly and we get the symptoms of jet stress. One solution to the problem is an electronic device I recommend that neutralizes this effect. It is called the Micro-Harmonizer and it puts out a 7.83-hertz frequency. Peter Lindeman's general impression is that when people wear the

Micro-Harmonizer device, no matter how many time zones they pass through, 90% do not suffer symptoms or symptoms are significantly minimized. For example, one person with multiple sclerosis who usually took two weeks to recover from her European trips found that with the Micro-Harmonizer it only took her one day. Wearing the device on the body gives a stronger normalizing input to the cells and counteracts the stress inputs due to the conditions in the airplane and the crossing of magnetic fields. In effect, this little 8-ounce device overrides both the vibrations of the jet and magnetic inputs with the healing Earth vibration. It creates a normalizing frequency effect on the cells.

Although jet stress is a complex condition that scientists do not fully comprehend, the unifying understanding in the two major approaches is that jet travel causes stress and chaos at the cellular level. The end result of all the stresses is essentially the same symptoms.

The strength of a person's vital force plays a role in how much jet stress they experience. This is the key in my approach to minimizing the effects of the jet stress. This would correlate with the finding that jet stress symptoms increase with the number of time zones one passes through, because the longer one is in the airplane passing through time zones, the more in-flight cellular stress one suffers from.

The ultimate prevention and treatment of jet stress is to become so healthy that one's cells **are strong enough to overcome the cellular stress of jet travel.** Research cited in *Overcoming Jet Lag* shows that babies and children are the least affected by jet stress. The older one gets, the more affected one is. *Overcoming Jet Lag* also points out that the more healthy and mentally calm one is, the less affected by jet stress symptoms. The same general principle is seen in those who do best against radiation exposure or exposure to any biological stressor. The healthier and calmer one is, the less affected by any sort of psycho-biological stress. In addition to maintaining a good state of health and vitality, the better we can protect our cells from cellular confusion and stress, the less affected they will be by jet travel.

# SEVEN STEPS TO PREVENT JET STRESS

The prevention of jet stress begins with maintaining good health as a prerequisite before traveling. The next level of prevention is stabilizing cellular, organ, endocrine, tissue, nervous system, and brain functioning while on the airplane. The stability and integrity of the subtle energy centers and acupuncture meridians also need support. Prevention of jet stress is accomplished using a blend of approaches that protect cellular integrity from both in-flight stress and the disruption of biological rhythms.

The jet stress program I have developed has seven steps. The fundamental idea is to keep healthy by living in a way that consistently enhances health under whatever psycho-biological stress one faces. Because I am involved in giving seminars in many parts of the world, it has been important for me to develop a comprehensive system to minimize jet stress. I don't remember the last time I felt any jet stress, even on trips going through nine time zones. I arrive fresh and ready to teach for four or seven days straight without any problem. The total system works for 95% of the people who try it. It seems significantly more effective than using any Micro-Harmonizer alone, particularly for longer flights.

The seven parts of the jet stress prevention program are synergistic and are based on general principles of health. Each part speaks to one aspect of the stress of flying. Jet stress is primarily the body-mind response to the totality of stress that the body undergoes while flying. The time it takes to heal from these stresses is part of it. The program is not meant to create an obsessive condition of worry about jet stress, but to encourage a more healthy and enjoyable trip and to minimize both the symptoms and the "lag" in recovery time. As you travel you will pick out the components that work best for you. Some people will utilize all seven steps and others may use just a few. On a short flight only a few of the approaches might be practiced such as using the jet stress device, only consuming juices on the flight, and doing what I call "airplane Yoga." On a long flight, superior results will more likely be obtained if the complete seven-step approach is used.

## STEP ONE

Use the Micro-Harmonizer that gives off the vibration of the Earth's resonance of 7.83 to 8 hertz. By wearing one of these on your body while on the airplane and for about one hour after leaving the plane, your cells get a message that they are in a normal, healing ground environment.

This device helps the cells minimize or even avoid the cellular stress that we are subjected to up in the air. The cells in effect use the device as a sort of pacemaker that overrides the micro-movement stress and confusion between the inner ear and the eyes created by the movement of the plane. To use a basic example, it is like tuning out the noise of the kids watching T.V. in another room by listening to a symphony with earphones.

This device also minimizes the effects of the body's magnetic fields cutting through the Earth's magnetic lines because the pulsing, healthy field is harder to disrupt than a non-pulsing field. One way to understand this protective effect is to remember how moving water is harder to freeze than stagnant water. A variety of researchers, including Dr. Andrija Puharich, a well-known medical physicist, have found that the healing vibration of hands-on healers also gives off an 8-hertz signal. This is another probable reason why this device seems to work. Using just the Micro-Harmonizer, several clients of mine who are airplane pilots, flight attendants, and frequent travelers found that the device really works to minimize jet stress.

## STEP TWO

Prevention of dehydration with water and healthy food intake helps maintain the vital force of the body. Drinking only fresh water or eating lightly also helps avoid the digestive upsets that often occur when the body is readjusting to the new time zone. As in any situation when the health of the body is challenged, it is better to eat lightly during the flight and at least until the next day after landing in order to maximize the body's ability to repair itself from the shock of flying. It is no accident that Dr. Peter Hansen, in his book *Stress for Success,* points out that 47% of the people with jet stress have poor digestion as a symptom.

Everyone knows that animals do not eat when they have been traumatized. Drinking only water or eating lightly (fresh live fruits, vegetables, and sea vegetables) allows all the body's energies to focus on repair and not be diverted to digestion. Consuming only liquids has been used for thousands of years to activate the vital life force that is so important in healing from any sort of cellular stress.

Additional research reported in *Overcoming Jet Lag* (Ehret and Scanlon) suggests that by eating sparingly or fasting one becomes more sensitive to the different time zone changes in a way that allows the body to more rapidly readjust its biological clock. Dr. Ehret conducted an interesting experiment with rats. First, the rats were not fed on the day before the experiment and were put through artificial time changes that were comparable to human beings on a long plane flight. Then they were fed the equivalent of breakfast in the new time zone, and they shifted to the new time frame faster than rats that were allowed to eat whenever they wanted.

I personally enjoy bringing my own fresh water for the full length of the trip. (Carbonated water is best avoided because it increases carbonic acid in the system and increases the tendency for gas.) Usually I do not eat until I have breakfast the next day at my destination. An additional fancy approach for the meticulous long-distance flyer is to time the taking of water so that it corresponds to the eating times of the new time zone. Generally, it is best to drink every few hours to keep hydrated and to drink when thirsty. For consistent clean water, I suggest using a portable filter on the plane. I use a system called the Wellness Portable water filtration system. I also use HydraCel (formerly called Crystal Energy), which is a liquid that reconstructs water to its highest biological potential.

STEP THREE

Oxygen is generally inadequate both in the airport and cabin of the plane. The oxygen is especially minimal if there is smoking on the airplane, as there still is on some international flights. This is further complicated by not being able to exercise, as one would be able to do traveling by car (stop the car and run around a bit). Exercise increases oxygen flow to the cells. When there is not enough oxygen in the system, cellular respiration and detoxification are limited. Under these circumstances, the red blood cells tend to clump and cause sludging in the blood. Dr. Hansen in *Stress for Success* cites a three-year research program at Heathrow Airport in London completed in 1986. They found sixty cases of sudden death during flights, and 18% of those deaths were from venous blood clots that traveled to the lungs. Blood clumping and sludging are made worse by low blood oxygen content.

To compensate for this I suggest some active breathing (which will be covered in the section on airplane Yoga) and some cardiovascular exercise such as walking before the flight. I also recommend taking some form of stabilized oxygen drops that are now available on the market. We use Vitamin O, a high-$O_2$ concentrated liquid, to increase the oxygen in the blood. HydraCel drops structure all drinking fluids and minimize clumping of the blood. This product also helps protect against this potential problem of low $O_2$ intake.

Another problem associated with cabin-recirculated air is that the atmosphere on the airplane has a low humidity that tends to dehydrate the system. This also leads to blood thickening and sludging. Drinking lots of fluids while flying helps prevent this. Salty foods and alcohol both contribute to the dehydration effect and therefore the blood sludging. Alcohol in significant amounts also creates red blood cell clumping and therefore leads toward blood sludging on its own. Because of this, alcohol should be avoided while flying.

STEP FOUR

Two supplements that help to minimize mind-body adrenal and brain stress and maximize cell integrity and overall body function are Siberian ginseng and AFA blue-green algae. I suggest thirty drops of Siberian ginseng in liquid every four hours. Siberian ginseng is excellent for minimizing the stress associated with all types of travel. AFA blue-green algae distinctly improves mind-brain-nervous system function as well as general body energy. It has a significant effect in preventing nervous system fatigue, one of the main symptoms of jet stress according to Dr. Peter Hansen. Dr. Hansen's jet stress findings show 69% of his subjects had poor concentration, 66% showed slowed reflexes, and 50% manifested irritability. OS-ADR Tachyonized Siberian ginseng is an excellent basic adrenal adaptogenic herbal extract.

## STEP FIVE

Because of the increased radiation exposure, there is an increase in free radical production in the system and hence more potential for cellular and intracellular membrane disruption. To minimize this effect I recommend ProGuard antioxidant enzyme tablets that are made from wheat sprouts. For the ProGuard, I suggest eight tablets the morning of the flight and six every four hours during the flight and through the next morning. These are best taken away from food. The second type of antioxidant I recommend is Antioxidant Supreme. Four of them can be taken every four hours with the ProGuard.

## STEP SIX

The disruption of the circadian and ultradian moment-to-moment rhythms of the body by crossing different time zones can be minimized by using a variety of biological stimulations that help to reestablish normal body rhythm synchronicity. The sun is the most important factor in reestablishing the body and mind biological rhythms. At night when the sun sets, the pineal gland releases melatonin, triggering a series of biochemical events that culminate in the organism feeling sleepy. In the morning when the sun hits our eyes, the sleep-producing melatonin secretio are shut off and one goes about the process of waking up. We strongly suggest using a Tachyonized melatonin called Sleepy Z. Take it one hour before going to sleep at the normal time in the new time zone. This will bring you most quickly into the day-night cycle of the time zone.

Minimizing the effect of light on the pineal secretions when applied to jet travel is rather simple. When starting the trip, especially if it is a long one, try to simulate the day/night pattern of the destination location by regulating the lighting in the airplane as much as possible. For example, if trying to simulate a nighttime situation, pull down the window shades or wear eyeshades or something to keep the light from your eyes.

To illustrate, if one is going to a place that is twelve time zones away, it would be nighttime in the place of destination if one starts out in the morning. To simulate the destination time zone "turn out" lights as if it were midnight at the place of one's destination and go to sleep. If this happens to be twelve noon of the time frame of one's home base, one may need to use some relaxation techniques. If the situation isn't right for sleep, then I'll meditate during this time. If you arrive the mid-afternoon before, try not to take a nap, as this will make it more difficult to go to sleep in the new time cycle. Wait until a reasonable hour such as 9 PM to go to sleep. Then get up as close to sunrise the next day as possible. Get out into the sunlight without sunglasses and do some exercise. The exercise provides a biological wake-up cue to the body. The eating rhythm is also a biological cue.

One concern about regulating the sleep and eating cycles is that it may turn our jet stress program into a mathematically calculated nervous experience, which could take the joy out of the trip. Although this highly organized approach may be more effective for international flights of six hours or more, for most people it is more relaxing to sleep when tired and eat or drink when hungry. The idea of the program is not to create more stress by demanding that one follow obsessive time schedules based on where one is going to be in twelve hours. Increasing $O_2$ intake is an excellent way to reprogram one's cellular biological clock to the new time zone of one's destination.

## STEP SEVEN

Exercise stimulates hormones and neurotransmitters that help to reset our biological clocks. Again for its biological cue value, it is advantageous to exercise during the time one would be active in the new time frame at the destination. For example, if one has not arrived at the destination by the morning, it is good to exercise (walk in the aisles or do airplane Yoga, as described below) before a fruit breakfast or juice while still on the plane. The idea would be to time breakfast on the plane to approximate the breakfast time of one's point of destination. By exercising before one eats, the body receives a biological cue to wake up. Mental activity at times that also correspond to when one would be mentally active at the new destination gives the body another entraining biological cue that helps one "be in sync" upon arrival.

Perhaps the best general exercise that one can do on the plane is to walk in the aisles to get the circulation going. This also helps prevent blood clotting by stimulating the movement of the venous fluid and lymph circulation. Exercise is one of the most effective antidotes to jet stress. It not only helps one reset the biological clock, but also breaks up lymph and blood stagnation, tones the organ and muscle systems, and awakens the mind. We feel airplane Yoga is a great way to get this exercise.

Let's summarize the seven-step process before presenting airplane Yoga:

1. Use the jet stress electronic device, Micro-Harmonizer, to give off a 7.83- to 8-hertz frequency and make the body feel as if it is still in the Earth's Schumann resonance field.

2. Drink one glass of clean water every hour with 8 drops of HydraCel. Use a high-quality water filter bottle if consuming the airplane water. Avoid liquids that clump the blood such as alcohol, and diuretics (soft drinks, coffee, and black tea) that further dehydrate the system.

3. Use a personal air ozone purifier (Personal Air Supply). Increase oxygen by breathing exercises before flying and using stabilized oxygen water. We use Vitamin O.

4. Take adaptogens such as Tachyonized Siberian Ginseng and Tachyon Klamath Lake Blue-Green Algae to minimize brain, body, and adrenal stress.

5. Use antioxidant supplements to minimize radiation and other free radical stress. I use ProGuard Plus, a wheat grass supplement high in sodium oxide dismutase, and Antioxidant Supreme.

6. Use melatonin for jet lag time zone adjustment. I suggest 1 tab of Sleepy Z, a Tachyonized low-dose melatonin, one hour before bed.

Also, go to bed at the normal time for the new time zone and awake to get early daylight.

7. Do airplane Yoga or any exercise you can just prior to and while flying.

The complete Jet Stress Kit includes the following products:
Micro-Harmonizer
HydraCel (formerly Crystal Energy)
Personal Air Supply
Vitamin O
Tachyonized Siberian Ginseng (called OS-GIN)
Tachyonized Klamath Lake Blue-Green Algae
Tachyonized Adrenal Support (called OS-ADR)
ProGuard Plus
Antioxidant Supreme
Tachyonized Sleepy Z

Purchase Individually:
The Wellness Portable water filtration system

You can purchase the Basic or Deluxe Jet Stress Kit at a discounted rate or buy the products individually from our online Health Store at www.tree-oflife.nu.

## AIRPLANE YOGA

In the process of working out the best overall exercise system for airplane travel I have sought the guidance and direct input of Kali Ray, a Master Yogini, who is the founder of Kali Ray TriYoga®. (See Resources Directory.)

It is said that yogis of old became so accomplished in their spiritual practices that they developed special powers, including the ability to fly. However, in the West, since the technology already exists for people to fly at high speeds and with a lot less personal self-mastery than the yogis of India exerted,

Westerners can at least learn airplane Yoga to help them preserve health while flying.

Most people think that Hatha Yoga is merely some sort of physical fitness exercise and stretch system, but it can be much more than that. Properly done, Yoga energizes and balances the total mind/body/spirit, including the seven subtle energy centers and the twelve meridians as described in the acupuncture system. According to acupuncture theory, the meridians are directly linked in two-hour cycles to our 24-hour day and night cycle. Yoga properly practiced and lived has the potential to take one beyond the limitations of the mind to the non-causal joy, love, and peace of the Self.

Kali Ray TriYoga® is a complete flowing Yoga system that energizes the body by linking breath to body movement and thus oxygenating the system. In addition, Yoga helps to calm the mind and increases body strength and flexibility. These qualities are important for nullifying the effects of in-flight stress and to avoid stiffness from several sitting hours on the airplane. The Kali Ray TriYoga® system is excellent for neutralizing and avoiding cellular stress while flying and also speeds up the synchronization of the body. The airplane Yoga sequence can be done several times while flying on long trips. It is also beneficial to do Yoga and walking before and after the flight. After the flight, one ideal way to ground oneself is to find some grass and connect with the earth by practicing Yoga there. For most people, just creating the space to take a gentle walk after arriving at their point of destination is sufficient.

Following is a sitting sequence of "airplane Yoga" with optional standing positions. These posture flows include seven groups of postures that Kali Ray TriYoga® uses to achieve full range of breath and body movement. They are: standing, lateral twist, forward bending, backward bending, balancing, inversion, and sitting.

It is best to not force the body into any postures beyond a point of comfort. The posture flows are meant to energize and gently activate the meridian and bone and muscle systems. These postures are obviously modified for airplane seating conditions. As each airplane is designed a little differently, a certain amount of creative common sense is required to modify the postures according to the particular space available. Who knows, perhaps some day in a more health-conscious future, flight attendants will lead passengers in in-flight Yoga synchronized with accompanying video demonstrations and timed to the new time zone activity cycles.

## SEAT SALUTATION: 10 MOVEMENTS AND BREATH PRACTICES

Seat Salutation is designed for an airplane seat. Since each plane is different in size, there may be one or two postures that will need to be modified according to the space around you.

Have a relaxed, seated posture. Remove your shoes and make your clothing comfortable. With the spine in natural alignment, allow the shoulders to roll back and down. Bring awareness to the breath. Aim to maintain rhythmical breathing throughout the Seat Salutation.

### NATURAL BREATH

*Technique* • To begin Natural Breath, first inhale, allowing the breath to flow into the lower lungs. The abdominal area expands, which allows the diaphragm to lower, giving more room for the lungs. Then exhale, allowing the abdominal area to pull in to release the air. When the abdominal area pulls in, the diaphragm naturally lifts up against the lower lungs, which allows the air to release.

*Benefit* • One benefit of Natural Breath is that it creates and maintains the natural way to breathe. In addition, it massages the internal organs, reduces stress and tension, and helps maintain a relaxed body and mind.

### COMPLETE BREATH

*Technique* • To begin Complete Breath, first exhale, releasing the air. Then inhale, filling the lungs to maximum capacity. Next, exhale, slowly releasing the air. The exhalation is complete when the abdominal area pulls in and the air is released. Continue with Complete Breath.

One option is to use Victory Breath (see below) with Complete Breath. The flow of air is the same throughout inhalation and exhalation, not speeded up or slowed down. It is even from beginning to end. With Complete Breath, use Victory Breath along with Balancing Breath, the breath ratio of 1:1, and gradually increase it to a 1:2 ratio.

## VICTORY BREATH

*Technique* · With Victory Breath, use Complete Breath. To begin, slightly close the glottis. Next, inhale and exhale with the gentle sound of the breath as it passes over the back of the throat. It is the friction of air around the glottis that produces the sound. This friction helps warm the air before it enters the lungs. The sound of the breath should be even and steady. By listening to the breath, one can easily hear if it is flowing or not flowing and make any necessary adjustments to maintain a rhythmic breath. Using Victory Breath deepens concentration by the act of listening to the sound of the breath.

## BALANCING BREATH

*Technique* · For Balancing Breath, begin by observing the flow of your breath. After a few rounds, count the length of your complete inhalation. Then use this number for your inhalation with the directions for the variations. The two variations that follow, however, will use the length of six seconds.

When Complete Breath becomes smooth, create the breathing ratio of 1:1 for kriya (movement) or 1:2 for asana (stillness). During the movement, make the inhalation and exhalation the same length. For example, if you inhale for six seconds, then exhale for six seconds. When sustaining a posture, eventually the exhalation becomes twice the length of the inhalation. If inhaling for six seconds, first aim toward exhaling for nine seconds, gradually developing the twelve-second exhalation. The breath should flow.

*Benefits* · Breathing practices are beneficial for both body and mind. They regulate the breath rhythm, providing steady oxygenation. Increasing the flow of air expands the chest and frees the breath. The exhalation eliminates toxins from the lungs while relaxing the body. The rhythmic breath strengthens the heart and lungs, and creates good communication between them. In addition, yoga breathing practices deepen concentration, calm the mind, and balance the subtle energies of the body and mind.

## PART 1: NECK MOVEMENTS

Keeping the spine lengthened and the body relaxed, rotate the shoulders in a forward circular movement several times. Next, rotate the shoulders in a backward circular movement. Remain with the shoulders relaxed back and down.

*Vertical* · On the next inhalation, lift the chin upward. Exhale and bend the head forward, bringing the chin to the dimple of the neck. Continue the movement; then sustain each position. While the chin is lifted up, an option is to place the bottom lip over the top lip to further stretch the front of neck. Take 3–5 breaths. Relax the lip. Exhale and bring the chin toward the dimple of the neck. With interlaced fingers behind the head, gently press the head down. Hold for 3–5 breaths; then release the hands. To include half circles, keep the head forward. Inhale as the head swings to the right. Exhale as the head swings to the left. Repeat several times. Then return the neck to natural alignment.

*Horizontal* · With the head and the back straight, inhale, turning the head to the right. Exhale to the left. Repeat a minimum of 3–5 times; then sustain each side for 3–5 breaths.

*Side-to-Side* · Exhale and bring the right ear toward the right shoulder. To deepen the stretch, externally rotate the left shoulder down away from the left ear. Inhale and return the head to the center. Exhale, turning the left ear toward the left shoulder. Alternate sides; then sustain each side 3–5 breaths. Return the neck to natural alignment.

*Clockwise/Counterclockwise* · Exhale and bring the chin toward the dimple of the neck. Rotate the head in a forward circular movement as if the nose were drawing a circle (do not take the head back). Repeat several times in each direction. Maintain continuous movement or hold one area longer if needed to release tension. When you complete, the head returns to the center with the chin toward the neck. Inhale and lift the head.

### PART 2: EYE MOVEMENTS

Eye movements soothe the eyes while toning and strengthening the eye muscles. During a flight the eyes may feel dry. Eye movements help restore lubrication. There are several variations. Rest between rounds if needed. The head should not move during the eye exercises. Maintain relaxation in the facial muscles, neck, and shoulders. Eye movements are performed slowly.

*Vertical* · Have a relaxed gaze with eyes facing forward. Inhale as the eyes gaze up. Exhale as the eyes move down and in as far as possible. Repeat several times; then hold each position. Return the eyes to center.

*Horizontal* · Inhale as the eyes move in a horizontal position to the right. On the exhalation, the eyes flow to the left. Repeat several times; then hold each side. Return the eyes to center.

*Diagonal* · Inhale as the eyes move to the upper right corner. Exhale as the eyes move diagonally down across the bridge of the nose to the lower left corner. Move from the upper right to the lower left. Complete 3–5 rounds. Repeat diagonal movements on the other side with the eyes flowing between the upper left corner and the lower right corner.

*Clockwise/Counterclockwise* · Lift the eyes up as if to see a number twelve on a clock. Make smooth clockwise circular movements. After several rounds, continue with counterclockwise movements.

*Inner Eye Gaze* · Close the eyes and focus on the space between the eyebrows, the seat of the mind. This eye gesture rests the eyes while calming the mind. During Seat Salutation the eyes may be open or closed.

### PART 3: OVER-ARM STRETCH

Inhale, interlace the fingers, and extend straight arms overhead, relaxing the shoulders down away from the ears with the palms facing up. Exhale, bending the elbows, and place interlaced fingers behind the head, keeping the elbows pulled back. Inhale and stretch the hands and arms overhead again. Repeat several times; then sustain each position for a few breaths. When completed, exhale, bringing palms together in front of the chest and the hands to the lap.

## PART 4: ARROW POSE

The shoulders remain rolled back and down. Exhale while bringing the left arm behind the back, reaching the left fingers up toward the neck. Inhale and extend the right arm overhead. Exhaling, bend the right elbow so the right and left hands come together. If you are unable to reach, use a tie between the hands or instead of having the right arm overhead, bring the right hand behind the back to support the left elbow. Another option is to bring the left side as high as you can; then sit back in your seat to support the arm position. Enjoy for 5 breaths. Exhale to release. Repeat on the other side. When completed, roll the shoulders back and down several times.

## PART 5: PALM TREE

Place the right forearm on the armrest. Inhale, lifting the left arm overhead. Exhale, lengthening the torso to the right while stretching the left side of the torso toward the right. Remain in this lateral flexion-spinal stretch for a few breaths. Inhale, lengthen the spine, and lift the arm overhead. Exhale, releasing the arm. Repeat on the other side.

## PART 6: SPINAL ROLLS

Some aircraft do not have room for this full spinal roll. If not, then modify accordingly by partially rolling forward or rolling to the side of the knees. Inhale, lengthening the spine. With your hands, hold onto the front of the chair. Exhaling, hinge from the hips, lengthening the spine out and over the thighs. The head is the last to come forward. After the torso completely relaxes onto the thighs, inhale. Then beginning at the base of the spine, roll up vertebra by vertebra. The head is the last to lift. The chest is open and the chin gently lifts. Both wave movements begin at the base of spine. While exhaling, keep the chest open until the torso completely relaxes onto the thighs. Then maintain a spinal flexion as you roll up. Repeat this wave-like movement through the spine several times. After the last exhalation, inhale and roll the spine into natural alignment.

### Part 7: Spinal Twist

Cross the right leg over the left leg. Inhaling, lengthen the spine as you prep for Spinal Twist. Place the right hand against the armrest on right side of the seat. Place the left forearm or hand against the outer right knee for leverage. Exhale, and beginning at the base of the spine rotate vertebra by vertebra, twisting the torso to your right. Use arm strength to take you deeper into the stretch. Hold for 5–10 breaths. Exhale and unwind, beginning at the base of the spine. After the spine unwinds, release the right foot to the ground. Repeat on the other side.

### Part 8: Ankle-Calf Leg Stretch

Inhale, stretching the right foot and leg out (under the front seat) as far as you can. Exhale, flexing the foot. Inhale and point the toes. Repeat a few times. Then circle the foot both clockwise and counterclockwise several times. Repeat with the left side.

### Part 9: Squat

Inhale, bringing the right knee toward the chest by lifting the foot onto the seat. Exhale, placing the right foot to the ground. Inhale and lift the left foot up. Exhale and put the left foot down. Repeat several times; then sustain each side. Place interlaced fingers around the knee to bring it closer to the chest. Sustain the knee close to the chest for 3–5 breaths. Exhale, lowering the foot to the ground. An option is to bring both knees to the chest for a few breaths.

### Part 10: Hip Opening/Ankle Rotations/Foot Massage

Inhale while placing the left foot across the thigh, directly above the right knee. To ensure that the ankle and knee are in line with one another, gently press the left hand on the left knee to aid in opening the left hip. If you are not wearing socks, place the right fingers between the toes for a toe stretch. With the right hand assisting the left foot in ankle rotations, make several clockwise and counterclockwise circles. When completed, enjoy a foot massage. There are vital points throughout the feet that help to energize the body when stimulated. Press each point on your foot with gentle, deep pressure. Do this for several minutes. Repeat on the other foot. Exhale, resting both feet on the floor.

This completes Seat Salutation. You may either add the wall postures after Seat Salutation or continue with Sun Moon Breath and Deep Relaxation.

## Sun Moon Breath

*Technique* · Use Complete Breath with Sun Moon. Exhale, and then begin with Variation 1 (1:1) of Balancing Breath, eventually progressing to Variation 2 (1:2).

Use *visnu mudra* (sustaining gesture) or *nasagra mudra* (nose gesture). For visnu mudra, lightly close the hand, extending the fourth and fifth fingers and thumb. With the right hand, the thumb closes the right nostril and the fourth finger closes the left nostril. For nasagra mudra, place the tips of the second and third fingers at the eyebrow center. When using the right hand, the thumb closes the right nostril and the fourth finger closes the left nostril. You may alternate hands so the arm doesn't tire, or support the elbow on the armrest so the upper body remains comfortable.

To control the airflow, the thumb and finger may be placed over the concave area. It is located on the side of the nostril next to the area that expands out. Inhale through the left nostril and then exhale through the right nostril. Next, inhale through the right nostril, and exhale through the left nostril. This completes one round. Begin with 5 to 10 minutes. Sun Moon completes with exhalation through the left nostril.

*Benefits* · The benefits of Sun Moon Breath are many. Sun Moon Breath increases lung capacity as well as purifies the blood through greater intake of oxygen. It relieves sinus congestion, headaches, nausea, and other imbalances. Sun Moon Breath also strengthens the nervous system and steadies the mind. It purifies *nadis,* the subtle nerve channels that carry the flow of *prana* (vital energy). In addition, this breath technique balances the male (rational) and the female (intuitive) energies, bringing good physical and mental health to the body and mind.

*Deep Relaxation* • The breath returns to Natural Breath. Close the eyes, gently focusing between the eyebrows. Remain the silent witness. Observe the flow of breath as the body relaxes. Maintain a calm mind and feel deep relaxation throughout the body. After meditation, allow the body to remain relaxed and the mind calm.

## STANDING POSTURES: FIVE MOVEMENTS AT THE WALL

### PART 1: STANDING TOE-CALF BALANCE

While standing in the aisle, inhale and lift onto the balls of the feet. Hold for 3–5 seconds. Exhale, lowering the feet to the ground. Continue for 5–10 rounds. You may hold onto the top of two seats or balance on your own. This stimulates lower leg circulation, which is important after sitting for a long time.

### PART 2: WALL HANG

Face the wall one arm's distance away. Place the feet beneath the hips and parallel to one another. Exhale Standing. Inhale Upward Salute, lifting the arms overhead and bringing palms together. Exhale Wall Hang. Place hands, fingers spread far apart, high up onto the wall with the shoulders in a diagonal line to the hips. Rotate the shoulders down and away from the ears. Lengthen the spine by moving the crown and the base of the spine in opposite directions. The chest remains extended outward toward the ground, with the head between the arms. Use a slow, even breath. This is an excellent posture to open the shoulders and back.

## PART 3: FLOWING WALL HANG

Exhale and bring the chin to the dimple of the neck. Inhale, flowing into Wall Lift. Press the pelvis forward and roll from the base of the spine vertebra by vertebra, creating a gentle backward bend. Exhale, pull the hips back and lengthen the spine, bringing the head between the arms. Repeat the flowing spinal roll. The movement is sequential from the base of the spine to the crown of the head. The aim is to create a wave-like motion through the spine. Flowing Wall Hang creates both a forward bend and a backward bending movement to energize the back. Repeat several times. To release, return to Wall Hang, exhale while slightly bending the knees, and roll the spine up as the arms relax to the side. Inhale Upward Salute, bringing the arms out from the side and overhead with palms together. Exhale Standing. Bring the palms together in front of the chest and arms to the side.

## PART 4: PALM TREE

Place the right side of the body facing the wall, one arm's distance away. To prep for Palm Tree, inhale, lifting the arms parallel to the ground, left palm facing up and right pahn facing down. Exhale as you lift the left arm overhead in line with the ear, stretching the torso to the right. Place the right hand on the wall. Extend the hips to the left in the opposite direction of the torso, stretching toward the wall. Inhale, returning to the prep position with the spine upright and the arms parallel to the ground. Repeat several rounds; then sustain Palm Tree. After sustaining, return to the prep position, exhale, and release the arms to the side. Repeat on the other side.

## PART 5: WATERFALL (FORWARD BEND AGAINST WALL)

The back faces the wall. With the feet placed approximately one foot away from the wall, rest the hips against the wall. For support, place the hands behind on the wall as you exhale, hinging forward from the hips into a forward bend. Keep the hips against the wall. Interlace the arms, hands resting in the crease of the elbows. Allow the head to relax toward the ground and the sit-bones toward the ceiling. Breathe slowly, allowing the posterior muscles of the body to relax. Hold for several breaths. Exhale, release the arms, slightly bend the knees, and roll up vertebra by vertebra. The head is the last to lift to Standing.

Take short walks throughout the flight and drink additional pure water. After the flight, enjoy a walk outdoors to feed the body/mind with life energy.

Kali Ray TriYoga® International copyright 2002.

## USING ESSENTIAL OILS TO PREVENT JET STRESS

Essential oils have very powerful healing properties. Certain essential oils help during and after the flight. The following essential oil blends are offered so that you may make your own therapeutic potions to prevent jet stress.

### JET LAG ESSENTIAL OIL BLEND

Lemon grass—5 drops

Black pepper—1 drop

Grapefruit—4 drops

Lavender—5 drops

Tea tree—3 drops

Add essential oils to a 10 mL glass bottle. Fill the remainder of the bottle with a carrier oil. We recommend jojoba oil, as it does not become rancid. Rub oil on soles of feet before or during plane ride. It is a simple but effective way to combat fatigue and to calm the mind. It is also antibacterial.

### ANTIBACTERIAL SPRAY

Tea Tree—3 drops

Lavender—3 drops

Sandalwood—3 drops

Eucalyptus—3 drops

Add essential oils to a small glass spray bottle. Fill bottle with water. Spray into the air around your seat. It is nice to explain to your seat mates that it is an all-natural antibacterial spray. This spray is an optional part of the protocol.

Putting into practice this seven-step jet stress prevention protocol, as well as incorporating the use of therapeutic essential oils, will help you arrive at your destination feeling vital and healthy. *Bon Voyage!*

*Appendix*

# Resources
# Directory

The resources in this section are those used by the Tree of Life Café and cover all the stored cupboard foods used in this book.

## RESOURCES FROM TREE OF LIFE CAFÉ

The Tree of Life Rejuvenation Center sells many of the products mentioned in this book:

FOODS

- Hemp Seeds
- Goji Berries
- Coconut Oil
- Mesquite Seed Pod Meal
- Golden Flax Seeds

- Olives
- Olive Oil
- Nut Butter
- Nori Sheets
- Celtic Sea Salt

## EQUIPMENT

- Green Star Juicer
- Champion Juicer
- Vitamix
- K-Tec Blender (professional, high-power blender)
- Tribest Travel Blender
- Wellness Water Filter
- Mandoline Plus
- Spiral Spaghetti Slicer
- Sprout Bags

## BOOKS BY GABRIEL COUSENS, M.D.

*Spiritual Nutrition and the Rainbow Diet*
*Conscious Eating,* revised edition
*Depression-Free for Life*
*Tachyon Energy: A New Paradigm in Holistic Healing*

*Sevenfold Peace*
*Modern Essene Way and Modern Essene Communions*
*Rainbow Green Live-Food Cuisine*

In addition to the products mentioned above, we also sell supplements, self-care products, and health products. You can view the latest products on our website, www.treeoflife.nu or give us a call at (520) 394-2520. You can also write to the Tree of Life Café if you have any questions about foods, products, or recipes at café@treeoflife.nu.

# OTHER RESOURCES

The following are excellent companies with products not available from The Tree of Life Rejuvenation Center:

## NUTS AND SEEDS

**Sun Organic Farm**
*Bulk Nuts and Seeds*
(888) 269-9888
www.sunorganic.com

**Big Tree Organic Farms**
*Bulk Certified and Transition Almonds*
(209) 669-3678
www.bigtreeorganic.com

**Living Tree Community Foods**
(800) 260-5534
www.livingtreecommunity.com

## HERBS

### Frontier Natural Foods
*Organic Bulk Herbs and Spices*
(800) 669-3275
www.frontiercoop.com

### Mountain Rose Herbs
*Bulk Wildcrafted Herbs*
(800) 879-3337
www.mountainroseherbs.com

### Ameri Herb
*Untreated herbs and spices*
P.O. Box 1968,
Ames, Iowa 50010-1968

### Primal Essence, Inc.
*Chai Spice and other liquid spice and herb extracts*
(877) 774-6253
(800) 267-6141

## SEA VEGETABLES

### Maine Coast Sea Vegetables
*Bulk sea vegetables*
(207) 565-2907
www.seaveg.com

### Mendocino Sea Vegetable Company
*Rare varieties of sea vegetables*
(707) 937-2050
www.seaweed.net

### Gold Mine
*Best source for nori*
(800) 475-3663
www.goldminenaturalfood.com

### Island Seaweed
*Sustainably wild-crafted seaweed*
(360) 398-1215
www.islandseaweed.com

### Ocean Harvest Sea Vegetable Company
*Wild-crafted and sun-dried*
(707) 937-0637 or
(707) 937-1923
www.ohsv.net

## OILS

### Omega Nutrition
*High-quality oil and raw apple cider vinegar*
(800) 661-FLAX (3529)
www.omegaflo.com

### Bariani Olive Oil
*Stone-pressed olive oil*
(415) 864-1917
bariani@aol.com

## COCONUTS

The Young Thai Coconut mentioned in the recipes can be found in Asian/Chinese supermarkets across the United States and U.K.

## MISO

**South River Miso**
(413) 369-4057
www.southrivermiso.com

## KEFIR GRAINS

**Dominic Anfiteatro**
*Offers kefir grains using either certified raw organic goat's milk, or certified raw bio-dynamic cow's milk; depending on availability. (Vegan kefir grains are not available.)*
10-B Harrow Avenue
Magill, 5072
Adelaide S.A.
Australia
61 0414 860 562
dna@chariot.net.au
http://users.chariot.net.au/~dna/kefirpage.html

**Lifeway, Inc.**
*Offers kefir grains (starter) derived from non-organic dairy. (Vegan kefir grains are not available.)*
(847) 967-1010
www.lifeway.net

## MISCELLANEOUS

**Kali Ray TriYoga International**™
P.O. Box 6367
Malibu, CA 90264
(310) 589-0600
fax: (310) 589-0783
info@triyoga.com
www.triyoga.com

**Elizabeth Van Buren Aromatherapy**
*High-quality essential oils*
(800) 710-7759
www.sub-aromatherapy.com

**Chad Sarno — Gourmet Raw Chef**
*Vital Creations*, book or video
www.rawchef.org.

**Super Oxy Powder**
*35% Food-grade $H_2O_2$ Powder*
(800) 253-2748

# RECOMMENDED CONNECTIONS

**Tree of Life Rejuvenation Center**

The Tree of Life Rejuvenation Center is open year round for workshops, rejuvenation treatments, and holistic medical evaluations. At the Tree of Life you can also experience the Rainbow Green Live-Food Cuisine outlined in this book and attend our daily food preparation classes.
(520) 394-2520
www.treeoflife.nu

**Nature's First Law**
Offers a large selection of books, events, and online communities covering all aspects of raw food.
(888) RAW-FOOD
www.rawfood.com

**The Fresh Network**
*Offers a large selection of books, events, and online communities covering all aspects of raw food.*
UK 870 800 7070
www.fresh-network.com
Europe

ORGANIZATION FOR WORLD FOOD SUPPLY ISSUES

**Food First: Institute for Food and Development Policies**
398 60th Street
Berkeley, California 94618
(510) 654-4400
www.foodfirst.com

*Appendix*

# Summary of Food Phases Chart

# Summary of Food Phases Chart

| Phase I | Phase I.5 | Phase II | Phase II Minimal Use | Rainbow Green Live-Food Cuisine Foods to Avoid |
|---|---|---|---|---|
| nuts & seeds | coconut water (diluted with other ingredients) | yams (raw) sweet potatoes (raw) pumpkin (raw) parsnips (raw) beets (raw) rutabaga (raw) | yams (cooked) sweet potatoes (cooked) pumpkin (cooked) parsnips (cooked) beets (cooked) rutabaga (cooked) hard squash (cooked) summer squash (cooked) | all processed foods |
| coconut pulp | | | | all animal products: flesh dairy eggs |
| all greens all vegetables (excepted those listed elsewhere) | carrots (raw) hard squash (raw) grapefruit | | | |
| | | oranges apples pears peaches plums pomegranates | straight carrot juice straight orange juice | all grains (except those listed) corn |
| summer squash (raw): zucchini patti pan yellow summer squash | raspberries blueberries strawberries cherries cranberries (fresh, unsweetened) goji berries | | high-glycemic fruits: apricots figs grapes raisins melons mangos bananas papaya pineapple kiwi sapote cherimoya rambutian durian dates | white potatoes white rice white flour honey sugar alcohol coffee caffeine tobacco |
| sea vegetables | | blackberries | | |
| tomatoes avocados cucumber red bell pepper | low-glycemic Tree of Life mesquite meal | grapefruit juice (diluted with water) raw carob | | |
| | | | | heated oil (except coconut oil) |
| flax oil hemp oil olive oil sesame oil almond oil sunflower oil coconut oil (butter) | non-stored grains: wild rice quinoa buckwheat millet amaranth spelt | bee pollen unfermented soy products (as a transition food) | | soy sauce & nama shoyu |
| | fermented foods: apple cider vinegar | | | yeast brewer's yeast |
| lemons limes | miso sauerkraut kefir | | dried fruits fresh, raw, fruit juices | nutritional yeast mushrooms |
| Klamath Lake algae | | | seed cheese | |
| super green powders | | | cooked, organic, whole foods | peanuts cashews cottonseed |
| stevia | | | | bottled juices |

# ABOUT THE AUTHORS

**Gabriel Cousens, M.D., M.D.(H), Diplomate in Ayurveda,** Founder and Director of the Tree of Life Rejuvenation Center in Patagonia, Arizona, is an internationally celebrated healer, spiritual facilitator, world peace-worker, and author. As a holistic medical physician, physician of the soul, a psychiatrist and family therapist, and a licensed homeopathic physician, Dr. Cousens uses the modalities of vegan live-food nutrition, naturopathy, Ayurveda, homeopathy, and acupuncture, blended with joyful spiritual awareness, in the healing of body, mind, and spirit. He is the University for Integrative Learning Provost of the world's first vegan, live-food Master of Arts program, hosted at the Tree of Life. A cum laude graduate of Amherst College, he received his M.D. degree from Columbia Medical School in 1969. He is a best-selling author. Titles include *Conscious Eating, Spiritual Nutrition and the Rainbow Diet, Sevenfold Peace, Tachyon Energy: A New Paradigm in Holistic Healing,* and *Depression-Free for Life.*

## TREE OF LIFE CAFÉ STAFF BIOGRAPHIES

**Shanti Golds Cousens** lives and serves at the Tree of Life Rejuvenation Center, where she shares her experiences teaching live-food preparation classes to guests, staff, and apprentices. For the "fragrant at heart," Shanti has created the Essential Oil Delicacies. The knowledge of aromatherapy was gained at Elizabeth Van Buren's college in Santa Cruz, California, completing the full spectrum of botany and chemistry. Shanti's support and strength into "Veganism" came from Kaliji, who shares her timeless wisdom of Kali Ray TriYoga®, in which Shanti is a Senior Teacher. She loves to teach TriYoga at the Tree of Life.

**Philip Madeley,** originally from Manchester, England, holds a Bachelor's degree in Environmental Management. He was an active promoter in the eco live-food movement in the United Kingdom. Philip is multi-talented, and as an integral member of the Tree of Life Community since May 2000, he has served in many capacities. In particular, Philip is the Tree of Life Café Manager. He specializes in teaching live-food preparation classes for Tree of Life guests, Chef Apprenticeship program participants, and Master's Degree program participants. Philip works directly with Dr. Cousens in researching high-quality foods and supplements, along with other health-enhancing products and their sources. He is an Essene Priest in the Essene Order of Light. Philip's radiant, heart-centered spirit is infectious and he brings delight to all who visit the Tree of Life. The food he serves is a reflection of the tremendous love and caring he brings to its preparation and presentation. Philip contributed greatly to this book, writing the "Secrets of Rainbow Green Live-Food Cuisine Preparation" and "Resources Directory" and taking the photographs of the food.

**Ivri Krzyz** is a dedicated spiritual student, an Essene Priestess, Yoga teacher, and sacred dance facilitator. She holds a Bachelor's degree in Environmental Policy. Along with her husband Anu Tarahum, she is a long-time member of the Tree of Life community. She "retired" from her position as Assistant to the Director of the Tree of Life to be a full-time mother to her son Israel, now a vibrant toddler. The uncharted, rewarding journey of nourishing a baby with 100% live foods from birth inspired her to write the section of this book entitled "Raising Rainbow Babies." She also served as compiler of the recipes and in-house editor of this book.

**Karen Parker** is the former Head Chef at the Tree of Life Café. Her culinary expertise combines the concepts of gourmet cuisine with Rainbow Green Live-Food Cuisine protocol. Karen is the lead instructor of food preparation for the culinary component of the Vegan Live-Food Nutrition Master's Program through the University of Integrative Learning at the Tree of Life. With equal parts enthusiasm and nutritional information, Karen also works with clients by conducting in-home dietary inventories, live-food menu planning, and instruction in food preparation through her website www.sunraw.com. She also consults with existing and start-up restaurants on the subject of gourmet raw-food dining operations. Before relocating to Arizona and the Tree of Life, she offered workshops in live-food nutrition and its preparation in the state of Washington, often in conjunction with yoga retreats. Karen holds a Bachelor's degree from the University of Nevada, where she did coursework in Environmental Management and in Nutrition (with field work in Costa Rica, Panama, and Guatemala).

**Chad Sarno** has been very active within the raw, vegan community for years. He is a certified Chef and Instructor and also the founder of Vital Creations Chef Services. Chad is a former Head Chef of the Tree of Life Café and former staff chef of the Living Light Culinary Arts Institute. He has been traveling the globe assisting in recipe, menu, and kitchen development for the opening of many restaurants and centers, including Vitalities Kauai and the world-renowned gourmet restaurant Roxanne's in Larkspur, California. Amidst this extensive traveling, Chad provides in-home personal trainings, group workshops, catering events, and restaurant consultation. He can be contacted through his website: www.RawChef.org.

**Rebecca Bosch,** former Head Chef at the Tree of Life Café, is a writer, raw-food chef, educator, and lifestyle consultant whose life is a testimony to the vitality of raw food, simplicity, and natural living. She has bicycled across two continents and run eight marathons—the better half totally raw! She and her mother Laurie are co-founders of "Good Stuff by Mom & Me," a multigenerational initiative dedicated to bringing food quality and nutrition issues into the public forum through the dissemination of informational materials and high-quality organic raw-food products. For more information please contact Good Stuff: (888) 797-6865 or foodalive@yahoo.com.

**Sita Rose,** former Head Chef at the Tree of Life Café, created the Spiritual Journal Writing course at the Tree of Life, authored *The Fasting Heart: a manual on journaling for fasting retreatants,* created and facilitated the Tree of Life Raw-Food Support Group, and coined her signature phrase, "Raw food is sacred, raw food is sexy!" Sita is a published poet and was recently awarded the Sue

Saniel Elkind Prize. She is currently in the developmental stages of founding her School of Ecstatic Embodiment, and writing its textbook to be entitled *Duh!* She resides in Manhattan and can be reached at Nothingwithoutjoy@hotmail.com.

**Rose Lee Calabro** is the author of *Living in the Raw* and worked at the Tree of Life for eight months while a client of Gabriel Cousens, M.D. She lives and teaches raw-food classes in Santa Cruz, California. Rose Lee was one of the creators of the Living Food Health Expo and produced it for three years. Her purpose in life is to inspire and motivate people to change their lifestyle and eat more raw living foods, and to help them understand that the body is self-healing. She has healed her own body of many health challenges; read about her life changes at www.rawlivingfoods.com. Rose Lee was responsible for compiling and formatting some of the recipes in the initial phase of the book. She also contributed a number of recipes.

**Ren Fisher** was an assistant chef at the Tree of Life Café. Her interest in nutrition began after working at several alternative health clinics, witnessing firsthand that the clients who saw health improvements were those who changed their diets. Living-food preparation is the perfect culmination of this awareness. Ren enjoys creating recipes that include nutritional powerhouses like kale and parsley. She also loves the challenge of recreating favorite ethnic dishes in a fresh-food fashion.

**Heather Thompson** worked at the Tree of Life Café as an apprentice and eventually Head Chef and contributed many recipes.

**Lucas Rockwood** is a raw-food chef, coach, and writer living between Los Angeles and New York City. He joined the Tree of Life Café as an apprentice, bringing with him a natural flair for creating delicious Rainbow Green Live-Food Cuisine. Lucas contributed a significant number of innovative recipes to this book.

**Alison Leigh Stern,** a Tree of Life Apprenticeship alumnus, has a flair for challah and desserts and contributed many delectable recipes to this book. Alison is a yoga instructor and live-food chef currently living in New York City.

Isaiah worked at the Tree of Life in the café, garden, and maintenance and contributed many recipes.

Others who contributed recipes:

**Tziona**

**Robert Dunlop**

**Richard Harvey** and **Mary Houston** have had a biological practice in New York since 1993. They have studied with such prominent figures in the world of biological medicine as Dr. Thomas Rau of the Paracelcus Klinik in Switzerland, and Dr. Maria Blecker, the successor of Dr. Enderlein, the progenitor of biological medicine. Richard has certification in biological medicine and Homeopathic homotoxicology and is a former psychotherapist. Mary is certified in Ayurvedic medicine. She has also studied with Dr. Dagmar Lattinger-Bolling, the leading exponent of Paracelsian medicine, an ancient form of alchemical medicine. Richard studied and worked with Dr. Robert Young, founder of Innerlight International, for several years and collaborated with Dr. Jack Lewin in the establishment of the first integrative medical facility in Hawaii. Mary had a weekly radio show on health and nutrition in New York for 17 years and pioneered the first global radio shows between the USA and USSR. Raw food is central to their practice of "biological alchemy." They train doctors and lay people in microscopy, biological medicine, and bringing the biological terrain back into balance. They contributed the dark-field and phase-contrast slides to this book. They can be contacted at (212) 932-8634.

# About Tree of Life Rejuvenation Center & Tree of Life Café

Tree of Life Rejuvenation Center in Patagonia, Arizona, is an innovative, spiritual, holistic healing, eco-retreat sanctuary for body, mind, and spirit and a holistic medical spa. We offer the art of physical rejuvenation, combined with psychological and spiritual development for complete body, mind and spiritual renewal. An oasis for awakening, Tree of Life is committed to the possibility and process of spiritual Liberation. We serve participants to awaken on all levels—to become free from all limitations, so that they may fully experience the natural, Divine joy of a life of "awakened normality."

The Tree of Life is located on 172 acres of a beautiful southern Arizona mesa 60 miles southeast of Tucson. Nestled in the Patagonia Mountains, the magnificent 360-degree view is awesome. In this inspirational setting, participants learn how to draw healing energies from the Divine and the elements of organic earth, clean air, radiant sun, pure water, and the living planet as a whole. Here on this blessed land we connect with the rhythms of nature and the Self though Rainbow Green Live-Food Cuisine and preparation instruction; "authentic" gardening; sunrise and sunset ceremonies; Kali Ray TriYoga®; meditation; breathing practices; Kabbalistic Shabbat Celebration; Spirit Dance drumming and chanting; Shaktipat/Ruah Hakodesh Meditation; Homa (purifying fire ceremony); sweat lodge; full moon ceremony; expressive dance; nature hikes; labyrinth walking; ecological living; and heartfelt human interaction. All of these contribute to creating, supporting, and sustaining the living of life in balance and the profound awakening of spiritual energies.

To support your journey, we offer a comprehensive synergy of the best elements of nutrition, Ayurveda, homeopathy, naturopathy, Tachyon technology, bodywork, colonics, state-of-the-art detoxification technologies, Pancha Karma (an ancient system of detoxification and balance), and medically supervised juice fasting. An integrated holistic approach, these modalities accelerate conscious physical, emotional, and spiritual evolution and often eliminate or greatly improve chronic disease.

Several levels of workshops on Rainbow Green Live-Food Cuisine preparation and lifestyle are available. These include: group Spiritual Fasting Retreats; Arizona Live!, a live-food education intensive; Conscious Eating, home-chef certification course; Zero Point Process, psychospiritual healing course; Sacred Relationships, embodying Divine Union in relationship; and Modern Essene Way Retreat, Levels I and II, which connect with the universal, core truths of the Essene way. For in-depth education in Rainbow Green Live-Food Cuisine lifestyle skills, the Tree of Life offers a Master's degree in Vegan Live-Food Nutrition and a four-month-long Apprenticeship Program in Vegan Live-Food Culinary Arts, in which participants become experts in preparing the Rainbow Green Live-Food Cuisine. We also offer a four-month to one-year Apprenticeship in "authentic" Spiritual Gardening.

At the Tree of Life we assist you in overcoming what we lovingly call "the dark chocolate side of healing"—the hidden resistance to healing. We skillfully and compassionately help you let go of your addictions to the unhealthy habits that bring on chronic disease and much misery. These addictions include negative lifestyle habits, poor food choices, the tendency to form unhealthy relationships, and addictions to such health-depleting substances such as coffee, tobacco, sugar, etc., all of which keep us from reaching our full potential. In many, we have helped release psychospiritual blocks that keep them stuck in self-defeating cycles of destructive habits.

For those who choose to participate in our Whole Person Healing optimal health medical evaluation (advance reservations required), we are able to detect often-overlooked biochemically based depression, as well as other biological imbalances of the brain and body. These imbalances may be caused by hypoglycemia, neurotransmitter deficiencies in brain chemistry, food allergies, previous alcohol and other substance abuse, or candida, among other causes. Helping people rebuild healthy biochemistry so they may be free of depression, chronic disease, addictions, prescription drugs, and other life addictions is a key to experiencing a life of joy, peace, and Freedom.

Intensive individual, couple, and family Zero Point Process psychospiritual healing sessions are facilitated by Dr. Cousens to catalyze and support the process of healing and awakening. (Advance reservations required.)

At the Tree of Life, we specialize in creating personalized programs to help you heal into health and happiness. All the healing modalities and programs that we offer systematically help you overcome life-force-depleting blocks to higher rejuvenation and awakening. Becoming free of addictions and chronic disease is just the first step in the rejuvenation process. We support you to become free on all levels, from all limitations—for only then can you fully experience the natural joy of being Divinely alive.

The Tree of Life Rejuvenation Center is home of the renowned Tree of Life Café—an innovative "authentic," organic, kosher, vegan-vegetarian, live-food restaurant. Guests of the Tree of Life, as well as the public, gather to experience delicious Rainbow Green Live-Food Cuisine. The Café is a completely ecological dining experience. Whether you are feasting in our straw bale structure or enjoying the fresh air and mountain views on the porch, you will be supported in conscious eating on all levels. We invite you to join us for a meal. Please call for reservations, meal times, and prices. We look forward to serving you.

The Tree of Life Rejuvenation Center is a fully operational center including the live-food café; eight simple, tasteful, residential Casitas; a meditation sanctuary; organic gardens and greenhouse; hiking trails; the world's largest Chartres labyrinth; a Mikvah, an Essene/Kabbalistic purification pool set in a "Garden of Eden"; hot tubs; detoxification treatment pavilions; healing arts room; Unity Room for Yoga and seminars; and an outdoor Yoga platform.

For those who are lovers of nature and pioneers at heart, there is much we have to offer that can create a powerful healing transformation in your life. Guests from 65 countries have come to share the "raw life" with us. They return to their homes around the globe rejuvenated, inspired, and empowered.

The key to shifting to a more positive lifestyle is inspiration for the commitment to change, rather than simply more intellectual education. This is where the real secret to healing happens. This inspiration is what we call *The Tree of Life Experience.* It is a pleasure to see people begin to drink deeply again from the fountain of joy within. It is your birthright that awaits reclaiming!

We invite you to visit us on the Internet at www.treeoflife.nu or schedule a tour of the Tree of Life Rejuvenation Center. We look forward to celebrating the joy of sacred living with you.

Contact us at:
P.O. Box 1080
Patagonia, Arizona 85624
(520) 394-2520
healing@treeoflife.nu
www.treeoflife.nu

# Bibliography

Alpert, M.E., Hutt, M.S.R., Wogan, G.N., Davidson, C.S. Association between aflatoxin content and hepatoma frequency in Uganda. *Cancer,* 1971; 28: 253.

Airola, Paavo. *Are You Confused?* Phoenix, Arizona: Health Plus Publishers, 1971.

_____. *How to Get Well.* Phoenix, Arizona: Health Plus Publishers, 1974.

_____. *Hypoglycemia: A Better Approach.* Phoenix, Arizona: Health Plus Publishers, 1977.

_____. *Worldwide Secrets for Staying Young.* Phoenix, Arizona: Health Plus Publishers, 1982.

Berger, Stewart M., M.D. *Forever Young.* New York: Avon Books, 1989.

Bland, Jeffrey S., Ph.D. *Genetic Nutritioneering.* Los Angeles: Keats Publishing, 1999.

Blecker, Dr. Maria. *Blood Examination in Darkfield According to Professor D. Günther Enderlein.* Gesamtherstellung, Germany: Semmelweiss-Verlag, 1993, p. 4.

Burkitt, D. Some disease characteristics of modern Western civilization. *British Medical Journal,* 1973; 1: 274.

Chen, F., Cole, P., Mi, Z., Xing, L.Y. Corn flour consumption and mortality from esophageal cancer in Shanxi, China. *International Journal of Cancer,* 1993; 4(2): 163–69.

Cichoke, Anthony J., D.C. *Enzymes and Enzyme Therapy.* New Canaan, Connecticut: Keates Publishing, Inc., 1994.

Cooper, L.A., and Gadd, G.M. Differentiation and melanin production in hyaline and pigmented strains of *Microdochium bolleyi.* In: Constantini, A.V., Weiland, H., Qvick, Lars I. *The Fungal/Microtoxin Etiology of Human Disease,* Vol. 2, Freiburg, Germany: Johann Friedrich Oberlin Verlag, 1994, pp. 63, 84, 89.

Costantini, Weiland, Qvick, op. cit. (above), p. 84.

Costantini, Weiland, Qvick, op. cit. (above), p. 63.

Cousens, Gabriel, M.D. *Conscious Eating*. Berkeley, California: North
    Atlantic Books, 2000.

_____. *Sevenfold Peace*. Tiburon, California: H.J. Kramer, 1990.

_____. *Spiritual Nutrition and the Rainbow Diet*. San Rafael, California:
    Cassandra Press, 1986.

Cousens, Gabriel, M.D., and Wagner, David. *Tachyon Energy: A New Paradigm in
    Holistic Healing*. Berkeley, California: North Atlantic Books, 1999.

Crook, William G., M.D. *The Yeast Connection, A Medical Breakthrough*. Jackson,
    Tennessee: Professional Books, 1984, pp. 352–55.

Culhane, J. "PCBs: The Poisons That Won't Go Away." *Reader's Digest*
    (December 1980): 113–15.

Culinary Institute of America. *Professional Chef's Knife Kit*. New York: John
    Wiley and Sons Inc., 2000.

D'Adamo, Peter, Dr. *Eat Right for Your Type*. New York: G.P. Putnam's Sons,
    1996.

Dickens, R., and Jones, H.E.H. Further studies on the carcinogenic action
    of patulin-induced mammary adenomas and local sarcomas or
    fibrosarcomas in mice and rats. *British Journal of Cancer*, 1965; 19: 392.

"Drinking water supplies before and after treatments." *Bulletin of
    Environmental and Contamination Toxicology* 34 (1985): 815–823.

Duggan, R. "Dietary Intake of Pesticide Chemicals in the United States
    (II), June 1966-April 1968," *Pesticides Monitoring Journal* 2 (1969):
    140–52.

Ehret, Charles, and Scanlon, Lynne. *Overcoming Jet Lag*. New York: Berkley
    Books, 1993.

Engel, Cindy. *Wild Health*. Boston, Massachusets: Houghton Mifflin
    Company, 2002.

"Environmental Quality—1975," The Sixth Annual Report of the Council
    on Environmental Quality, Washington, D.C., December 1979.

Galland, Leo, M.D. *Superimmunity for Kids*. New York: Copestone Press, Inc.,
    1988.

Gates, Donna. *The Body Ecology Diet.* Atlanta, Georgia: B.E.D. Publications, Inc., 1996.

Ghadirian, P. "Thermal irritation and esophageal cancer in northern Iran." *Cancer,* 1987; 60(8): 1909–14.

Goster-Powell, K., and Miller, J.B. "International tables of glycemic index." *American Journal of Clinical Nutrition* 62 (1995): 871S–91S.

Graham, Douglas N., D.C., *Grain Damage.* Marathon, Florida: self-published, 1998.

Gray, Robert. *The Colon Health Handbook.* Reno, Nevada: Emerald Publishing, 1991.

Guillette, Elizabeth A., Meza, Maria Mercedes, Aquilar, Maria Guadalupe, Soto, Alma Delia, and Garcia, Idalia Enedina. An Anthropological Approach to the Evaluation of Preschool Children Exposed to Pesticides in Mexico. *Environmental Health Perspectives,* 1998; Vol. 106, No. 6.

Hansen, Peter, Dr. *Stress for Success.* New York: Ballantine Books, 1991.

Harris, S. "Organochlorine Contamination of Breast Milk." Environmental Defense Fund, Washington, D.C., November 7, 1979.

Higa, Teruo, Dr. *An Earth-Saving Revolution.* Tokyo, Japan: Sunmark Publishing Inc., 1993.

Higa, Teruo, Dr. *An Earth-Saving Revolution II.* Tokyo, Japan: Sunmark Publishing Inc., 1994.

Howell, Edward. *Enzyme Nutrition, The Food Enzyme Concept.* Wayne, New Jersey: Avery Publishing Group, Inc., 1986.

Howell, Edward. *Food Enzymes for Health and Longevity.* Woodstock Valley, Connecticut: Omangod Press, 1946.

Hume, E. Douglas. *Béchamp or Pasteur? A Lost Chapter in the History of Biology.* First edition. Ashingdon, Rochford, Essex, England: The C.W. Daniel Company, 1923, p. 150; second edition (London: C.W. Daniel Company, 1932) reprinted by Health Research, Pomeroy, Washington, 1989; pp. 173–74.

"Infant Abnormalities Linked to PCB-Contaminated Fish." *Vegetarian Times* 8 (November 1984).

Ingram, D.M., Nottage, E., Roberts, T. The Role of *Saccharomyces cerevisiae*—baker's, or brewer's, yeast—in the development of breast cancer: A case-control study of patients with breast cancer, benign epithelial hyperplasia and fibrocystic disease of the breast. *British Journal of Cancer,* 1991; 64(1): 187-91.

Jacobson, S. "The Effect of Intrauterine PCB Exposure on Visual Recognition Memory." *Child Development* 56 (1985).

Jensen, Bernard. *The Healing Power of Chlorophyll from Plant Life.* Escondido, California: Bernard Jensen Enterprises, 1984, p. 51.

*Journal of Medical Biological Research,* 1986; 19(6):771–74.

Klaper, Michael. *Pregnancy, Children and the Vegan Diet.* Maui, Hawaii: Gentle World, Inc., 1994.

Kent, Saul. "Aging Research Becomes A Science." *Life Extension.* December 2001: 13–18.

Kramer, Penny. "Health and Longevity: What Centenarians Can Teach Us." *Yoga Journal,* Sept/Oct 1983: 26–30.

Kulvinskas, Viktoras, *Survival into the 21st Century.* Woodstock Valley, Connecticut: Omangod Press, 1981.

Liebman, James. *Rising Toxic Tide: Pesticide Use in California 1991–95.* San Francisco: Pesticide Action Network, 1997.

Linderfelser, L.A., Lillehoj, E.B., Burmeister, H.R. Aflatoxin and trichothecene toxins: skin tumor induction and synergistic acute toxicity in white mice. *Journal of the National Cancer Institute,* 1974; 52: 113.

Livingston-Wheeler, Virginia, M.D. *The Conquest of Cancer.* New York: Franklin Watts, 1984, p. 54.

Lopez, D.A., Williams, R.M., and Miehlke, K. *Enzymes: The Fountain of Youth.* München, Germany: The Neville Press, 1994.

McCay, Clive, Dr. "Life Span of Rats." *Arch. Biochem.* Vol. 2, 1943: 469–76.

Mott, Laurie, and Snyder, Karen. "Pesticide Alert," *Amicus Journal,* Spring 1988.

*New England Journal of Medicine.* "A Study on Contamination in Mother's Breast Milk." March 26, 1981.

Nison, Paul. *Raw Knowledge.* New York: 343 Publishing Company, 2002.

_____. *The Raw Life.* New York: 343 Publishing Company, 2000.

Norden, Michael J., M.D. *Beyond Prozac.* New York: Regan Books, 1995.

Peska, J.J., Bondy, G.S. Alteration of immune function following dietary mycotoxin exposure. *Canadian Journal of Physiology and Pharmacology,* 1990; (68)7: 1009–16.

Popp, F.A. "Biophoton Emission: New Evidence for Coherence in DNA." *Cell Biophysics,* March 1984, Vol 6: 32–52.

Pottenger, Francis M. *Pottenger's Cats: A Study in Nutrition.* San Diego, CA: Price-Pottenger Nutrition Foundation Inc., 1995.

Price, Weston A. *Nutrition and Physical Degeneration.* New Canaan, Connecticut: Keats Publishing, 1989.

Robbins, John. *Diet for a New America.* Walpole, New Hampshire: Stillpoint, 1987.

_____. *The Food Revolution.* Berkeley, California: Conari Press, 2001.

Rogers, Sherry A. *Detox or Die.* Sarasota, Florida: Sam Key, 2002.

Rosen, Ruth. "Polluted Bodies," *San Francisco Chronicle.* February 3, 2003.

Santillo, Humbart. *Food Enzymes, The Missing Link.* Prescott Valley, Arizona: Hohm Press, 1987.

Sears, Barry, Ph.D. *Enter the Zone.* New York: Regan Books, 1995.

Spindler, Stephen, Dr. *Proceedings of the National Academy of Sciences,* September 11, 2001.

Steinman, David. *Diet for a Poisoned Planet.* New York: Harmony Books, 1990.

Stoll, Andrew L., M.D. *The Omega-3 Connection.* New York: Simon & Schuster, 2001.

*Surgeon General's Report on Nutrition and Health.* Washington, D.C.: U.S. Department of Health and Human Services, Public Health Service, 1988.

Svoboda, Dr. Robert E. *Prakruti, Your Ayurvedic Constitution*. Albuquerque, New Mexico: Geocom, 1989.

Toth, B., Patil, K., Erikson, J., Kupper, R. False morel mushroom *Gyromitra esculenta* toxin: N-methyl-N-formylhydrazone carcinogenesis in mice. *Mycopathologia*, 1979; 68(2): 121–28.

Toth, B., Gannett, P. Carcinogenesis study in mice by 3-methylbutanol methylformylhydrazone of *Gyromitra esculenta*, in vivo. *Mycopathologia*, 1990; 4(5): 283–88.

Toth, B., Taylor, J., Gannett, P. Tumor induction with hexanol methylformylhydrazone of *Gyromitra esculenta*. *Mycopathologia*, 1991; 115(2): 65–71.

Toth, B., Patil, K., Pyssalo, H., Stessman, C., Gannett, P. Cancer induction in mice by feeding the raw morel mushroom *Gyromitra esculenta*. *Cancer Research*, 1992; 52(8): 2279-84.

Walford, Roy, M.D. *120-Year Diet*. New York: Pocket Books, 1986.

Weindruch, Richard, Dr., and Prolla, Tomas, Dr. *Science*. August 27, 1999.

Weissberg, Steven M., M.D., and Christiano, Joseph, A.P.P.T. *The Answer is in Your Blood Type*. Lake Mary, Florida: Personal Nutrition USA, Inc, 1999.

Wigmore, Ann. *The Hippocrates Diet*. Wayne, New Jersey: Avery Publishing Group, 1984.

Wolfe, David. *Sunfood Diet Success System*. San Diego, California: Maul Brothers Publishing, 1999.

Yarron, Ruth. *Super Baby Food*. Archbald, Pennsylvania: F.J. Roberts Publishing Company, 1996.

Young, Robert, O., Ph.D., D.Sc. *Sick and Tired?* Pleasant Grove, Utah: Woodland Publishing, 1999.

# Continuing Education
# Opportunities

## RAINBOW GREEN LIVE-FOOD CUISINE VIDEO/DVD

This dynamic, hands-on video has been created to support you in the journey of healing and awakening with Rainbow Green Live-Food Cuisine. This full-length video includes:

An in-depth interview with author and holistic physician Gabriel Cousens, M.D., which highlights the key principles of Rainbow Green Live-Food Cuisine.

A series of Rainbow Green Live-Food Cuisine recipe demonstrations with the personable and talented Tree of Life Café Chefs.

VIDEO/DVD
Introduction to the Tree of Life Rejuvenation Center & the Secrets of Rejuvenation

BOOKS BY GABRIEL COUSENS, M.D.
*Rainbow Green Live-Food Cuisine*
*Conscious Eating, revised edition*
*Spiritual Nutrition and the Rainbow Diet*
*Depression-Free for Life*
*Sevenfold Peace*
*Tachyon Energy: A New Paradigm in Holistic Healing*
*Modern Essene Way and Modern Essene Communions*

## ORDERING INFORMATION

To order books and videos/DVDs, please contact the Tree of Life:

Website: www.treeoflife.nu
e-mail: orders@treeoflife.nu
Phone: (520) 394-2520 x 203

## TREE OF LIFE'S FREE E-WELLNESS NEWSLETTER

Subscribe online at www.treeoflife.nu and receive holistic healing, socio-political, spiritually uplifting articles by Gabriel Cousens, M.D., and news from the Tree of Life every month.

## SPIRITUAL AND NUTRITIONAL WORKSHOPS

We invite you to join us at the Tree of Life Rejuvenation Center to be supported in living the Rainbow Green Live-Food Cuisine. We offer a variety of workshops, detoxification programs, and lifestyle learning opportunities. Please visit us on line at www.treeoflife.nu or call us at (520) 394-2520 x 206.

## VEGAN LIVE-FOOD CULINARY ARTS APPRENTICESHIP PTOGRAM

This unique three- to four-month apprenticeship program offers those interested in the art and science of live-food preparation an opportunity to receive personal and career training with the talented Tree of Life Café chefs. Participants become certified chefs in the sophisticated Rainbow Green Live-Food Cuisine.

## MASTER'S DEGREE PROGRAM IN VEGAN LIVE-FOOD NUTRITION

This two-year correspondence program with a four-week residency intensive is offered through the University of Integrative Learning under the Provostship of Gabriel Cousens, M.D., at the Tree of Life Rejuvenation Center. Facility staff includes Gabriel Cousens, M.D., M.D. (H.), Diplomate in Ayurveda, David Wolfe, J.D., Christopher "Yashpal" Jayne, N.D., John Phillips, M.S., Shanti Golds Cousens, Philip Madeley, and Karen Parker.

# INDEX

Page numbers in *italics* indicate a photograph; page numbers followed by "t" indicate a table (e.g. 474t).